Modern and Contemporary Poetry and Poetics

Modern and Contemporary Poetry and Poetics promotes and pursues topics in the burgeoning field of twentieth- and twenty-first-century poetics. Critical and scholarly work on poetry and poetics of interest to the series includes social location in its relationships to subjectivity, to the construction of authorship, to oeuvres, and to careers; poetic reception and dissemination (groups, movements, formations, institutions); the intersection of poetry and theory; questions about language, poetic authority, and the goals of writing; claims in poetics, impacts of social life, and the dynamics of the poetic career as these are staged and debated by poets and inside poems. Topics that are bibliographic, pedagogic, that concern the social field of poetry, and reflect on the history of poetry studies are valued as well. This series focuses both on individual poets and texts and on larger movements, poetic institutions, and questions about poetic authority, social identifications, and aesthetics.

Language and the Renewal of Society in Walt Whitman, Laura (Riding) Jackson, and Charles Olson
The American Cratylus
Carla Billitteri

Modernism and Poetic Inspiration
The Shadow Mouth
Jed Rasula

The Social Life of Poetry
Appalachia, Race, and Radical Modernism
Chris Green

Procedural Form in Postmodern American Poetry
Berrigan, Antin, Silliman, and Hejinian
David W. Huntsperger

Modernist Writings and Religio-scientific Discourse
H. D., Loy, and Toomer
Lara Vetter

Male Subjectivity and Poetic Form in "New American" Poetry
Andrew Mossin

The Poetry of Susan Howe
History, Theology, Authority
Will Montgomery

Ronald Johnson's Modernist Collage Poetry
Ross Hair

Pastoral, Pragmatism, and Twentieth-Century American Poetry
Ann Marie Mikkelsen

(Re:)Working the Ground
Essays on the Late Writings of Robert Duncan
edited by James Maynard

Women's Poetry and Popular Culture
Marsha Bryant

Delmore Schwartz
A Critical Reassessment

Alex Runchman

palgrave
macmillan

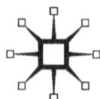

DELMORE SCHWARTZ
Copyright © Alex Runchman, 2014.

First published in 2014 by
PALGRAVE MACMILLAN®
in the United States—a division of St. Martin's Press LLC,
175 Fifth Avenue, New York, NY 10010.

Where this book is distributed in the UK, Europe and the rest of the world,
this is by Palgrave Macmillan, a division of Macmillan Publishers Limited,
registered in England, company number 785998, of Houndmills,
Basingstoke, Hampshire RG21 6XS.

Palgrave Macmillan is the global academic imprint of the above companies
and has companies and representatives throughout the world.

Palgrave® and Macmillan® are registered trademarks in the United States,
the United Kingdom, Europe and other countries.

ISBN: 978–1–137–39437–8

Library of Congress Cataloging-in-Publication Data

Runchman, Alex, 1981–
    Delmore Schwartz : a critical reassessment / Alex Runchman.
        pages cm. — (Modern and contemporary poetry and poetics)
    Includes bibliographical references and index.
    ISBN 978–1–137–39437–8 (hardback : alk. paper)
        1. Schwartz, Delmore, 1913–1966—Criticism and interpretation.
    2. American poetry—Jewish authors—History and criticism. I. Title.

PS3537.C79Z86 2014
811'.52—dc23   2013046410

A catalogue record of the book is available from the British Library.

Design by Newgen Knowledge Works (P) Ltd., Chennai, India.

First edition: May 2014

10 9 8 7 6 5 4 3 2 1

For Joanne: "animula, vagula, blandula"

Contents

Permissions

Some portions of chapters 1 and 2 appeared previously, in an earlier version, as "'The Greatest Thing in North America': Delmore Schwartz and Europe," *Comparative American Studies* 11, no. 1 (March 2013), 37–51. URLS: www.maneypublishing.com/journals/cas and www.ingentaconnect.com/content/maney/cas. © W. S. Maney & Son Limited. Reprinted with permission from Maney Publishing.

Some portions of chapter 3 appeared previously, in an earlier version, as "Delmore Schwartz's *Genesis* and 'International Consciousness,'" *IJASonline* 2 (Summer 2010). URL: www.ijasonline.com. Reprinted with permission of the editor, Stephen Matterson.

Some portions of chapters 2 and 4 appeared previously, in an earlier version, in "Delmore Schwartz and Education," *POST* 2 (2010). URL: www.post.materdei.ie. Reprinted with permission of the editor, Michael Hinds.

Acknowledgments

This study has its origins in a PhD thesis undertaken at Trinity College Dublin under the supervision of Philip Coleman. For his support, advice, belief in my research, and, most of all, his friendship, I am enormously appreciative.

I was able to revise the thesis for monograph publication with the help of a Donald C. Gallup Fellowship at the Beinecke Rare Book and Manuscripts Library, Yale. An earlier trip also aided my research. I would especially like to thank Nancy Kuhl, Mary Ellen Budney, and Molly Wheeler, Schwartz's archivist. Robert Phillips, executor of the Schwartz estate, encouraged the project and granted me permission to quote from unpublished archival material.

I am grateful to Rachel Blau DuPlessis, editor of this series on Modern and Contemporary Poetry and Poetics, whose insights have been valuable at every stage; to my commissioning editor, Brigitte Shull; and to my editorial assistant, Ryan Jenkins, for his patience and efficiency in guiding me through the publication process. Two exacting peer reviews of an initial manuscript helped to turn this into a much-improved book. At an earlier stage, the contributions of my PhD examiners, Stephen Matterson and David Herd, were also enormously constructive.

Harold Bloom and Langdon Hammer made time to meet with me when I was at Yale, and I have also benefited from discussions with numerous colleagues at TCD including Sam Slote, Nicholas Grene, and Gerald Dawe. I owe particular debts to Darryl Jones and Eve Patten, head and former head of the School of English, for helping to keep me solvent by providing teaching while I completed the manuscript; I am likewise thankful to Anne Fogarty, Ron Callan, and Nerys Williams of University College Dublin, and especially to Michael Hinds at the Mater Dei Institute of Education, Dublin City University. Meanwhile, more friends than I can list have offered suggestions, pints, and proofreading services along the way, among them Gillian Groszewski, Dara Downey, Derek Dunne, Clare Hayes-Brady, Niamh NicGhabbhan, Guy Woodward, Marcus Mucha, and Johnny Lee, who must also take credit for first encouraging me to read Schwartz.

Most important of all have been my parents, Phil and Roz, and my sister, Felicity, for being there at every stage—not just while writing this book, but always.

Finally, to my most severe—but also most astute—critic, Joanne O'Leary, much love and many thanks.

Abbreviations

The poems from *In Dreams Begin Responsibilities,* which I discuss in chapter 2, are all reprinted in the more easily available *Selected Poems (1938–1958): Summer Knowledge.* However, because I am concerned with the unity of the earlier collection, that is the one to which I refer. In discussing stories published in the now out-of-print *The World Is a Wedding: And Other Stories,* however, I use James Atlas's *In Dreams Begin Responsibilities, and Other Stories,* with the exception of the title story, "A Bitter Farce" (which was not recollected), and "The Statues" (which is reprinted in *Screeno: Stories and Poems).*

The following abbreviations are used throughout:

In Dreams Begin Responsibilities—IDBR
Genesis—G
The World Is a Wedding, and Other Stories—WW
Vaudeville for a Princess, and Other Poems—V
Selected Poems (1938–1958): Summer Knowledge—SK
Last & Lost Poems—LL
Screeno: Stories and Poems—Screeno
Selected Essays of Delmore Schwartz—Essays
Letters of Delmore Schwartz—Letters
Portrait of Delmore: Journals and Notes of Delmore Schwartz: 1939–1959—
    Portrait Delmore Schwartz and James Laughlin: Selected Letters—DS &
    JL Letters
Eliot, T. S., *The Complete Poems and Plays*—Eliot, *CPP.*

Introduction

In the posthumously published poem "America, America!," Delmore Schwartz announces himself to be "a poet of the Hudson River and the heights above it, / the lights, the stars, the bridges."[1] In so doing, he is claiming, metonymically, to be a poet of the American Dream—of New York and its literal skyscrapers, but also of the heights of ambition that they represent; of actual city lights, but also of hope and mental lucidity; of Broadway celebrities, shining as brightly as stars in the sky; and of bridges, both concrete, joining separate districts, and metaphorical, uniting peoples separated from each other by culture and race. But Schwartz then reformulates this assertion, escalating his claims: "I am also by self-appointment the laureate of the Atlantic /—of the peoples' hearts, crossing it / to new America" (*LL*, 4). Moving from "a" to "the" (from one among many to the only one), from "poet" to "laureate," and from the Hudson River to the unimaginably vaster Atlantic Ocean, he performs a rhetorical maneuver that seems to grant him totemic authority. His self-promotion aligns him with the foremost New York poet, Walt Whitman, who had described the United States as a "teeming nation of nations."[2] Schwartz's emphasis upon the Atlantic itself, however, the protean expanse between two continents, rather than upon the solid land of the United States or any European nation, belies a sense of indeterminacy. He is confidently declaring himself to be the poet of uncertainty and transition.

Being an Atlantic poet is not incompatible with being an American poet: Schwartz's "also" insists that he sees himself as both. Born in Brooklyn on December 8, 1913, he repeatedly employs a US perspective in examining a European heritage both personal (as the child of Russian-Romanian parents) and literary (as a writer who had self-consciously absorbed the Western canon). James Atlas's 1977 biography is subtitled *The Life of an American Poet*, but for the "European Son" of Jewish immigrants such unambiguous nationality was not easily achieved or even desirable.[3] It could only be understood in terms of a broader, transatlantic identity, one capable of recognizing New York City as "Europe's last capital."[4] Schwartz was far more interested, throughout his career, in US historical and cultural relation to Europe than he was in ideas of independent nationhood. Although Europe and America often represent conflicting ideologies for him, he recognizes their relationship as symbiotic, and, by explicitly orienting his oeuvre between them, resists stating a stronger affinity to either.

It is in his long, unfinished 1943 work, *Genesis* (which he had briefly considered titling *An Atlantic Boy*) that Schwartz writes most directly about the mass immigration at the end of the nineteenth century. The subject is as important to him, however, for its symbolic value as its actuality, becoming paradigmatic, in poems, stories, and essays alike, of other instances of upheaval or displacement. Similarly, the Atlantic Ocean itself becomes a favorite metaphor for separation. In the story "America! America!," for example (as opposed to the poem of almost the same title), the protagonist Shenandoah Fish—one of Schwartz's many versions of himself—comes to the conclusion that "the separation, the contempt, and the gulf" between his generation and his parents' might in fact be the center or starting point of his writing, compelling "the innermost motion of the work to be flight, or criticism, or denial, or rejection."[5] Shenandoah eventually accepts, however, that "his separation was actual enough, but there existed also an unbreakable unity" ("America! America!," 32). In reaching this conclusion, he is emulating his parents' own ongoing relationship with Europe: they have crossed the gulf of the Atlantic, but remain bound to their past just as he remains bound to them in his attempted independence.

More broadly, the state of in-between-ness represented by the Atlantic Ocean characterizes Schwartz's entire corpus. The poles of Europe and the United States, Jewishness and Americanness, are only the most determined of the dialectical oppositions that Schwartz routinely sets up, blurs, and partially breaks down without ever fully reconciling. His commitment to the international is undermined by his acute sense of individual isolation and alienation. Dreams and actuality become indistinguishable. Audience members at movies and plays find themselves acting leading roles. Characters attempt to exert free will within a world in which so much is predetermined. The typical Schwartz protagonist is an adolescent or young adult, caught between childhood and maturity. Meanwhile, poems rich in literary reference seem to condemn themselves by advocating intuitive knowledge over book learning. Schwartz poses generic challenges too: narrative, lyric, and drama jostle against each other. On one hand, he espouses the stylistic complexities of modernism and symbolism; on the other, he aspires toward naturalistic directness. Initially suspicious of popular culture, his high cultural allusions fail to conceal his attraction to it, while his later attempts to embrace popular culture betray a lingering attachment to the more refined. Even as a figure of influence for his contemporaries, Schwartz is claimed by both Robert Lowell and John Ashbery, poets whose ideologies would seem to be in opposition. Schwartz's belief, as stated in the "Author's Note" to *Selected Poems: Summer Knowledge*, that "every point of view, every kind of knowledge and every kind of experience is limited and ignorant," no matter how true, leaves him in a perpetual limbo, unable to commit to any clearly defined position.

At worst, this amounts to a weakness of conviction. Schwartz's articulations of uncertain purpose and liminality, however, make him a spokesman not only for other intellectually minded sons of the diaspora, but for *all* those invested in the promise of the American Dream and forced to contend with its inevitable disappointment. Admitting, in a 1955 essay on Hemingway, that Hollywood's popularization of the American Dream has at once vulgarized it and made it increasingly difficult to define, Schwartz nonetheless regularly employs the term as shorthand for thinking about cultural nationalism. The very concept, he suggests, "is formulated in the American Constitution as every human being's inalienable right to life, liberty, and the pursuit of happiness" ("The Fiction of Ernest Hemingway," 271); but far from accepting it simply as what James Truslow Adams had, in 1931, famously called "that American dream of a better, richer, and happier life for all our citizens of every rank," Schwartz insists, too, on its nightmarish potential. Because the dream is based upon a false promise—of converting "the pursuit of happiness into the guarantee of a happy ending"—it gives rise to anxiety as well as ambition: "disillusion is inseparable from illusion and despair from hope." Equally, the dream becomes "insomnia when it is not fulfilled" (one reason, perhaps, why so many of Schwartz's characters are caught between sleep and wakefulness). It causes "endless fear and insecurity."[6]

Schwartz's most enduring correlative for this feeling is the "sick-excited passage" (*LL*, 4) undertaken by the transatlantic immigrants. In the face of such trials, courage—a quality more available to Hemingway's characters than Schwartz's own—becomes an "obsession" and a "necessity." It cannot, however, overcome what Schwartz describes as "the American Dream's giddy, unpredictable, magical, tragic, and fabulous juggernaut." Schwartz concludes that "the dream, the hope, the anxiety, and the courage began with the discovery of America."[7] The origins of the American Dream, then, lie in Europe with Columbus's initial fantasy of wealth. Columbus's voyage is reenacted, in a more or less literal sense, by nineteenth and early twentieth-century Jews seeking a new life in America, but an approximation of it is also carried out by every US citizen in their own pursuit of happiness. Schwartz's writing about success and failure, and about departure and transit keeps both historical precedents clearly in mind.

This book reappraises Schwartz's work in relation to his self-definition as both Atlantic poet and poet of the American Dream. To use the words of a character in one of his most experimental later works, "Kilroy's Carnival: A Poetic Prologue for TV," the "underlying unity of purpose" in Schwartz's various writings is his "infinite interest" in the American Dream, the ultimate image of that which is desired but unattainable (*LL*, 97). It is a subject that, of necessity, also concerned Schwartz's contemporaries, from his coeditors and fellow critics at *Partisan Review*, to onetime friends including the novelist Saul Bellow and the "middle generation" poets, Lowell and John Berryman, to the younger New York poets, Frank O'Hara and Ashbery. While admitting the contradictions in Schwartz's ideology, and acknowledging that his debts to T. S. Eliot in particular are never fully resolved, this study examines why his writing mattered to his peers and why it might still matter.

For better or worse, many of those Schwartz influenced (O'Hara and Ashbery excepted) played a role in turning his own life and career into a parable of the American Dream. Along with Atlas's biography, their accounts of his early critical acclaim and tragic demise brought Schwartz a degree of posthumous fame in the decade or so after his death, but this was largely to the neglect of his writing. All the same, the success and the disappointment were genuine. The publication of his short story, "In Dreams Begin Responsibilities," as the leading feature in the revived *Partisan Review* in December 1937—ahead of contributions by Wallace Stevens, Edmund Wilson, Lionel Abel, Dwight MacDonald, and even Picasso—established him immediately as the literary wunderkind of the mostly Jewish American New York intellectuals. Irving Howe thrilled at the "shock of recognition" he experienced on reading it, while Alfred Kazin remembered it as "the greatest fable I was ever to read of 'our experience.'"[8] When Schwartz's first book, of the same title, appeared the following year, Allen Tate described his poetic style as "the only genuine innovation we've had since Pound and Eliot came upon the scene twenty-five years ago," praising his "wholly new feeling for language" and use of "a new metrical system of great subtlety and originality."[9] There were similar accolades from John Crowe Ransom and Mark Van Doren. Eliot himself wrote Schwartz that he "was much impressed."[10] W. H. Auden, meanwhile, thought him "very promising" and Stevens told his friend Henry Church "there is no one in whom I believe as much as I believe in Delmore Schwartz."[11]

This was the "young & gift-strong" Schwartz commemorated by Berryman in fourteen elegiac *Dream Songs*, Schwartz "In the brightness of his promise, //unstained,.../ blazing with insight."[12] It was a promise achieved against considerable odds. Schwartz endured an unhappy childhood, which he was to revisit often in his writing. Following numerous affairs, his father left the family when Schwartz was nine, leaving him and his brother to be brought up by a suffocating mother whom he did not love. When Harry Schwartz died, in 1930, Schwartz expected to receive a large inheritance, but this had been devalued as a consequence of the Depression and the corruption of an unscrupulous executor. Schwartz had to borrow money to study philosophy, first at the University of Wisconsin, and then at New York University before undertaking some graduate study at Harvard under Alfred North Whitehead. He was never financially secure thereafter, more than once stressing that his greatest influences as a writer were "Shakespeare and the depression of 1929–1937," the social impetus behind his work jostling with its purely literary aspirations.[13]

Schwartz immediately consolidated his reputation by writing regular reviews and essays for *The Kenyon Review*, *The Southern Review*, and especially *Partisan Review*, of which he became poetry editor in 1943.[14] A verse play, *Shenandoah* (1940), and a short-story collection, *The World Is a Wedding* (1948), were each met with plaudits, capturing—in Howe's words—

the quality of New York life in the 1930's and 1940's with a fine comic intensity—not, of course, the whole of New York life but that interesting point where intellectual children of immigrant Jews are finding their way into the larger world while casting uneasy, rueful glances over their backs.[15]

By this stage, Schwartz was so associated with *Partisan Review* that William Phillips, one of the founding editors along with Philip Rahv, could suggest in a later memoir that Schwartz was "the most extreme representative of the new intellectual grouping"—not because he was the most central or typical, but because he "embod[ied] most of the strains that came together" (William Phillips, 75).[16] Schwartz undoubtedly shared many of the magazine's values: he was, above all, cosmopolitan in outlook, earnest in his attempts to bring together Marx and Freud, and (to evoke Lionel Trilling's characterization of *Partisan Review*'s achievement) intent upon forging a union between politics and the imagination.[17] For Atlas, "It was as if the self-constituted intelligentsia with which [Schwartz] had allied himself required a spokesman to dramatize its cultural dilemmas."[18] *Partisan Review*'s readership was not, however, uniquely Jewish American, and reading Schwartz only in terms of his "representative relationship to Jewishness," as Benjamin Schreier has argued, has led to overdetermined readings of Schwartz's works—many of them perpetuated by the memoirs of the likes of Kazin and Phillips.[19] The magazine might, all the same, be regarded, to adapt Lawrence Rainey's phrase, as an institution of late modernism, both creating an appreciative coterie for Schwartz's talent but perhaps also limiting him in his later attempts to recreate himself as a different kind of writer. Similarly, James Laughlin, Schwartz's publisher at New Directions, can be seen as an unofficial patron, providing Schwartz with financial support and even giving secretarial work to his first wife, Gertrude Buckman. Between them, Laughlin and *Partisan Review* sustained Schwartz in his early career.

After *In Dreams Begin Responsibilities,* Schwartz never enjoyed the same critical applause as a poet. His translation of Rimbaud's *A Season in Hell,* hurriedly published in 1939, was derided for its inaccuracies, while the muted response to *Genesis: Book I* in 1943—an intended magnum opus of immigration and developing selfhood—was a greater disappointment still. *Books II* and *III,* though roughly drafted, remained unpublished. Countless other works, including several novels and critical studies of Eliot and Heinrich Heine, were started and left unfinished. Some of the reviews of *Vaudeville for a Princess* (1950), meanwhile, were overtly hostile, and when Schwartz became the youngest poet ever to win the Bollingen Prize for *Summer Knowledge: Selected Poems* in 1959, it was tacitly agreed that this was mainly on the strength of his reprinted early poems, not the hundred-odd effusive new poems that made up the book's second half. In Berryman's words, "His throat ached, and he could sing no more. / All ears closed."[20]

But Schwartz continued to write: a few further poems and essays appeared in journals, and a further book of stories, *Successful Love and Other Stories* (1961), breezily extended the satirical scope of his earlier works, taking on the liberal society of the 1950s. Further unfinished drafts accumulated. By this time, however, Schwartz was ravaged by mental illness, paranoia, and addictions to Nembutal, Dexedrine, and alcohol, all of which had begun to affect him as early as the early-1940s. His personal life was in disarray following his separation, in 1958, from his second wife, Elizabeth Pollet. He was briefly committed to Bellevue after threatening Pollet's supposed lover, Hilton Kramer; and the years up to Schwartz's untimely death are blighted by false accusations against friends, hopeless lawsuits, and increasing alienation. When he died of a heart attack, aged 52, on July 11, 1966, he had left his teaching position at Syracuse University unannounced and was living in a cheap West Forty-sixth Street hotel. His body was unclaimed for three days.

Atlas tells the tale comprehensively and uncompromisingly, although, as David Lehman has remarked, his readings of Schwartz's works are often too perfunctory to advance their own interest over that of the life.[21] But the aura around Schwartz's self-destructive genius had already been articulated by John Berryman, Robert Lowell, and William Barrett in his memoir, *The Truants*, and Saul Bellow, for whom Schwartz inspired the fictional poet Von Humboldt Fleisher in *Humboldt's Gift*. Bellow's narrator, Charlie Citrine, speaks with occasional reverence of Humboldt: he was "an avant-garde writer, the first of a new generation"; he was a pioneer in the use of the word "sensibility"; and his early ballads were "pure, musical, witty, radiant, humane"—Platonic even, evoking an original state of perfection.[22] But the enduring image is of Humboldt reeling off into insanity. He "passionately lived out the theme of Success," Citrine remarks. "Naturally he died a Failure."[23] Berryman, although he idealizes the youthful Schwartz, presents Delmore "out of his mind," besieged by the failure of his "administration." "I'd bleed to say his lovely work improved," he laments, "but it is not so."[24] Lowell sounds a similar note, regretting, in his own "In Dreams Begin Responsibilities," how the genius of Schwartz's dream "thickened," and characterizing his former friend's surname as "one vowel bedevilled by seven consonants."[25] Lowell is ambiguous as to whether he regards Schwartz's bedevilment to have been self-inflicted or caused by factors beyond his personal control, as exemplified by having to bear a name that he himself could never have chosen.

Dwight MacDonald, for his part, blamed America. "Poetry is a dangerous occupation in this country," he contended in his memorial to Schwartz—a position condemned by Karl Shapiro as betraying a "dismal, sociologically oriented view of poetry...shared neither by Schwartz nor by [Randall] Jarrell nor myself nor by any of the poets I know of."[26] To say that "America got Delmore" is an easy way out, a "facile aesthetic lie" that denies his individual agency.[27] Kazin's view of Schwartz as "a prophecy of the last literary generation to believe in the authority of culture, the logic of tradition...the poet on the cross of culture, every muscle contorted; Brooklyn's best, nailed down" similarly presents Schwartz as victim rather than perpetrator of his own destiny.[28] There are numerous possible reasons, none of them definitive, why those who knew Schwartz found it necessary to mythologize him after death—perhaps as a salutary warning, or to palliate their own experiences of failure, or because it enabled them to make failure one of their own central subjects; and perhaps even out of rivalry, as a means of vindicating their own diversions from Schwartz's aesthetic, or of suggesting how they had surpassed what he might once have been expected to achieve. Whatever its reasons, such mythologizing turns Schwartz into something both more and less than a writer, often resulting in overdetermined readings that over-look much of what he actually wrote.[29]

"He had followers but they could not find him": Berryman ascribed to Schwartz not just messianic intensity, but also the devotion of disciples who, at times, esteemed him more highly than he esteemed himself.[30] "I went to Harvard mainly with the idea of studying with him, which I ended up never doing," recalls Ashbery.[31] A 2010 poem by Charles Simic also captures Schwartz's elusiveness: "Where's the poet Delmore Schwartz I once saw sit-ting / In Washington Square Park gesturing theatrically to himself?"[32] This fittingly evokes how, nearly 50 years after his death, we seem to have lost sight of Schwartz's achievement. It was not always easy for his peers to grasp either. He refused—or failed—to settle upon a single definitive worldview or literary form, starting off by writing, in Kazin's words, "stories and poems that astonished everyone by being impeccably formally *right* in the prevail-ing Eliot tradition—emotional ingenuity tuned to perfect pitch by gravity of manner," only then to take up arms against that tradition, never wholly conquering it, but nonetheless suggesting ways, in *Genesis*, of returning the individual self to the center of the poem and extending the traditional scope of the lyric, and, in his *Summer Knowledge* poems, of adopting a more incan-tatory style as possible directions out of modernism.[33] Schwartz's poetic development, observed Anthony Hecht in a review of *Summer Knowledge*, "has not been smooth and gradual; it has been filled with sudden breaks and new starts that are rash and audacious and unbelievably risky."[34]

It was partly because of this erratic trajectory, and partly because of the already fixed notion of Schwartz's decline, that Berryman was able to declare him, as early as 1970, "the most underrated poet of the twentieth century." Not the most consistent—Berryman thought the later work "*absolutely* no good." But, in common with other followers who have anticipated a revival in Schwartz's reputation, Berryman was adamant that "the early poetry will come back—no question": "The young will read his young verse / for as long as such things go."[35] Ashbery, meanwhile, has no hesitation in call-ing Schwartz a "neglected major poet" and attributes his fall from critical standing primarily to the fickleness of literary fashion: he is "but one, albeit perhaps the most distinguished one, of a group of poets of his time whom a revolution in taste...has swept from view, perhaps to be swept back in by some future revolution when his time has come."[36] Like Berryman, Ashbery expresses reservations about the later poems, which seem to him "to lack the electric compressions and simplifications that animate his early writ-ing, tending toward bald assertiveness." But Ashbery is more prepared than Berryman to admit the possibility of a reevaluation, conceding that "critics were premature in condemning the late work of Picasso and Stravinsky" and wondering whether "Delmore will one day get a similar reprieve." [37] Schwartz's literary executor, Robert Phillips, who has overseen the publication of letters, "bagatelles," plays and, most importantly, poems uncollected or unpublished during Schwartz's lifetime, has begun to make a case for the later poetry, celebrating its accuracy in recreating sensuous experiences (*LL*, "Introduction," xiv).[38] My fifth chapter seeks to develop this case further. But even Schwartz's most-acclaimed works are now little read, and it is for this reason that his oeuvre in its entirety (and particularly his poetry) requires reappraisal.[39]

* * *

In examining the "Atlantic" character of Schwartz's writing, my first chapter establishes the conflicting concepts of "international consciousness" and "the isolation of modern poetry," which influence everything he wrote. This chapter concentrates upon the principles Schwartz sets up in his most prominent critical writings—notably "The Isolation of Modern Poetry" and "T. S. Eliot as the International Hero"—thinking about how these provide a framework within which to read the poetry. It also examines Schwartz's interpretation of his Jewish inheritance and how this informs his identity as a poet, making particular reference to his anxious attempts to account for the anti-Semitic strains in Eliot's poetry and to the story "A Bitter Farce."

Chapter 2 offers a detailed analysis of *In Dreams Begin Responsibilities*, linking Schwartz's allusive practice throughout to his interest in genealogy, and considering how he both advertises his relation to a European literary tradition and adapts this to a contemporary US context. Drawing upon what Ralph Barton Perry called the "egocentric predicament"—the difficulty of experiencing the world except through one's own perceptions—I also analyze the volume's challenges to the distinctions between dream and actuality, and between the individual and the world in which he lives.

Chapter 3, meanwhile, makes a case for *Genesis*, Schwartz's most sustained attempt to articulate "international consciousness," outlining its influences, the role played by its chorus of ghost commentators (who offer Freudian and Marxist interpretations), and its conflation of different genres and forms. I analyze the poem's use of language and voice, as well as its attempts to extrapolate universal and historical truths from the individual experience of its hero, Hershey Green. This chapter also addresses the poem's engagement with the dialectics of success and failure, and concludes with a discussion of alienation and misimagining in the story "America! America!"

Chapter 4 addresses Schwartz's response to Oswald Spengler's *The Decline of the West* and reads *Vaudeville for a Princess* in relation to Schwartz's vacillation between societal engagement and withdrawal, epitomized by his ambivalent position on American involvement in the Second World War. "Starlight Like Intuition Pierced the Twelve" and the sequence titled "The True, The Good, and the Beautiful" are, I argue, poems of guilty witness that are helpfully read alongside Schwartz's attempts to justify his status as an intellectual during wartime. This chapter also compares Schwartz's conception of responsibility to Dwight MacDonald's, and considers his turn away from the American Dream, and toward American "actuality," in his postwar cultural criticism

Finally, Chapter 5 reevaluates Schwartz's later poems, arguing for their continuity with his earlier work (despite surface differences) and assessing the phoenix and ripe fruit as symbols of hope and natural cycles of regeneration. This chapter also considers Schwartz's engagements, late in his career, with US history, and outlines the principles of "Summer Knowledge." I conclude by reading "Seurat's Sunday Afternoon along the Seine" as the culmination of Schwartz's investigations into the potentialities of art.

A short Conclusion revisits the dual impulses in Schwartz's writing: toward both high and low culture; toward both the purely lyrical and the socially engaged; and toward both the individual and the universal. In particular, I consider—with recourse to Eliot's lectures on *The Use of Poetry and the Use of Criticism*—how Schwartz attempts to reconcile a desire to represent his contemporary moment with an equally strong aspiration toward the timeless.

Except in the first chapter, I focus principally on Schwartz's poetry. Each of his volumes, however, contains passages that are in prose, and all of my readings are undertaken in the awareness that there is a fundamental, if sometimes uneasy, interdependency between Schwartz's poetry, his fiction, and his criticism.

CHAPTER 1

"The Greatest Thing in North America": "International Consciousness" or "The Isolation of Modern Poetry?"

New Europe

In the summer of 1943, in the midst of the Second World War, Schwartz wrote to his publisher, James Laughlin, embracing Laughlin's proposal that they set up a magazine together. It should be titled *New Europe*, Schwartz suggested, and it should be based upon the hypothesis "that Europe is through, but that something has to be done to carry on the greatness of European culture." Its articles would carry out a "large-scale attack on popular culture" and would attempt to "overcome the gulf between popular culture and advance guard culture" by taking seriously "Hollywood, Broadway, popular novels, comic strips, *NY Times* editorials and poems, the prose of *Time*, and the photos of *Life*." The whole project would be founded upon the assumption that "Europe is the greatest thing in America...but the next greatest thing in America is Hollywood; and between these two large-scale cultural factors, the future of culture lies" (*DS & JL Letters*, 214–215). Ultimately, Schwartz implies, establishing the new magazine would constitute a stage in enabling America to become the sanctuary of Western civilization.

New Europe never came to anything. Schwartz's manifesto is worth taking seriously, however, because it epitomizes his lifelong preoccupation with the ways in which American culture might be able to extend and develop European culture while retaining a distinct character of its own.

In proposing such a course, Schwartz was restating views already well-established among the *Partisan Review* circle.[1] As early as 1937, shortly before their official break from the Communist Party and their founding of the revived *Partisan Review*, William Phillips and Philip Rahv had called for "the Europeanization of American literature."[2] The efforts of the American Communist Party to "create a literature in one country" were futile, they argued, "because inevitably a contradiction arises between the international consciousness of intellectual life and the provincial smugness of the literature itself" (Cooney, 92). As Terry Cooney has explained, "the goal was not to imitate Europe and thus to remain its province" but "to bring a new sophistication to *American* literature, to broaden the national culture by making it more international and more cosmopolitan without discarding its particular qualities" (Cooney, 93). The model for Rahv and Phillips was Thomas Mann whose work, though "deeply rooted in the German soil" also generalized "the intellectual experience of Europe" (Cooney, 93). The American writer, they hoped, "rising to a high level of consciousness," would similarly "carry the particulars of American life into the main stream of world culture" (Cooney, 93).

Implicit in Rahv and Phillips's essay on "Literature in a Political Decade" is a belief that to be intellectual is, by definition, to be internationally minded. Calls for internationalism are common among thinkers on the Left in the 1930s, Sidney Hook, for example, proposing in 1933 that "the time has come to build a new communist party and a new communist international": again, the implication is that progress cannot be confined to a single nation, although there is equally no call to give up national characteristics.[3] Cooney explains that "cosmopolitanism as interpreted in *Partisan Review* meant that secularism, urbanism, intellectuality, and international-mindedness would generally be taken to represent positive cultural and political values, whereas rural, religious, nationalistic, and anti-theoretical attitudes would commonly be regarded as evidence of backwardness or bad faith" (Cooney, 150). The cause was as cultural as it was political, perhaps even more so; and its most iconic figure was Leon Trotsky who, despite privately criticizing the journal's overrespectability, contributed an article on "Art and Politics" and an open letter to André Breton to *Partisan Review* in the late 1930s. As a revolutionary in exile—"Intellectual, International, Jewish, Secular, Literary, Classicist, Modernist"—Trotsky was, in Christopher Hitchens's account, "the ideal-type, of the cosmopolitan, the modernist, the essayist and the man of action yearned for by the diaspora of *Partisan Review*." Even regardless of his Jewishness and his Marxism, Trotsky remains "the [twentieth] century's most arresting instance of the aesthete and the intellectual in politics."[4]

Trotsky had himself contended, in *Literature and Revolution*, that "the development of art is the highest test of the vitality and significance of each epoch" (Trotsky, 9). He also argued, in his letter to Breton, that, "In our epoch of convulsive reaction, of cultural decline and return to savagery, truly independent creation cannot but be revolutionary by its very nature, for it cannot but seek an outlet from intolerable social suffocation."[5] On these terms, the emergence of a sophisticated and cosmopolitan literature would be the justification of the radical politics championed by *Partisan Review*'s editors. They knew, however, that literature written to conform to a prescribed ideology, even a radical one, must inevitably lack vitality. They saw the anti-intellectual, anti-international proletarian literature sponsored by the American Communist Party and published in journals such as *New Masses* as evidence of this, its purposes more political than they were literary. The extent to which a writer's politics and social attitudes may or may not be extricable from his or her writing is a problem recurrently suggested in the pages of *Partisan Review*.[6] It is one, however, that the magazine's editors, on its relaunch, insisted would have no bearing upon their editorial principles. "Conformity to a given social ideology or to a prescribed attitude or technique, will not be asked of our writers," they insisted. "On the contrary, our pages will be open to any tendency which is relevant to literature in our time."[7] As will be seen, such a policy of openness itself amounts to an ideological stance, entailing complications of its own. But it also made *Partisan Review*, in Irving Howe's words, "the first journal in which it was not merely respectable but a matter of pride to print one of Eliot's *Four Quartets* side by side with Marxist criticism."[8] It established for the journal a crucial role in the "process of internationalizing American culture (also, by the way, Americanizing international culture)," the "international" suggesting not just a willingness to publish writers of all nationalities, but also a catholicity of taste, a preparedness to recognize the artistic or literary merit of writers regardless of their extraliterary views.[9]

For Schwartz, as he wrote to Dwight MacDonald following Trotsky's assassination, the Soviet revolutionary had "created in his writing alone a kind of international consciousness, an instrument like the electric light"[10]— a modern, far-reaching consciousness that became indispensable as soon as it had been created. The same idea finds different expression in a short piece Schwartz quickly abandoned entitled "Funeral Oration." "The biggest thing in America is Europe," Schwartz writes, "and the biggest thing in Europe is Russia and the biggest thing in Russia was this small bearded gesticulating angry man in Mexico."[11] If this is ultimately an America-centric way of putting it—a disingenuous means of claiming Trotsky for the United States and suggesting that Russia and Europe only exist for US sustenance—it nonetheless delineates how Schwartz perceived the transmission of that electric light, projected from individual to nation to continent and beyond.

"International consciousness" is a condition toward which Schwartz consistently aspired in his own writing. He picks up the idea again in an October 1940 letter to his friend, Robert Hivnor, this time using it in relation to his writing of *Genesis* and referring not just to an ideological position but also to a formal consideration. "My main problem right along," he explains,

> has been to get the kind of structure which would make reasonable and articulate and symmetrical the kind of international consciousness which keeps growing bigger all the time in the world—in such strange plants as the radio and the newspaper—and which is the only point of view from which I can see my subject.[12]

What exactly is this "kind of international consciousness?" In its simplest sense, it amounts to an awareness of one's position in the world, in relation to others, in relation to both temporally and physically distant events, and in relation to surroundings both immediate and remote. Schwartz repeatedly stresses that it is impossible for anyone—not just poets—to overlook the internationality of modern experience, but this is not the same as being internationally "conscious," which for Schwartz also involves a hard-earned ability to find universal principles in particular events. In his essay, "Delmore Schwartz's Strange Times," Jim Keller recognizes Schwartz 's aspiration toward "international consciousness" but describes it in slightly different terms when he argues that Schwartz, in *Genesis* in particular, "was guided by an epic sensibility to rewrite history within a bold new Eliotic structure, one that he increasingly despaired of ever finding." It is a sensibility that makes him strive to transform personal history "into epochal history"—or to transform the local into the international, the particular into the universal.[13]

The language Schwartz uses to describe "international consciousness" suggests, however, that transformation was less his intent than assimilation. Uncomfortable about admitting the tensions and difficulties that result when two or more national cultures intersect, his solution was to try to incorporate European culture—even though it may retain its specifically European qualities—into American culture. "Europe is the greatest thing *in* North America": playing upon both the concrete and the abstract senses of "greatest," the statement conflates a sense of physical or geographical conditions (most appositely, the fact that a majority of North America's population can claim some kind of European ancestry) with an evaluation of cultural importance that sees Europe as the source of all that is great in America but also as now subsidiary to America. Even the colloquial idiom—"the greatest thing"—usurps notions of European refinement, and often enough "Europe" seems to be simply synonymous for Schwartz with the Jewish cosmopolitan culture of his native New York City. All the same, the will to preserve a European heritage is greater than the will to change it, even if the means of preservation within another culture turns it, of necessity, into something new.

Attempting to "overcome the gulf between popular culture and advance guard culture" (*DS & JL Letters*, 214) and attempting to recast personal history within an international framework, are different facets of the same project of assimilation. To counter the threat posed by popular culture, the avant-garde can simply absorb it, as Joyce had demonstrated in *Ulysses*, as Eliot had shown in *The Waste Land* by incorporating jazz motifs and the song about Mrs. Porter and her daughter, and as Schwartz himself does in his frequent exploitation of cinematic techniques. And yet, paradoxically, in each of these cases, assimilation, even when successful, heightens the distinctions between the two entities to be combined. The contrast between popular song and "pure" poetry is intensified when one is used in the service of the other; self-consciousness is heightened when the individual recognizes his or her relation to a world that diminishes individual agency; and Europe and America come to seem all the more separate when one tries to merge them. It is for this reason that Schwartz's allusions to European works, and his depictions of "Old World" Jewish customs, often end up accentuating his modern American identity. The very premise of "international consciousness" would seem to unsettle the idea of a purely American poetry, and yet Schwartz's own engagements with European thought and writing also provided a standard against and alongside which he could establish his *national* consciousness.

Schwartz's commitment to internationality and his "infinite interest" in the American Dream, though interdependent, often jostle against each other uneasily. Europe and America, whatever Schwartz's claims about European culture infiltrating American culture, figure as polarities in his writing. Europe represents, on one hand, the apex of literary and artistic civilization, and on the other the backward and parochial traditions that the first generation of Jewish immigrants failed to leave behind. America, in contrast, represents modernity and cosmopolitanism, but also (with a few crucial exceptions) a cultural morass. This view is only heightened by Schwartz's refusal to look, except occasionally, much beyond New York City. His "international consciousness" might more accurately be regarded as a transatlantic consciousness, and his national consciousness an East Coast consciousness (each accentuated by his "Atlantic" self-identification). The various contradictions arising between his ideology and his practice, and even within the ideology itself, account for Schwartz's difficulties in finding "the right structure" within which to express his "international consciousness." How could an internationally conscious poet, for example, allow a single point of view—albeit one that purports to be all-encompassing—block out other points of view that might have their own validity? Most pressingly, how might being "internationally conscious" be contingent upon the experience of the possibly biased or prejudiced individual whose particular perceptions must inevitably color the nature of his or her consciousness? Such problems—many of them inherited from the modernist mentors he so ambivalently admired—animate Schwartz's work as much as they hinder it. His oeuvre can be read as an ongoing attempt to work them through.

"International Heroes": Eliot, Yeats, Pound, and Joyce

The question of how a poet might express universal themes while also addressing actual and localized experiences dominates Schwartz's critical essays throughout his career. In an early piece, written soon after Yeats's death, Schwartz maintains that Yeats became a European (as opposed to merely Anglo-Irish) poet despite himself. Yeats's young poetry, for Schwartz, is all subjectivity and aestheticism. As he became more involved in political and social affairs, Yeats was increasingly forced to confront the difficulty of sustaining such an attitude, but he did not give it up. "The substance of the later poetry is, then," says Schwartz, "the *emotion* of the Poet as Poet (in the romantic sense) when faced with modern times, when forced to exist and to practice his art in the circumstances of the last forty years."[14] In a further essay Schwartz argues that neither Yeats's attempts to write "sub specie aeternitatis," nor his supposedly localized political poetry, can conceal the wider influence of European history upon his writing: "as Yeats follows what interests him, in his poems and in his autobiographies, he is following, in his own way, the effect of Europe upon his own life."[15] The change in Yeats's style, far from just having a personal or even political cause, is attributable to "the character and changes in European civilization"; and this is also the source of the transformation from "the pre-Raphaelites to Picasso, from Debussy to Stravinsky, from Swinburne, Symons and Dowson, to the Imagists, Pound and Eliot" ("An Unwritten Book," 86). This is such a complex shift, Schwartz explains, that it can perhaps only be understood "from an angel's point of view" (85)—the all-encompassing point of view toward which "international consciousness" must always aspire, even if it cannot be attained.

The most important aspect of this, for Schwartz, is that "the history" about which Yeats writes "has become poetry in that the particular event signifies a typical kind of event" (88). To write atemporally, without a foundation in actual experience, is to deny poetry any kind of social import and to risk excessive abstraction. Schwartz requires poetry to present either a particular truth from which universal truths can be drawn, or a universal truth that can illuminate each particular truth. Schwartz's own poetry, at its best, makes the move from particular incident to worldwide general principle seem inevitable. On other occasions, however, as Helen Vendler has remarked, there is too conspicuous a strain, and either the local detail is sacrificed in the service of a generalization or the universal law, drawn from too minor an occurrence, seems preposterous.[16]

Schwartz accepts that "international consciousness" cannot always compensate for a lack of local consciousness; or rather, he implies that it should ideally *incorporate* local consciousness. American critics are likely to misconstrue the political connotations of Yeats's poetry, he suggests, because they can at best "understand, knowing that [they] cannot feel, what names like Parnell, O'Leary, Pearse and Connally [*sic*] mean to the Irish nationalists." If this is problematic, however, Schwartz is also alert to how difficult it would be for an Irish critic to write an unprejudiced critique of Yeats without being blinkered by "many native feelings about Ireland" ("An Unwritten Book," 88). Some degree of critical distance may be advantageous insofar as it allows one to take a wider perspective and to limit bias, or at least to admit the ways in which one's individual perspective might be distorted.[17]

Much as he admired Yeats, Schwartz's exemplary international poet was Eliot. Eliot's principles provided Schwartz with the justification not just for attempting to assimilate a European literary tradition into an American one, but also for attempting to assimilate (despite Eliot's caveats about personality in poetry) the whole of history into one's individual experience. "Eliot's work is important," Schwartz argues, "in relation to the fact that experience has become international":

> We are able to understand the character of our lives only when we are aware of all history, of the philosophy of history, of primitive peoples, and the Russian Revolution, of ancient Egypt and the unconscious mind.[18]

This position incorporates Eliot's own famous advocacy of "the historical sense," which "involves a perception, not only of the pastness of the past, but of its presence" and which

> compels a man to write not merely with his own generation in his bones, but with a feeling that the whole of the literature of Europe from Homer

and within it the whole of the literature of his own country has a simultaneous existence and composes a simultaneous order.[19]

Both views endorse a principle of relativity, a recognition that nothing has meaning in isolation and that whatever meaning a work of literature, or a person's life, might have becomes unclear if it is removed from wider historical or cultural contexts. Schwartz differs from Eliot only in the emphasis that he gives to social history: the Russian Revolution and advances in psychology matter to him as much as the canon of Western literature (and perhaps matter to Eliot, Schwartz seems to be suggesting, more than Eliot himself admits). It is a small but crucial divergence, symptomatic of the ways in which the New York intellectuals managed to promote, despite their apparent incompatibility, both Marxist criticism and modernist literature.

Like Schwartz's other chief departure from Eliotic doctrine—his refocusing of attention onto the individual as the one who perceives, and whose life is conditioned by, the international—the further broadening of focus is an attempted extension of Eliot's principles as much as it is a refutation. And yet, in his unpublished critical study of Eliot, drafted in the early 1940s, Schwartz admits to finding Eliot's own terms too broad. Addressing the elder poet's belief that every new poem modifies every previous poem, Schwartz quibbles that "by the same argument, every event would change the character of all previous events: but an explosion in the Milky Way or a herdsman who bites his nails in Thibet [*sic*] does not really alter universal history."[20] Or, rather, they do so in such distant and minute ways that the effects are imperceptible. A soon-abandoned poetic draft further admits to the circumscription of "international consciousness":

You can, although you do not know Swahili,
Go to the grave serene and not depressed;
You will not feel that at life's feast you missed
The real McCoy. The same for Uruguay—
However, Abraham should be well known[21]

If the terms "international" and "universal" imply a lack of differentiation, Schwartz still believes in a hierarchy: Hebraic scripture matters to him more than minority African or South American cultures, if only because it did more to shape Western civilization than they did. Similarly, although the Russian Revolution, ancient Egypt, and an increased understanding of the unconscious mind very distinctly affected the course of "all history," their importance to Schwartz is as personal as it is representative. "International consciousness" is, and cannot help but be, selective.

These instances suggest that Schwartz was less resolved on the topic than his more confident assertions would suggest. On a couple of points, however, he remains convinced. One is that the international perspective is distinctively modern, vastly accentuated in an era of travel, media, increased psychological insight, and the kinds of technological advance (like the radio) that make time and distance seem to contract. "The reader of T. S. Eliot," Schwartz notes, "by turning the dials of his radio can hear the capitals of the world, London, Vienna, Athens, Alexandria, Jerusalem" ("T. S. Eliot as the International Hero," 120). Much earlier readers, interested though they may also have been in events in these cities, could not have had such direct or immediate access to them. Meanwhile, Joyce, no less an "international hero" than Eliot, read the New York *Herald Tribune* while in Paris and Zurich, and owned a short wave radio. This explains, Schwartz argues, how echoes of American radio comedy and Yiddish humor make their way into *Finnegans Wake*, a book which

> exhibits in the smallest detail and in the entire scope of the work the internationality of the modern poet, his involvement in all history, and his consciousness of the impingement of any foreign language from Hebrew to Esperanto upon the poet's use of the English language.[22]

Such a "clear and explicit consciousness of the international span of experience, and a pan-historical sense of culture, art, and literature" had become commonplace in writing, Schwartz argued in a 1958 lecture, even though it "did not and indeed could not exist in the past."[23]

Schwartz is also consistent in maintaining that a heightened sense of internationality coincides with feelings of homelessness and alienation. The international poet, he argues, must be "cosmopolitan and expatriated": "To be international is to be a citizen of the world and thus a citizen of no particular city" ("T. S. Eliot as the International Hero," 122, 127). It is to recognize one's individual insignificance, isolation, and status as an exile. Such a view affirms what Stephen Hahn has described as "the paradox that the modern self participates most in the collective life of the time through its isolation."[24] For the international poet, detachment from society and nation makes it possible to comment impartially, to observe the world through a wide-angle lens. But it also means that the lyric detachment Schwartz criticizes in early Yeats becomes an attractive refuge: the poet risks introversion. Unable to conceive of the world except from his own unique perspective, he risks imposing too subjective an interpretation onto history and society. This is one of the problems that Schwartz finds in Pound's *Cantos*. At their best, he notes in a late essay, they create

> the sense that all history is relevant to any moment of history, and the profound belief that the entire past, at any moment and in any place, is capable of illuminating the present and the whole nature of historical experience.[25]

At their weakest, however, the *Cantos* too often read, Schwartz argues, like "Pound's discursive monologue about his own *personal* experience of history," and it is a failing that he appeared never to have asked himself "what would have happened to Western civilization, America, modern literature and his own poetry, if Germany had won the Second World War" ("Ezra Pound and History," 113, Schwartz's emphasis). Aside from the issue of Pound's anti-Semitism (to be discussed shortly), Schwartz is accusing Pound of an abnegation of social responsibility.

"The Isolation of Modern Poetry"

One of the reasons Schwartz esteems "international consciousness" so highly is that it suggests how a poet might resume his role as a spokesman for society in an era when the arts have found themselves increasingly "out of key" with communal values.[26] "Some poets are fortunate," he remarks in his note "To the Reader" at the beginning of *Genesis*:

> They live in an age when their beliefs and values are embodied in great institutions and in the way of life of many human beings. These authors do not have to bring in their beliefs and values from the outside; they have only to examine their experience with love in order to find particular beings and actions which are significant of their beliefs and values. (*G*, vii)

Although he goes on to suggest that perhaps only the Gospel writers ever enjoyed this advantage to the utmost, Schwartz emphasizes that the poet in 1943, writing at "a time of much variety of belief" (viii), is especially unlikely to find his convictions shared by his readers. It is a more somber assessment of the same modernist conundrum that W. H. Auden contrasts, in "Letter to Lord Byron," with the patron-sponsored literature of the Augustan Age when "Each poet knew for whom he had to write, / Because their life was still the same as his."[27] In the early twentieth century, however, Schwartz laments that "no author can assume a community of ideas and values between himself and his audience" (*G*, viii). No poet can wholly overcome his separation from the rest of society, and this is a situation that he must either embrace—by writing solely for himself, with no regard for an audience—or attempt to overcome—by trying to address society more broadly, but at the possible risk of his aesthetic integrity.

For Schwartz, the "isolation" of modern poetry, rather than "its difficulty, its famous obscurity," was its most salient characteristic.[28] "The modern poet," he suggests, "has been very much affected by the condition and the circumstance that he has been separated from the whole life of society" ("The Isolation of Modern Poetry," 5). This separation takes a number of forms. One is

> a break between intellect and sensibility; the intellect finds unreasonable what the sensibility and the imagination cannot help but accept because of centuries of imagining and feeling in terms of definite images of the world. (5)

Of equal, if not greater, importance is the fact that the modern poet has been "separated by poetry from the rest of society," a consequence, Schwartz argues, of "the whole way of life of modern society" (5). It is not so much the poet who is isolated, as "poetry, culture, sensibility, [and] imagination" (7) themselves. One of the reasons Schwartz idealized Europe so greatly, and the reason he supposes James and Eliot chose to live there, is his belief that "the divorce between culture and the rest of life, although it had begun, had by no means reached the point which was unavoidable in America" (8). Europe could boast a relative resistance to modernization and the demands of a mass audience.

The break between intellect and sensibility to which Schwartz refers evokes Eliot's discussion of the "dissociation of sensibility" in "The Metaphysical Poets." Schwartz refutes Eliot's view in that essay that modern(ist) poetry must necessarily be difficult, since it reflects the "great variety and complexity" of modern civilization. This, Schwartz insists, is superficial, because

> the complexity of modern life, the disorder of the traffic on a business street or the variety of reference in the daily newspaper is far from being the same thing as the difficulties of syntax, tone, diction, metaphor, and allusion which face the reader in the modern poem. ("The Isolation of Modern Poetry," 4)

One of the problems for the modern poet, he maintains, is that there is no such "simple causal relationship" between the life around him and the poetry that he writes (4). Despite this quarrel, Schwartz is indebted to "The

Metaphysical Poets" when he discusses sensibility.[29] The central point of Eliot's essay is that for poets such as Donne, Marvell, Herbert, Vaughan and Crashaw, thought and feeling were not distinct: "their mode of feeling was directly and freshly altered by their reading and thought."[30] This is not true, in general, of Romantic and Victorian poets. "Tennyson and Browning are poets, and they think," Eliot remarks, "but they do not feel their thought as immediately as the odour of a rose. A thought to Donne was an experience; it modified his sensibility" ("The Metaphysical Poets," 287). Schwartz does not take issue with any of this, but whereas Eliot regarded the "dissociation of sensibility" principally as a question of style, attributing what he regarded as the disjunction between increasingly refined language and increasingly crude feeling in English poetry to the domineering influence of Milton and Dryden, Schwartz's discussion is, once again, more alert to broader historical factors. The break between intellect and sensibility, Schwartz argues, begins with "the gradual destruction of...the traditional world picture of Western culture" ("The Isolation of Modern Poetry," 5) presented by the Bible; by the time of Blake, this world picture and the one provided by the physical sciences are in overt conflict, and the rift has continued to widen since.

Schwartz is particularly conscious of how late-nineteenth-century poets, writing at a time when evolutionary theory was challenging the most fundamental principles of Christian doctrine and exposing the insignificance of the individual in an infinite universe, must have endured this conflict between "the very images which [they] viewed as the world, and the evolving and blank and empty universe of nineteenth century science" ("The Isolation of Modern Poetry," 6). In an earlier essay, he had considered Hardy as a poet whose sensibility was Christian but whose intellect made it impossible for him to accept the Christian belief he had inherited. Hardy holds the old and new views of life "in a dialectical tension," Schwartz argues, and his most successful poems convey this tension as a lived experience.[31] A poet such as Yeats, meanwhile, on learning of the immensity of the universe, must have "felt a fundamental incongruity between his own sense of the importance of human lives and their physical smallness in the universe"—and it was in an attempt to "restore dignity to both man and the universe," Schwartz maintains, that Yeats occupied himself for so long with theosophy and what Schwartz misleadingly describes as "black magic" ("The Isolation of Modern Poetry," 6). These pursuits enabled him to ignore the empirical findings of modern science, which were too bleak to be of use to him as a poet.

Given Schwartz's own fascination with the illusory lure of the American Dream, the emphasis he gives here to images and to the difficulty of imagining a universe so starkly at odds with the inherited images of Christianity assumes particular importance. The poet, who deals in images and who "must see," cannot help but regard his condition in visual terms, seeing more keenly than the philosopher and theologian the incongruity between "the importance man attributes to himself and his smallness against the background of the physical world of nineteenth century science" (6). The long-established and "definite" images of the world that humanity has become accustomed to seeing are not easily eradicated, even when proven to be inaccurate. It is perhaps harder to imagine the known and uncertain reality than the more hopeful, but illusory, world picture that had previously been accepted. As Schwartz puts it in "Rimbaud in Our Time,"

> Man cannot live without an interpretation of the whole of life which will tell him or seem to tell him what is good, what is right, what is important, and which will relate nature, man, man's economy, and man's art, so that they are not opposed in a conflict in which one or the other is abused and denied.[32]

However, no such interpretation can ever be definitive and, consequently, whatever one believes is likely to be at odds with life as one actually experiences it. There is a disparity between dream and actuality, between the images we view "as the world" ("The Isolation of Modern Poetry," 6) and the world itself. The modern poet confronts an equivalent disparity: he depends upon images and dreams to define his sense of himself, even though his society may not sanction them. Therefore he must try to find alternative images to those that have become discredited.

Schwartz's view of Yeats in "The Isolation of Modern Poetry" is informed by Edmund Wilson's discussion of the poet in *Axel's Castle*, his 1931 study of literary modernism's origins in French symbolist poetry. In a 1942 overview of Wilson's work, Schwartz disputes the elder critic's presentation of Yeats as a late symbolist.[33] However, his own attitude echoes Wilson's certainty that Yeats was "conscious from the start of an antagonism between the actual world of industry, politics and science, on the one hand, and the imaginative poetic life on the other"—an antagonism that the symbolists had been the first to feel so acutely.[34] In his chapter on Yeats, Wilson asks, "What *is* the consequence of living for beauty…, of cultivating the imagination, the enjoyment of aesthetic sensations, as a supreme end in itself?"[35] "The Isolation of Modern Poetry" is Schwartz's answer to that question: the consequence is that the modern poet distances himself from the actual world (although his work may still criticize it), and thus risks, in turn, being entirely ignored by it.

The poet also became isolated, Schwartz argues, because there was no place for cultivated man in an increasingly industrialized society and, as a result, culture "fed upon itself" and was forced to create "its own autono-mous satisfactions, removing itself further all the time from any essential part in the organic life of society" ("The Isolation of Modern Poetry," 7). Ultimately, he suggests, "the modern poet has had nothing to do, no serious activity other than the cultivation of his own sensibility" (10). Schwartz's use of the word "cultivation" (which again picks up on Wilson) alerts us to the element of artifice involved in this process, and he associates the ten-dency with the aestheticism of Walter Pater and his doctrine of Art for Art's Sake—"a doctrine which is meaningful only when viewed in the context [of]...a society which had no use and no need for Art, other than as a super-fluous amusement or decoration" (9).[36] The need to "cultivate" sensibility also reinforces Eliot's view that sensibility had become increasingly "dissoci-ated": lacking any instinctive sensitivity to kinds of feeling, or to art, modern poets had to teach themselves by immersing themselves in other poetry and works of art, thereby distancing themselves further from society in general.

One consequence of poets cultivating their own sensibilities rather than engaging with society is "a failure or an absence of narrative or dramatic writing in verse": these forms "require a grasp of the lives of other men, and it is precisely these lives...that are outside the orbit of poetic style and poetic sensibility" ("The Isolation of Modern Poetry," 8, 11). The isolated poet, Schwartz contends, "can only write lyric poetry" (11). The obscurity of mod-ern poetry (which, despite disputing it as a defining characteristic, Schwartz does not deny) also arises from the poet's cultivation of his own sensibility. This causes his subject, method, and especially language to become "more unique and special" (11). Although Schwartz, as Atlas has noted, manages to critique "the whole enterprise of Modernism" here, he also makes clear that such increased introspection and specialization have not been wholly nega-tive.[37] Despite its consequences for narrative and dramatic verse, and for the poet himself in relation to his society, the isolation of the poet in the mod-ern period—"the age which begins with Baudelaire"—"increased the uses and powers of languages in the most amazing and most valuable directions" (12). Nonetheless, Schwartz concludes his essay by conceding that isolation "haunts" modern poetry and that it is a state from which many poets "have been trying to escape" (13).

What could the poet in 1941 do about such a heritage of isolation? Wilson, a decade earlier, offers two possibilities. One is to follow the way of Axel (the eponymous protagonist of the dramatic poem by Villiers de l'Isle-Adam) and remain isolated—to shut oneself up "in one's private world, cul-tivating one's private fantasies" and "ultimately mistaking one's chimeras for realities."[38] The other alternative is to choose the way of Rimbaud and to try "to leave the twentieth century behind—to find the good life in some country where modern manufacturing methods and modern democratic institutions do not present any problems to the artist because they haven't yet arrived" (Wilson, *Axel's Castle,* 227). Although this seems, initially, a more international, socially engaged position, it, too, is isolating—and Rimbaud entirely forsook literature soon after pursuing this aim. Wilson concludes that neither course is wholly viable, suggesting instead that "we may see Naturalism and Symbolism combine to provide us with a vision of human life and its universe, richer, more subtle, more complex and more complete than any man has yet known" (232). Both courses, Axel's and Rimbaud's, hold some appeal for Schwartz, and his work is often concerned with how to reconcile such contrary impulses. Equally, a desire to unite Naturalism and Symbolism is apparent in his simultaneous attraction to narrative and to the purely aesthetic. However, he more commonly sets these tendencies against each other, holding them in equilibrium, than he actively combines them.

The Figure of the Jew

Toward the end of "The Isolation of Modern Poetry," Schwartz cites Baudelaire's prose poem "The Stranger," in which the stranger of the title rejects family, friends, country, and gold, proclaiming instead his love of Beauty and the clouds. Schwartz takes this as typifying the deepest feelings of the modern poet.

> He does feel that he is a stranger, an alien, an outsider; he finds himself without a father or mother, or he is separated from them by the opposition between his values as an artist and their values as respectable members of modern society. ("The Isolation of Modern Poetry," 9)

Given Schwartz's position here, and throughout the essay, it follows that whenever he writes about alienation from family, homeland, or lovers, he also has in mind the role of the poet in the early to mid-twentieth century.

Also implicit—and sometimes explicit—is an identification of the immigrant Jew with the unaccepted artist. Lacking a nation of their own until 1948, the Jews were the most "cosmopolitan and expatriated" of people, like Schwartz's ideal international poet ("T. S. Eliot as the International Hero," 122). In a 1951 essay on "The Vocation of the Poet," in which he considers why Joyce may have identified himself with Jews in *Ulysses* and *Finnegans Wake,* Schwartz spells out the connection:

> The Jew is at once alienated and indestructible, he is an exile from his own country and an exile even from himself, yet he survives the annihilating

fury of history. In the unpredictable and fearful future that awaits civilization, the poet must prepare to be alienated and indestructible.[39]

There is a necessarily veiled reference to the Holocaust here: to make it more direct would render the comparison preposterous. The suffering of the poet, real enough perhaps, is not proportionate to the torture undergone in the concentration camps.

Similarly, when Schwartz writes of the international poet as a citizen of no city, though he can point to several instances of artistic expatriation, he never approaches the plight of those actually stateless citizens about whom Hannah Arendt wrote in the 1950s. Alienation seems to be an ideological position for him as much as it is a reality.

All the same, Schwartz certainly did endure "the antagonism of the stranger" (G, 90) himself, notably at Harvard in the 1940s where he once received a note from a student saying "FUCK THE JEWS."[40] In "Under Forty: A Symposium on American Literature and the Younger Generation of American Jews," published in the *Contemporary Jewish Record* in February 1944, Schwartz discusses how his Judaism "became available" to him as a "central symbol" of the "alienation, bias, point of view, and certain other characteristics which are the peculiar marks of modern life."[41] He suggests, as Benjamin Schreier has elucidated, that it was only his increasing experience of anti-Semitism—as opposed to social exclusion for reasons unrelated to race, a far more general experience of alienation with which Schwartz was already familiar—that made his Jewish identity in any way distinctive for him. For this reason, Schreier explains, "Alienation alone will not suffice as a proxy for Jewish identity; the historically specific intervention of a gentile seems to be necessary."[42] Be this as it may, the formula *can* work the other way and Schwartz often makes Jewish identity emblematic of both the modern poet's alienation and of alienation more generally.

Schwartz is only one of many poets—Jewish American or not—to have insisted upon the relation between artist and wandering Jew. More recently, John Hollander, for example, has stated that "every true poet is in a kind of diaspora in his own language"—a comparison which Maeera Y. Schreiber has argued "potentially leads to the problematic erasure of the specificity of Jewish poetic practice, as the Jew becomes but a trope for the universalized poet."[43] Certainly the *idea* of the Jew seems to have resonated with Schwartz at least as much as the actual Jewish traditions into which he had been born. This concords with Berryman's revelation, in his story "The Imaginary Jew," that imaginary Jew and real Jew are one and the same: Jewishness, in Bryan Cheyette's phrase, is a "construction," a state of mind as much as an identifiable racial or religious distinction. This is as true for the person who is born Jewish as for the person who identifies him or herself with the Jews. When, in *Genesis*, for example, the protagonist, Hershey Green, recounts how his circumcision made him "even unto coitus fully a member of the people chosen for wandering and alienation" (*G*, 69), he is constructing an identity, imposing an interpretation onto a ritual that God commanded *before* the Exodus and using this to account for his uneasiness about sex. Hershey is also nostalgic for a time before his Jewish identity had been constructed, wishing he could regain a pre-Third-Reich innocence when he did not know that to be a Jew was to be an outsider or even realize that Jews and Germans were different (90).

Schwartz may have felt alienated from American society on account of being a Jew, but he felt just as acutely alienated from his own heritage. He also felt that being a poet made him as much of a stranger as being Jewish. Because of this, the anti-Semitic attitudes sometimes expressed by Pound and Eliot, two of the poets he most admired, troubled him even more than they did other readers. Schwartz was so affronted by Pound's claim, in *Introduction to Kulcher*, that "race prejudice is red herring" that he wrote to him and tendered his "resignation" as his disciple. "A race cannot commit a moral act," he insisted.

> Only an individual can be moral or immoral. No generalization from a sum of particulars is possible, which will render a moral judgment. In a court of law, the criminal is always one individual, and when he is condemned, his whole family is not, qua family, condemned. This is not to deny, however, that there are such entities as races. (*Letters*, 68)

There is courage in such a belief in individual agency, an agency that Schwartz himself exercises here by refusing to overlook the misguided convictions of a poet who had been one of his heroes. The rebuke also finds Schwartz checking his own instinct toward generalization and holding off his obsessive self-consciousness regarding those traits he had inherited from his family. It is a mark of Schwartz's perhaps excessive generosity as a critic that he later suggests that although some passages of the *Cantos* show that Pound is, "at times, anti-Semitic, he is also, at other times, philo-Semitic."[44]

Eliot's hostile references to Jews throughout *Poems 1920*, and especially in "The Idea of a Christian Society," discomfited Schwartz even more than Pound's. That Eliot should argue, "in the spring when Hitler came to power in Germany," that "a large number of free-thinking Jews would be undesirable" in an ideal society creates a particularly unfavorable impression.[45]

Nonetheless, Schwartz did not reject Eliot as he had rejected Pound. In the drafts of his unpublished critical book on Eliot, written in the early 1940s, Schwartz tentatively titles one chapter "The Anti-Semitic Theme" and underlines his belief that race prejudice of any kind is "an unspeakable abomination."[46] All the same, in analyzing how Eliot's views nuance his literary output, Schwartz is more apologist than prosecutor. Racial prejudice is "one of the barriers to understanding Eliot," he argues, but the prejudice cannot be discounted, and neither can it be used to damn the whole oeuvre.[47] However distasteful and immoral the attitude may be, "from the point of view of the criticism of poetry, we must recognize the poet is expressing a genuine and significant feeling."[48] Furthermore, this feeling is consistent with Eliot's eventual espousal of Anglo-Catholic royalism. Eliot's stance is therefore quite different to dismissing all race prejudice as "red herring": race prejudice is of utmost importance to him even though it leads him toward views that are repugnant.

Anthony Julius has stated outright that Eliot's poems "insult Jews" and that "to ignore these insults is to misread the poems."[49] Julius criticizes Schwartz for not attacking Eliot's anti-Semitism in any of his published essays, despite commenting upon it privately at a time when it had not yet been widely discussed.[50] Schwartz did not ignore the insults, but he never goes further in his unfinished book than to compare the way Eliot's anti-Semitism affects his poetry to a squint. "If one squints, it is inevitable that one sees certain things in a given way," Schwartz argues. Mann, Joyce, and Proust, whose circumstances were very different to Eliot's, were able to present Jews in a much more sympathetic light.

> Since Proust was Jewish himself, since Joyce was Irish, and suffered his own kind of alienation, and since Mann suffered—and celebrated the alienation of the artist, there is a sympathy to be remarked which we cannot expect of James and Eliot; and this sympathy too must be considered as a possible squint and distortion.[51]

A decade later, Schwartz's attitude had hardened. In a 1954 letter to Karl Shapiro, he scoffs at his naïve belief, as a young man, that it was "a wonderful advantage" for a poet "to be a Jew and have a Jewish name" (*Letters*, 292) (as he had claimed in the "Under Forty" symposium), wondering how he ever managed to overlook the anti-Jewish sentiment in Eliot's poetry. More euphemistically, but perhaps more tellingly, he wrote to Van Wyck Brooks in 1952 and admitted that, like Brooks, he now believed the leading social attitudes in the work of Eliot and James to be "vicious and destructive." Again maintaining that "one cannot condemn a literary work because some of its elements are reactionary and despairing," Schwartz nonetheless concedes

> [I] perceived how much more fruitful as a creative writer I might have been, had I not suffered from too uncritical an admiration of Eliot in particular. For personal reasons which will be obvious to you as well as for principled ones, I think, no authors more than James and Eliot would be likely to create so many feelings of self-distrust and conflict in a person existing in my own social and literary situation.[52]

Why, even here, can Schwartz not spell out what those personal reasons are: his own malaise, as a Jew, at being unable to explain away such lines as "The rats are underneath the piles. / The Jew is underneath the lot" (Eliot, *CPP*, 41) in his idol's poems?

The reason is surely that to do so would cause Schwartz's whole infrastructure of "international consciousness" to collapse. How, given the connection made earlier between immigrant Jew and international poet, could he justify the exemplary international poet, Eliot, expressing views that were anti-Semitic? It is not enough to say—as Schwartz does—that even Marx, despite himself being Jewish, was also anti-Semitic in his criticisms of financiers.[53] That is a deflection of the question. Nor can the attitude be justified by noting its inevitability for someone concerned about the fate of "European civilization at a particular moment in time when social strata were being broken down and entered by outsiders."[54] And yet, Schwartz, knowing that Eliot, an American and therefore an outsider himself, had infiltrated those strata, comes close here to anticipating persuasive arguments by Maud Ellman and Bryan Cheyette that present Eliot's "extreme racialization of 'the Jew'" as arising from conflicts within his own psyche.[55]

"The Jew," Cheyette explains, had become an "ideal objective correlative for [a] lack of absolute knowledge." Whereas a writer such as Joyce was able to embrace such indeterminacy in his "greekjewish" hero Leopold Bloom, Eliot was intent upon maintaining distinctions between "Hebrew and Hellene" and establishing "a clear and unequivocal relationship with the European past." Eliot's "repressed fear of being Judaized," Cheyette argues, his determination to ward off a "shocking identification" with "the Jew" and a "fearful recognition" of "the Jew" within himself, prompts the denigrating presentations in *Poems 1920* in particular.[56] Ellman further advances the case by suggesting that "Eliot's distrust of Jews corresponds to his distrust of writing. Sooner or later, written words are destined to desert the place of their origination; like Jews, they refuse to remain in the place where they were born." Although Eliot's own poetry exploits this tendency—*The*

Waste Land, says Ellman, is "a textual diaspora"—Eliot, "by banishing free-thinking Jews from his utopia, was attempting to banish from himself the forces of displacement exemplified in both his life and his art."[57] Schwartz admired the nomadic errancy in Eliot's poetry; but the international poet himself craved fixity.

Schwartz's leniency in discussing the anti-Semitic strains of Eliot's poetry may have its own psychological basis. By emphasizing Eliot's international-ity, and thus his alienation, Schwartz brings Eliot's experience closer to his own. He creates a point of identification between himself and Eliot, bring-ing Eliot's achievement within closer reach. If one alienated poet can write such poems, why shouldn't another? As we shall see, Schwartz's relentless allusions to the elder poet, even when trying to resist adulation, are another means of achieving the same end. Although, later in his life, Schwartz was increasingly able to criticize Eliot, disliking much of *Four Quartets* and espe-cially *The Family Reunion*, and demoting the elder poet from "culture hero" to "literary dictator," he was never able to overcome his overcathexis to him. Perhaps, ultimately, a problem of choice was at stake. Schwartz had not cho-sen to be born Jewish, and often resented the fact that he had been, even though it provided him with "the hard identity felt in the bone" that is "the basis of the art of poetry" (*G*, 70). He had, however, consciously fashioned himself as a disciple of Eliot: to reject him would therefore be to reject his own decision to become a poet.

"A Bitter Farce"

A further obstacle to successfully attaining "international consciousness" is Schwartz's own ambivalence toward non-Jewish ethnic groups in America. The New York intellectuals in general took little interest in racial politics until at least the late 1950s, barely registering the contribution the Harlem Renaissance had made to modernism and cagily avoiding involvement with what would become the civil rights movement—partly because, in Harvey M. Teres's assessment, affirmative action "seemed to challenge the very uni-versalist, color-blind principles responsible for their own successful integra-tion into mainstream American life."[58] Howe, alluding to Schwartz on Eliot, recalls how the New York intellectuals "meant to declare themselves citizens of the world and, that succeeding, perhaps consider becoming writers of this country."[59] Many African Americans, however, did not want to be citizens of the world, which would mean giving up their own roots and adopting an indeterminate identity. They wanted to reassert an African heritage that American society had suppressed, to claim equal rights but not simply to be assimilated.

Schwartz's own unease in response to this distinction can be discerned, first, from an episode in his unpublished novel, *A Child's Universal History*, in which his protagonist, Bertholde Cannon (another of Schwartz's versions of himself), announces "that it was highly likely that at least one of his great-grandchildren would be a pickaninny."[60] This is presented as a progressive statement, an acceptance of "inter marriage" and racial mixing becoming the norm: from the perspective of "international consciousness," this, rather than being a racist attitude, would be something to celebrate, a stage toward entirely eradicating racial differences and one form of alienation. But the term "pickaninny" itself—along with "Creoles," used shortly afterward—emphatically reaffirms difference, not to mention a condescending attitude toward those who are black or of mixed race. In 1952, meanwhile, reviewing Ralph Ellison's *Invisible Man* for *Partisan Review*, Schwartz, though impressed by the novel, evades discussing its racial politics: "It is somehow dishonest or hypocritical or irreverent to speak of such books merely in the language of literary criticism."[61] Even though his own criticism generally had a more social or historicist bent than that of several New Critical contemporaries, he seems, at times, to have wished that literature should exist in a realm apart from real social problems and that the two should never intersect.

The story "A Bitter Farce," published in *The World Is a Wedding* in 1948, is Schwartz's most sustained consideration of race and immigrant status in mid-twentieth-century America. It resolves none of the contradictions that foxed Schwartz's attempts to declare an uncomplicated "international consciousness," but it puts them candidly and admits the polarities that come into play throughout Schwartz's oeuvre. The story recounts the encounters of Shenandoah Fish as he teaches composition to a class of navy students and a class of girls—as Schwartz himself had done—during the Second World War. Faced with expressions of anti-Semitism from his students, both direct and indirect, Fish reflects upon his Jewish heritage and attempts to explain (to himself as well as to his students) that if America's glory was a consequence of the diversity of its races, then this was also one of the reasons why so many of its citizens "feared that [they were] a stranger or [were] conscious of a fear of the stranger."[62] The cosmopolitan nature of life in America provokes social insecurity and worsens individual alienation.

"A Bitter Farce" also explores Fish's growing understanding that his interest in "the ways to use the powerful English language" ("A Bitter Farce," 108) cannot be separated from wider societal concerns. As a teacher of largely reluctant students, his position is similar to that of the modern poet in relation to an uncomprehending public.[63] Time and again he regrets allowing himself to be sidetracked from teaching about "choice of words, sentence structure, and clear thought" (113) into discussions about the "topics of the day" (104). But he comes to accept, distinguishing himself from the kind of poet who is only concerned with cultivating his own sensibility, that "language [is] involved in all things" (108): the poet-teacher's responsibility is to show how it might be used directly and frankly. Fish, however, indulges in mere "verbalism—ratiocination..., just playing a game with facts and words" (119), and this, as much as his uneasiness about his Jewish heritage, is a source of his anxiety and frustration at the end.

Fish's sense of his own racial identity is complicated when he is made to confront his uneasy views about black Americans. When, following the Detroit race riots, he is asked his view on "the Negro problem" (105), he is unable to give a direct answer. The solution that he does propose with regard to easing racial tension in the South would today seem inflammatory: "for the Negroes to depart from the South. Any other course would result in a resumption of the Civil War" (105). Fish's lack of empathy with black Americans can be evinced by his inability to consider the tensions in the South in anything other than theoretical and hypothetical terms. He does not, as one might expect, make any connection here between exiling black Americans from the South and the fate of his own Jewish ancestors. Perhaps such a connection would be impossible, given the very different circumstances under which a majority of black Americans and Jews came to America—one race brought to America from Africa unwillingly, as slaves, and the other, at a much later historical moment, coming in search of prosperity and a better life.

Fish goes on to propose that a region might be selected in which "a strict equality would be enforced," but almost immediately dismisses the idea, admitting that "equality cannot be dictated merely by signing a bill" (105). And to "enforce" equality would be self-defeating. By denying the possibility of such a "strict equality," Fish also undermines the principles on which America's independence had been declared over one hundred and fifty years previously. The race riots, Fish implies, provide just one example of the ways in which man's equality is anything but "self-evident." To believe that all men should be treated equally and to believe that they actually are equal are quite different beliefs. The distinction is the same as that between believing in the pursuit of happiness as a legal right and believing in the guarantee of happiness, as Schwartz points out in his essay on Hemingway ("The Fiction of Ernest Hemingway," 271). Behind Fish's comments is probably an acknowledgment that he, as a Jew, is not treated equally either.

The question of the black American's position in society remains in the background of Fish's later discussion about America's "universal" and "pan-human culture" (113), a discussion in which he is more personally invested because of his self-consciousness about being Jewish. This is heightened by an earlier discussion with a female student, Miss Lucy Eberhart, who suggests that even the best Jews are "demanding, grasping, almost unscrupulous about the way they get what they want" (111), and explains that for this reason she would prefer, hypothetically, to marry "a Chinaman...or a Negro" (110). When Fish is himself asked, earlier in the story, whether or not he would marry a black woman, he is evasive; and although Miss Eberhart's response is more simplistic it is perhaps also more honest. She is open about her prejudices, whereas Fish's uncertainty regarding his attitude to black Americans reveals a confrontation between his intellectual, ethical position—that all men should be treated equally—and an instinctive distrust of those who are different, and who might therefore be competitors. Such prejudice, his own version of Eliot's "squint," is an inescapable part of his sensibility.

Fish's sensitivity about his racial identity is apparent in his response to Miss Eberhart's suggestion that the Chinese, America's allies in the War, tend to be friendly and intelligent (111). The history of postwar American-Chinese relations makes this view seem naïve, and Fish cannot resist pointing out that "on the Pacific Coast, the Chinese are disliked very much too, or were for a time, until the Exclusion Act was passed" (112). This is a complex statement, as it amounts to a simultaneous assertion of difference and of identification. For the oppressed Jew in the East, it may be consoling to know that there is a different race that is equally subject to prejudice in the West. By referring to the Johnson-Reed Act of 1924, Fish gestures toward how unaccommodating to immigrants of all races America had become during the interwar years, a fact that may account for the illiberal attitudes of some of his students. Between 1933 and 1941 tens of thousands of German Jews were refused immigration rights to the United States, evidence of the nation's blindness to the world situation at the time.[64] Fish does not discuss the consequences of this directly, but he is perhaps trying to suggest that the Jews suffered more on account of this law than the Chinese.

The question of Jewish affinity with other races occurs relatively rarely in Schwartz's writing, but whenever it does, such a consciousness of a similarity of situation but difference in almost every other respect is also present. In *Genesis*, when Hershey is taunted for being a Jew, it is his "colored maid" (*G*, 90) who drives away his tormentors: she has perhaps suffered similarly before. Later, Hershey recalls how

Al Jolson sang for them of going to the sunny South, where the Negro, the enslaved peasant, and Dixie, the defeated nation,
    Furnished for the immigrant Jewish genius metaphors for his maternal emotion. (117)

Jolson, the first successful Jewish crooner in America, often performed in blackface, and was influential in introducing African American music to a white audience. There is nostalgia, even sentimentality, in this account, but what is most remarkable is that, listening to Jolson, Hershey empathizes with both the black slaves and with the Southerners defeated in the Civil War who would have owned them. Actual questions of nationality or ideology are less important to him than the fact of having been defeated or oppressed in one way or another.

The central episode in "A Bitter Farce" is a discussion of an assigned essay by Louis Adamic, entitled "Plymouth Rock and Ellis Island," on the immigrant in America. Adamic argues that "the hope of the world...was [in America] just because of [its] diversity of peoples," and claims that this made possible "a universal culture, a pan-human culture such as had never before existed on the globe." This, he says, is "the American Dream and the American Tradition" ("A Bitter Farce," 113). Fish does not contradict this, but feels compelled to add that

> if America has always been the land of liberty, it has also been the land of the witch-hunt and the lynching party, the land of persecution and the land where everyone feared that he was a stranger or was conscious of a fear of the stranger. (114)

The race riots would not occur if America "were not also the land of liberty" (114), because democracy, even if it is the fairest method of government, will always favor the majority and underrepresent minorities. The rhetoric of the American Constitution, however, does not distinguish between minorities and the majority: life, liberty, and the pursuit of happiness are the right of all, meaning that those to whom they are denied have genuine grounds for protest. The problem that most ruffles Schwartz, both here and elsewhere, is that the kind of democratic and capitalist society upon which the American Dream is based must necessarily be competitive. Such a society allows for the possibility of liberty and success, but, realistically, there will always be those whose possibility is greater and those whose possibility is lesser. The ideal of a universal "pan-human" culture is in fact at odds with the dream of individual success because success can only be measured in relation to others. Schwartz is most explicit about the dilemma in his essay on Hemingway and the American Dream, pointing out that

> a society committed to the American Dream is one which creates perpetual social mobility but also one in which the individual must suffer

perpetual insecurity of status as the price of being free of fixed status. ("The Fiction of Ernest Hemingway," 273)

Not all individuals can be equally successful or accepted, and, the fact that everyone has the opportunity to succeed means that they must also accept that they might fail.

The discussion of Adamic's essay prompts one of Fish's students, an Irishman (and thus of immigrant stock himself) named Murphy, to declare that a lot of Jews are not "all right" ("A Bitter Farce," 115). Fish points out to Murphy, a Catholic, that the Jews have been "a commercial people...because that is all they were permitted to be by the decree of the Catholic Church"; and when Murphy goes on to suggest that the Jews are nonetheless "traitors by inheritance" (116), Fish's response is an assertion that no moral decision can be predetermined by one's nationality or by one's parents. "Can a moral act be inherited?" he asks. "Can anyone be condemned to death as a murderer because his father is a murderer?" (117). Confident though these rhetorical questions sound, they in fact betray Fish's unease about those aspects of his own character that are inherited—not so much, perhaps, the fact of being Jewish, as the fact that so much of his character is determined simply by who his parents are and when and where he was born.

There is greater conviction in Fish's argument as he goes on, putting the case in a tone similar to Schwartz's "resignation" letter to Pound:

Even if we grant that there are inherited patterns of behaviour, like inherited diseases and inherited features, no one can be sure in advance that any person, starting from the moment of his birth, is bound to have a certain kind of character... even if we grant a certain tendency to behave as one's parents, it is an abomination to condemn any man before he has committed a crime. And this is exactly what race prejudice does: it is a denial of the freedom of the will and of moral responsibility. (117)

Taken alongside the anxieties expressed elsewhere in Schwartz's oeuvre regarding the extent to which personality is conditioned by one's family, one's nationality, and unalterable events in the past, this is a strong statement that free will is in fact possible for everyone. And yet, the very existence of such freedom of the will admits the possibility of acting immorally or of attempting to deny the free will of others.

Despite Fish's refusal to attribute present-day characteristics to past occurrences or genes, he admits to his students that he takes pride, "but not personal pride" in his ancestors, who were "scholars, prophets and students of God when most of Europe worshipped sticks and stones" (118). This is clearly reasoned, but that he feels affronted by his students' attitudes is suggested by the barbed nature of some of his comments: "it is not your fault if your forebears were barbarians grovelling and groping about for peat or something" (118). Despite all that he has just said, he is impelled to mock his students' ancestors, and in this respect he appears to be as prejudiced as they are.

Fish goes on to explain that a great-grandmother of his was raped by a Mongolian and that he is therefore a "mongrel Mongol." He claims to be ashamed of this, even though his own earlier argument would imply that it is illogical to be ashamed of events in the past that he could never have altered. However, he adds, "it appears to be likely that the Mongolians are the ancestors of the American Indians, who are the only true natives of this country of ours, America" (119). Fish concludes from this that he is, in fact, "a hundred and fifty per cent American," turning the tables on the Irish Murphy and suggesting that he can "go back where [he] came from" if he doesn't like the class of people in America (119). Fish's use of the word "mongrel," with its offensive implications, has been used earlier in the story by Murphy, who says of the tensions between black and white in the South that "the thoroughbred dogs will always fight with the mongrels" (106). Fish makes it seem, however, that in being "mongrel," miscegenated, he is in fact purer in blood than any but true Native Americans. He is able to use his superior ability at manipulating language and arguing from every conceivable point of view to make an untenable state (being "a hundred and fifty per cent American") seem tenable. But when he returns home he remains subject to "innumerable anxiety feelings which had their source in events which had occurred for the past five thousand years" (121).

Implicitly, this is the source of the bitterness in the title: all of the ratiocination in front of his class has proved nothing and Fish remains just as uncertain about his own twentieth-century Jewish American identity as ever. He feels that he has managed to trivialize a topic of the utmost importance to him, doing little to engage directly with and thus challenge the prejudices of his students and, at the same time, little to improve their grammar. As in many of Schwartz's other works, evasion is a preoccupation of this story. Fish has evaded the draft, evaded frankness in his discussion of race, and evaded coming to any definite conclusions. While skepticism of all views, a predominant Schwartz trait, is arguably the most intelligent approach to such issues, Fish cannot help but be irritated that nothing has been resolved by the end.

Nonetheless, "A Bitter Farce" remains Schwartz's most direct confrontation of these questions, its tergiversations between the ideal of embracing a broad international outlook and the actuality of being hampered by one's own prejudices and grievances epitomizing a conflict that is ever-present in Schwartz's oeuvre. The chapters that follow probe how the conflict between "international consciousness" and "the isolation of modern poetry" is enacted in Schwartz's poetic works.

CHAPTER 2

In Dreams Begin Responsibilities: "The Egocentric Predicament"

Allusion and Imitation

In Dreams Begin Responsibilities begins with an allusion that positions Schwartz's contemporary American moment within the wider context of the history of Western civilization. The book's personal dedication, "For Gertrude," is followed by an epigraph, "*animula, vagula, blandula . . . ,*" the first words of a lyric composed by the Emperor Hadrian on his deathbed.[1] They gesture forward in the collection to Schwartz's poem "Prothalamion," which has as its own epigraph a translation of Hadrian's lyric by the Scottish poet Joseph Gordon MacLeod: "*little soul, little flirting, / little perverse one*" (*IDBR*, 105). They also evoke Eliot's "Animula," one of the *Ariel Poems* of 1927. Eliot's meditation on "The heavy burden of the growing soul" gives Schwartz the cue for a book replete with images of labor and carrying. The youthful soul in Eliot's poem "Confounds the actual and the fanciful"; as it grows, it stalls in the face of "The pain of living and the drug of dreams / . . . Fearing the warm reality, the offered good" (Eliot, *CPP*, 107).[2] This difficulty of accepting the disparity between dreams and actuality—and of knowing which is which—underlies Schwartz's entire corpus, but especially *In Dreams Begin Responsibilities*. The prompts for Schwartz's speculations on the topic are often personal and immediate, and include his family background and his uneasy hopes for his marriage. His simultaneous evocation of Eliot and Hadrian before the book proper has even begun creates a broad historical—and transatlantic—canvas against which to address these concerns.

The volume is divided into four parts. The title story is followed by the long "narrative poem," "Coriolanus and His Mother," which is in turn followed by a series of lyrics under the heading "Poems of Experiment and Imitation." This comprises two subsections, "The Repetitive Heart: Eleven Poems in Imitation of the Fugue Form" and "Twenty-four Poems." The collection concludes with "Dr. Bergen's Belief," "a play in prose and verse." While this is the weakest of the book's offerings, the title character's efforts to understand "what mediates between the divine and the human, the infinite and the finite" (*IDBR*, 165) reiterate the book's overall anxieties about how we can distinguish between phenomenological experience and objective reality, the worlds of the imagination and of the body.

The title, *In Dreams Begin Responsibilities*, itself establishes these dialectics. An alteration of "In dreams begins responsibility," the epigraph to Yeats's 1914 collection, *Responsibilities* (enigmatically attributed by Yeats only to an "Old Play"), it sends us back not just to 1914, but also to a past so distant that it cannot be defined by date.[3] This helps to make the volume appear timeless, but its contemporaneity is also advertised through self-conscious references to cinema, Freudian and Marxist criticism, and city life. Throughout, Schwartz has his speakers turn away from private reverie and toward direct involvement with the world in which they live, subordinating their seemingly atemporal lyric perceptions to a time-bound order over which they have no control. Their dreams, to employ Sharon Cameron's terminology, break on "touch[ing] the surface of reality."[4] This is not to discredit them. To a follower of Stevens—with his belief in poetry as "the supreme fiction"—to persist with a faith in the lyric as somehow *beyond* the ordinary temporal order, while conscious that this position is, in fact, untenable, might serve to validate, rather than undermine, what it can achieve. Put Cameron's way, "In order to maintain its status as fiction the lyric must assert its deviance from the strictures of reality and, at the same time, assert the unreliability of the adherence to the impossible."[5] It must convince us to suspend our disbelief, but not trick us into doing so unknowingly, which would wreck its very status as an artwork.

As both title and book, *In Dreams Begin Responsibilities* also supports Theodor Adorno's paradoxical understanding of the lyric as "essentially social in nature," the very solitude of its expression containing "the voice of humanity": "indeed," Adorno argues, "the loneliness of the lyric expression itself is latent in our individualistic and, ultimately, atomistic society—just as, by contrast, its general binding validity derives from the denseness of its individuation."[6] This is not to say that a resolution between the private and the social is always possible: the later collection, *Vaudeville for a Princess*, in particular, evidences the difficulty Schwartz sometimes had in reconciling the two. It does suggest, however, that sometimes dreaming may itself be responsible.

Read allegorically, *In Dreams Begin Responsibilities* presents the collision of the American Dream with the actuality of American life in all its social inequality. Recognizing the national impetus behind Schwartz's works brings into play another aspect of his titular allusion: the plural "responsibilities" calls up *both* the epigraph to Yeats's collection *and*, via its title, the collection as a whole, throughout which Yeats combines aesthetic craft and politically engaged cultural nationalism. *Responsibilities* regularly questions what the writer owes to his nation, its prefatory poem, for example, asking pardon of "old fathers" and concluding: "I have no child, I have nothing but a book, / Nothing but that to prove your blood and mine" (Yeats, 102). Although "nation" is a less stable category for Schwartz than it was for Yeats, and although Schwartz more commonly imitates his poetic ancestors than apostrophizes them, Yeats nonetheless provides a crucial transatlantic context for the interrogations of genealogy, fatherhood, and nationality that Schwartz's own volume undertakes.

This aspect of the allusion would have been attractive to the editors of *Partisan Review* when publishing the title story the previous year. "In Dreams Begin Responsibilities" appears there immediately after an "Editorial Statement" that declares the journal's "responsibility to the revolutionary movement in general" while disclaiming "obligation to any of its organized political expressions" and that criticizes the American Communist Party for "grow[ing] automatic in their political responses but increasingly less responsible in an artistic sense."[7] Aside from implicitly derogatory references to the Republican capitalists William Randolph Hearst and President William Howard Taft, "In Dreams Begin Responsibilities" makes no political comment. As such, it exemplifies the editors' claims that they will publish works solely on the grounds of literary quality, not ideology. But it is not hard, either, to see how the placement of Schwartz's story politicizes it. The title begins to sound propagandist: the dream of Marxism, the editors want their readers to deduce, has engendered responsibilities—among them, the responsibility to cultivate a literature worthy of Marx's socialist vision—that official bastions of Communism are ignoring, but that *Partisan Review* is not. *PR*'s need to prove itself culturally worthy of Marx's original ideals is no less urgent than Yeats's desire to justify himself to his "old fathers": implications from a quite different context are easily transposed.

Such political connotations are more muted within the context of Schwartz's collection. The literary heritage borne by the title makes it impossible to accept it simply as an axiomatic piece of social wisdom: it has also to be read in terms of the relationship it seeks to establish with another writer. Schwartz is the most allusive of poets, and allusion—the "calling into play of another writer's words"[8]—is one of his means of being "internationally conscious": it deflates the illusion that one's own poetry exists independent of a tradition. Within a book that begins with a son's reaction to watching his parents' engagement in a movie, charts numerous further parent-child relationships, and ends, in "Dr. Bergen's Belief," with a daughter's suicide, committed out of loyalty to her deluded father, allusion can be seen as Schwartz's way of paying homage to fathers that he has deliberately chosen as opposed to those that he has reluctantly inherited. It is a kind of bridge-building, a way of traversing the distance between one writer and another, but it declares the distance as well as the connection: Schwartz's incorporation of Yeats into an American context, and his breaking down of the collective "responsibility" into individual "responsibilities," transforms the phrase.

This being the case, Schwartz defeats one of the usual purposes of allusion—that the attentive reader should recognize it unaided—by overexplicitly admitting his looting of Yeats in the first of nine "Acknowledgments." These conjure up intimations of Eliot's "Notes on the Waste Land," but are half-hearted in comparison: "Several other quotations are at second hand also" (*IDBR*, 172), Schwartz explains, as if concerned that his readers might not otherwise discern his Eliotic practice, but also unwilling to spell out each instance. This suggests that he is not quite easy about his poetry's relation to that of his predecessors: is he straining too hard to declare his kinship while also trying to be independent?

At his best, Schwartz, in the spirit of Eliot's well-known dictum that "immature poets imitate; mature poets steal; bad poets deface what they take, and good poets make it into something better, or at least something different," is a genuine thief.[9] But, on the evidence of his note to his title, he is liable, no sooner than he has committed his crime, to hand himself in. He also takes implicit issue with Eliot (or deliberately plays the immature apprentice) by titling the third section of *In Dreams Begin Responsibilities* "Poems of Experiment and Imitation," beginning with "Eleven Poems in Imitation of the Fugue Form." Although Schwartz has in mind here the emulation of a musical form in language rather than the aping of an elder's style (an Aristotelian rather than Dionysian conception of mimesis), it is evident that he regards imitation of all kinds not as plain copying but as the origin of independent artistic creation.

Schwartz's willingness to use the term "imitation" also underlines his disregard for Yvor Winters's criticism of "the fallacy of imitative form." Winters, Schwartz argues in a 1938 review of *Primitivism and Decadence*, oversimplifies in arguing that a poet's use of "a disintegrated form in order to express a feeling of disintegration, is merely a sophistical justification of bad poetry."[10] Schwartz's overall point is that since form (and, specifically, meter) lacks meaning by itself, it can only be regarded as "imitative" when fused with style and diction in the service of expressing a particular experience—"and this will be a different problem in every case" ("Primitivism and Decadence," 343). For Schwartz himself, form is one component of successful imitation, but only one.

In a 1936 Harvard essay, "Poetry as Imitation," Schwartz suggests—again echoing Aristotle's views in the *Poetics*—that the purpose of all art is the imitation of "disguised emotions and motives": "The medium of each art," he argues, "is the looking-glass" (a recurring symbol in his poems) "which by imitation shows us what we could not see in any other way."[11] Successful imitation is revelatory; and it is by stylistic imitation that poets first tend to discover their own distinctive styles. "Most poets," Schwartz would suggest in a 1943 review of Karl Shapiro's *Person, Place and Thing* that imitates Eliot on imitation,

> begin by taking fire from other poets, and most poets end, sadly enough, in self-imitation. But between the time when the poet is an echoing novice and the time when he is a self-infatuated and tired master, there occurs, if the poet has genuine gifts, a period during which the borrowed or imitated style is gradually altered into something new and strange—as the glove is shaped by the hand, day by day—through the constant pressure of the poet's own and unique subject matter, his own experience.[12]

This is partly a veiled attack on Eliot, whose *Four Quartets* Schwartz thought were marred by "self-consciousness" and "falsity of tone."[13] But it also tells us something about his own development. Sometimes, as "echoing novice," his references are so direct, relentless, and self-conscious that they choke his poems.[14] His liftings are effective, however—and often more "mature" in *In Dreams Begin Responsibilities* than in later works—when, as in the case of his adaptation to Yeats's epigraph, they turn their sources into something, if not better, at least different, new or strange.

Eliot further contends that "a good poet will usually borrow from authors remote in time, or alien in language, or diverse in interest."[15] This is not always true of Schwartz; but his most successfully transformative borrowings tend to subject European or English sources to the pressures of an American idiom. His best-known poem, "The Heavy Bear Who Goes with Me," for example, has its origins in a line from Apollinaire's

"La Tzigane": "l'amour lourd comme un ours privé."[16] Schwartz's heavy bear, however, far from being a simile for love, is an obstruction to it, and a rival even for the beloved, stretching as he does "to embrace the very dear / With whom I would walk without him near" (*IDBR*, 101). These lines of yearning, with their note of late-Victorian sentimentality, contrast starkly to the poem's growling colloquialisms: it is as though the howling bear, as well as corrupting the speaker's love, also forestalls his attempts at achieving an aesthetic purity of speech. The speaker wants to cultivate a European sensibility, but his alter ego, the American "show-off" with his love of "candy," bulging "pants," football-kicking, and scrimmages refuses to let him do so.

The majority of Schwartz's poems are in conversation with previous poems, but almost always in the service of illuminating his own identity in the American present. Schwartz once wrote of Stevens that "his intimate relationship with his own generation in Europe did not diminish but rather intensified the way in which he was a purely American poet."[17] The same is true of Schwartz's relationship with his own, and previous, generations in Europe. Although he alludes to American poets as well, the effect of this is as often to bolster an international sensibility as it is to promote a national one. In "Prothalamion," for example, when he writes "Summon the children eating ice cream . . . / Summon the florist! And the tobacconist!" (*IDBR*, 106, 107), Schwartz also summons Stevens, who had called for flowers and tobacco (in the form of "big cigars") in "The Emperor of Ice-Cream."[18] Schwartz's evocation of a poem about a wake both casts a pall over his fantasy of possible wedding guests and acknowledges the strange levity of Stevens's poem. But Stevens keeps company with a host of international guests in "Prothalamion," among them Freud, Marx, Mozart, Athena, Crusoe, Chaplin, and—like Stevens, alluded to rather than named directly—Eliot, Saint-Exupéry, and Hadrian. Stevens is just one of many figures to charm Schwartz's "various tongue" (105). And yet, as the only "native" US citizen among the congregation, Schwartz's special affinity to him is conspicuous. The line "I am my father's father" (*IDBR*, 114) in "The Ballad of the Children of the Czar" represents a similarly unnationalistic instance of allusion to a fellow American. It is taken from Hart Crane's "You are your father's father" in "The River"; but this, in its turn, has a European source highly pertinent to Schwartz in Wordsworth's "The child is the father of the man."[19] Such secondhand allusions to European poems allow Schwartz to proclaim his own poetry's far-reaching ancestry, to insist that he is not an orphan. They enable him to admit that his poetry is derivative while also drawing attention to the ways in which it is different and American.

"In Dreams Begin Responsibilities"

The story "In Dreams Begin Responsibilities" establishes Schwartz's central topics: the disharmony between immigrant parents and intellectual son, the experience of being at once in the audience and a participant in a performance, and the binaries of dream and actuality. Schwartz's narrator recounts his experience of watching his parents' engagement, from the perspective of the future, on a cinema screen before waking, in the story's final sentence, "into the bleak winter morning of [his] twenty-first birthday" (*IDBR*, 20). The situation may owe something to Auden's *The Orators*, published in 1932, whose airman hero describes his first memories of his uncle as being like "images cast on the screen of a television set, maternally induced." [20]

Schwartz's narrator witnesses the scene at at least three removes—temporal, audio-visual, and oneiric, this distance acknowledging the three removes from nature that Socrates ascribes to all imitative art in Book X of *The Republic*.[21] The poor quality of the film further abets the distancing: it is a "silent picture," full of "sudden jumps" and "rays and dots," the organist only able to peal out "obvious approximate emotions" (11) which fall short of the narrator's own. The various removes cannot, however, prevent the overidentification that leads him to shout a warning of the marriage's failure at the screen, and this forestalls any possibility of catharsis. The reader, positioned at one further remove, is in an analogous position, sharing the narrator's experience but regularly reminded of the story's artifice, even at the end when the metaphor of the "lip of snow" (20) on the windowsill reminds us that, despite the narrator's renewed confrontation with reality on waking up, we remain in a fictional realm.

The story is concerned, above all, with the ways in which a viewer or reader might participate in a work of art or entertainment and help to create its meaning. Apperception—the mind's ability to *interpret* what it perceives, its being conscious of its own consciousness—matters to Schwartz as much as the perception itself, and he was intuitive enough to recognize (as Walter Benjamin did in the same year) how film was a medium that, as well as enhancing our "optical" and "acoustical" perception, had also "brought about a similar deepening of apperception."[22] Benjamin argues that in film "the audience's identification with the actor is really an identification with the camera. Consequently, the audience takes the position of the camera" (Benjamin, 222), and thus that of the amateur-critic in the audience. But Schwartz's narrator veers between such a conscious awareness of himself as audience member-cum-critic and an unconscious conquest of the camera that sees him become personally involved in the scene he is watching.

At first, while he is able to remain a disinterested observer, he experiences a loss of self, enacted in the move from "I" to "one" to an indistinct "they": "I am anonymous. I have forgotten myself: it is always so when one goes to a movie, it is, as they say, a drug" (11). This recalls Eliot's contrasting of "the drug of dreams" with the "pain of living"—a pain that returns to Schwartz's dreamer when, at a jolt in the film, he succumbs again to a self-consciousness which, in turn, leads to the other viewers becoming conscious of him. When, at the moment of his father's proposal, he shouts, "Don't do it! It's not too late to change your minds, both of you," the audience turns to look at him, "annoyed" (17), and he, rather than the performance on the screen, has become the center of attention. It is at the moment at which he most wants to negate his own individuality that he is least able to escape it.

This involuntary shift from audience member to chief spectacle represents "a return of what has been repressed" on a magnified scale.[23] According to Schelling's definition, as cited by Freud, the uncanny "applies to everything that was intended to remain secret, hidden away, and has come into the open" ("The Uncanny," 132). The narrator's anxiety about his origins, despite his attempts to conceal it, is strong enough—as the "*compulsion to repeat*, which proceeds from instinctual impulses" must be—"to override the pleasure principle" represented by his escape to the movies ("The Uncanny," 145, emphasis in original). As Freud later explains, "an uncanny effect often arises when the boundary between fantasy and reality is blurred, when we are faced with the reality of something that we have until now considered imaginary" ("The Uncanny," 150). This is precisely the confusion suffered by the narrator who, despite his insistence on the obstacles to believing in the reality of the onscreen performance, turns it into something real through his climactic outburst. We might remember that in one of Freud's case studies, Hoffmann's "The Sand-Man," an eavesdropping child gives away his presence by letting out a scream ("The Uncanny," 137). "In Dreams Begin Responsibilities" enacts a similar self-betrayal. Until his interruption, the narrator had remained anonymous and there was no reason for anybody else to believe that the movie had anything to do with him.

Even before this, however, the dreamer's sense of self has swollen to such an extent that it seems to have taken over the film itself. "I stare at the terrible sun which breaks up sight" (*IDBR*, 15), he states. His belief that he is himself a terrible son overwhelmingly distorts his vision, and it is this projection of his own self into the film that shatters his anonymity within the audience. When he describes his father as proposing "with awful daring" we realize, too, that he is bringing his reading of Eliot to bear upon the scene, remembering "the awful daring of a moment's surrender" and perhaps granting a literal meaning to the line that follows it in *The Waste Land*: "By this, and only this, have we existed" (Eliot, *CPP*, 74).

These punning and allusive instances indicate that the narrator of "In Dreams Begin Responsibilities" is in thrall to what one of Eliot's Harvard professors, Ralph Barton Perry, had termed "the egocentric predicament." Perry invented the phrase, Schwartz explains in his unpublished study of Eliot, "to state the impossibility of knowing anything *except through* the medium of one's own perceptions (which is not the same thing as saying it is impossible to know anything *but* one's own perceptions)."[24] In other words, one may be conscious of the way in which one's own perceptions tincture a particular experience, but, even with this knowledge, still be unable to overcome them and achieve perfect objectivity. F. H. Bradley, in the passage from *Appearance and Reality* to which Eliot refers in the "Notes on the Waste Land," observes how "my external sensations are no less private to myself than are my thoughts or my feelings…In brief, regarded as an existence which appears in a soul, the whole world for each is peculiar and private to that soul" (Eliot, *CPP*, 80). Schwartz's position is closer to Perry's in that he never disputes the existence of a world beyond one's own senses even if he believes experiencing that world independent of them to be impossible.

The "egocentric predicament" makes it difficult to distinguish between dream and actuality, but to experience something egocentrically neither invalidates that experience nor one's subjective interpretation of it. "Poetry," Eliot claimed, "is not a turning loose of emotion, but an escape from emotion; it is not the expression of personality, but an escape from personality."[25] Schwartz's depiction, here and elsewhere, of how an individual might impose a highly subjective interpretation onto a scene that is not obviously about him can be read as an implicit corrective to Eliot's insistence on leaving personality and emotions out of poetry. To attempt to do so, Schwartz suggests, is to falsify experience: for events or impressions to be meaningful one must acknowledge the centrality of the person who perceives them.

Eliot goes on to say, however, that "only those who have personality and emotions know what it means to want to escape from these things" ("Tradition and the Individual Talent," 49). This is something that Schwartz acutely recognizes, even though his narrator's attempt to escape personality leads to an intensified confrontation with it. When he is removed from the cinema at the end, it is suggested that he should be concerned not with his parents' past actions, over which he has no control, but with his own in the present, over which he does. "What are *you* doing?" the usher asks him,

> Don't you know you can't do things like this, you can't do whatever you want to do, even if other people aren't about? You will be sorry if you do

not do what you should do. You can't carry on like this, it is not right, you will find that out soon enough, everything you do matters too much (*IDBR*, 20, Schwartz's emphasis).

If, however, the usher's disapprobation seems to encapsulate the moral suggested in the title of "In Dreams Begin Responsibilities," the story's ending creates a couple of subverting complications. First of all, in being cast out of the movie theater, the narrator is relieved from having to face his origins any further. The external world, with its snow on the windowsill, has become the place of respite, a world more idealized than that of the movie-dream. There is genuine ambiguity as to whether the world shown on the screen or the barely depicted world outside is the more real. For Laurence Goldstein, the Freudian implication of "In Dreams Begin Responsibilities" that "the unconscious or dream life is the *true* life, and the external world is seemingly a fictive shadow, an artful simulation derived from the iconography of the artistic tradition...inverts the Platonic parable [of the cave] with a vengeance."[26] In the world of the story, actuality itself might be something subjective.

It is not, however, an absolute inversion.[27] Schwartz is more concerned with the interplay between internal and external worlds, the ways in which they might act upon one another, than he is in asserting the primacy of either one. The sufferer of the "egocentric predicament" is aware that an objective world exists beyond, and influences, his own perceptions, even though he cannot understand it independently of them. Schwartz never forgets that the images his narrator watches are created by a projector and would look entirely different were it not for the artificial frame of the screen. The poem "Metro-Goldwyn-Mayer"—written in 1937 but only published posthumously—concludes with a desire to ignore that Hollywood's "happily ever after" is "always played out // By an ignorant arm, which crosses the dark / And lights up a thin sheet with a shadow's mark" (*LL*, 22). It is this awareness of the mechanisms of film that breaks the dream, the curtailed reference to Matthew Arnold's "ignorant armies" at the end of "Dover Beach" intimating that there may also be a wider issue of religious belief in question.[28] The situation of "In Dreams Begin Responsibilities" is more complex, however, since the projection upon the screen is not merely idealized and because the mechanical hindrances do so little to obstruct the narrator's sense of personal involvement.

Distinctions between internal and external worlds in "In Dreams Begin Responsibilites" are further muddied by the recognition that the narrator's encounter with his prehistory is, at least partly, self-created. As Elisa New explains, "The dreamer is not mere spectator, but also producer; not passive but culpable."[29] This is because, by the very act of telling the story—and especially of publishing it—he turns it *knowingly* into something for public consumption. The projection of his family romance onto the screen may have been involuntarily induced by repressed feelings, but his recasting of it into a coherent narrative cannot be anything but conscious. This remains true regardless of whether or not we identify Schwartz himself with his narrator, since we are still to assume that the narrator is addressing an audience beyond the one that supposedly watched the movie with him. The reader only encounters the story at a point when its teller has already begun to interpret it.

Another problem is that, despite the usher's reproach, the narrator does seem to be at least partly vindicated in his belief that his parents are the source of his unhappiness. He shares many of their traits, and his attempt to lose himself in the "common dream" (*LL*, 22) can be seen as a symbolic reenactment of his parents' own pursuit of the American Dream and their own flights, as immigrants, from an oppressive past. The father is someone for whom "actualities somehow fall short" (*IDBR*, 14), disturbed when his fiancée weeps on accepting his proposal, since it is "scarcely as he thought it would be, on his long walks over Brooklyn Bridge in the revery of a fine cigar" (17). His son likewise discovers that things are not as he would have them. New further accentuates the similarities between parents and son by reading the story as an allegory for the displacement, more generally, of Jewish American life in mass culture and technology. She argues that the couple on the screen is seduced by media—the merry-go-round, the photographer's booth, and the crystal ball—"whose enticements are nothing less than those of the film in embryo." They "submit to a series of temptations, making, in effect, a greenhorn pilgrimage into the mass monster in whose grip their son already struggles."[30] It is a further irony, then, that this "mass monster"— the epitome of American modernity—was a largely Jewish American enterprise: most of the early Hollywood producers—Samuel Goldwyn, Louis B. Mayer, William Fox, and the Warner brothers among them—had been immigrants themselves.[31] For Jewish Americans, then, the very experience of going to the pictures in the early years of Hollywood would have both reinforced their own aspirations in coming to America and acted as a gauge of their own distance from achieving such success themselves. "In Dreams Begin Responsibilities" may be an unresolved illustration of philosophical problems regarding self, perception, and apperception, and it may be a psychological study into the Freudian principles of the uncanny and the family romance, but it is also, symbolically, a response to a particular historical moment and social context. It has the virtue of rendering abstract problems in concrete terms.

Dream and Actuality

Almost all of Schwartz's other creative works revisit the preoccupations of "In Dreams Begin Responsibilities," particularly the genealogical relation of the individual to the past, attempts to flee from personality, and the distinctions between dream and actuality. The rest of the volume needs to be read in explicit relation to the title story. Variations on the usher's chiding speech, for example, occur in several of the poems that follow: "It is time to shake yourself! and break this / Banal dream" (*IDBR*, 131), the poet warns the addressee (presumably himself) in "Tired and Unhappy, You Think of Houses." Breaking the dream necessitates a confrontation with the self, but this is a noble course, at least according to the father in "Father and Son," who warns, "You will try to escape / From melting time and your dissipating soul" when it would be more honorable to "Face yourself, constantly go back / To what you were, your own history" (110, 111)—not with a view to changing what cannot be changed but to accepting it. "Be guilty of yourself in the full looking-glass" (112), he advises. Or, as Schwartz puts it at the end of "Pleasure," from "Coriolanus and His Mother," with a possible nod to Rimbaud: "Let us require of ourselves the strength and power to view ourselves and the heart of man *with* disgust" (38, Schwartz's emphasis).

All of this is in the service of acquiring enough self-knowledge to understand how the self distorts one's experience of actuality. It is Schwartz's perpetual hope, as stated in "Prothalamion," to "gain once more / The look of actuality, the certainty / Of those who run down stairs and drive a car" (108). But even here he can only conceive the "the *look* of actuality." Is the best that we can attain a mere simulacrum? At his most apparently affirmative, in the sonnet "The Beautiful American Word, Sure," Schwartz can still only figure surety by way of an extended simile through which light temporarily illuminates a room at the touch of a button, defining things that had previously been indistinguishable in the darkness. "Sure" is an "American" word insofar as it signifies a conviction that anything can be done, a lack of self-doubt, and no ambiguity. The poem itself is more hesitant, and concludes with the poet hoping, by no means confidently, "for day when the whole world has that face: / For what assures her present every year? / In dark accidents the mind's sufficient grace" (136). Whether we take "her" here to refer to a specific loved one, to light, hope, actuality, or even the American Dream itself, these enigmatic lines concede that "her" presence can only be experienced as a consequence of fate ("dark accidents") and acceptance ("grace").

Often those things that would seem to enable our perception of actuality also hinder it. The screens and mirrors found throughout Schwartz's writing make it possible to see things that could otherwise not be seen, but at the same time they accentuate the impossibility of experiencing the things that they show firsthand. Observation always implies a degree of removal from the thing observed, and in Schwartz's poetry this often reinforces the individual's detachment from the community at large. All the same, he strives to overcome obstructions to direct experience or actuality (partly by admitting their existence) and to achieve a purity of perception whereby things can be known in their essence. Schwartz never abandons hope of eventually reaching an empirical understanding of his world, which he most often equates with intuitive knowledge—the "summer" knowledge that will be so important to his later poetry but that is also so difficult to articulate.

The story "An Argument in 1934"—published in the *Kenyon Review* in 1942 but never collected—sets out the problems as clearly as any of the poems. Here, it is the mistake of the idealist, Bradley Brown (whose name suggests an association with F. H. Bradley) to insist that the world can only exist in the mind. "It is as if the senses were stained-glass windows," he argues,

> and one only saw the light through the stained-glass windows of one's senses. What the light is beyond the stained-glass windows, you do not know. What a thing is, apart from the way you see it, you do not know, do you? How can you? [32]

The conceit is taken from Shelley's "Adonais": "Life, like a dome of many-coloured glass, / Stains the white radiance of Eternity."[33] Bradley, though, rejecting Shelley's Platonism, refuses to believe in a world existing outside of his own mind, an objective, external reality. This is made to look foolish by his companion Noah Gottlieb's rebuff: "'It is December in New York in 1934. The weather is cold and it is going to snow'" ("An Argument in 1934," 70). Even when given a bloody nose by a drunkard for inadvertently bumping into the latter's girl at a pedestrian crossing, Bradley remains in his own dream, leading his companions to remark on how "'he will never wake up to this',... pointing to the great city moving about them in 1934" (74). Schwartz, typically, does not allow us to discredit Bradley's view entirely: the self-proclaimed intellectuals, Gottlieb and Harry Morton, are themselves guilty of imposing their own prejudices onto a neutral scene. They perceive the "crowd which flowed ignorantly by them" (74), for example, as flowing because they know how "A crowd flowed over London Bridge" in *The Waste Land* (Eliot, *CPP*, 62) and regard their knowledge of modern poetry as a gauge of their separation. Their criticism of Bradley, then, is partly negated by the fact that they are no less guilty than he is of letting the stained glass windows of their own senses distort the light beyond.

Schwartz's "In the Naked Bed, in Plato's Cave" similarly resists the view that actuality is either entirely external to the self or solely internal. Plato's metaphorical cave becomes a bedroom, the insomniac speaker only able to experience the city life outside through reflections seen on the walls and sounds heard through the window. When he looks out at the "winter sky's pure capital"—representing "actuality"—it is too much for him to bear: he turns "back to bed with exhausted eyes" (*IDBR*, 134). In contrast to Plato, however, Schwartz suggests that the speaker's sense-bound experience inside his "cave" may be actual too. First of all, the description of the bed as "naked," stripped down to its basic elements, is a further evocation of Plato—this time of his philosophy of forms. Is this a stark manifestation of the original "idea" of a bed? The speaker's anxiety colors everything he perceives: wind "troubles" the curtains, and trucks "strain" and "grind" uphill because these verbs reflect his own sense of burden. Images are projected, movie-like, onto his wall, but he also projects his own feelings onto *them* (or else, he is such a representative of modern urban life that his own emotions and those of the city automatically match one another). As in "In Dreams Begin Responsibilities," the observer is complicit in the creation of what he sees. The headlights, trucks, and freights outside the window have an external reality independent of him, but he is responsible for how he perceives (and apperceives) them, giving them meaning and thereby making it possible for them to be thought of as actual.

One way of countering the "egocentric predicament" is to seek for the universal aspects of one's experience: isolation may be palliated by "international consciousness." The poem's ending attempts such a gesture. The speaker's sleepless night, he suggests, is emblematic of the human condition, and all of the concrete details accrued earlier in the poem are transcended:

> So, so
> O son of man, the ignorant night, the travail
> Of early morning, the mystery of beginning
> Again and again,
> > while History is unforgiven. (*IDBR*, 134)

As in "Metro-Goldwyn-Mayer," the allusion to Arnold's "ignorant armies" who "clash by night" casts the vagaries of mimesis as a problem of religious faith. If it is impossible to trust one's own perceptions, how can one believe in the authenticity of one's experience? The recognition that "the travail / Of early morning" is common to all, and always has been, is not a consolation, but it does make the speaker in his Spartan room seem less isolated. The mystery and ignorance remain, but the experience "of beginning / Again and again" is no less true, no less real, for that, and its truth is not only subjective.

"Sonnet: O City, City," the last of the lyric poems in *In Dreams Begin Responsibilities*, is a response to Wordsworth's "Composed upon Westminster Bridge, September 3, 1802."[34] But while that poem praises London's deep calm and celebrates clarity of vision, Schwartz's presents death's "loud picture" in the depths of the New York subway and laments the impossibility of experiencing things "as they are"[35] rather than at a remove. His sestet yearns for a cure:

> Whence, if ever, shall come the actuality
> Of a voice speaking the mind's knowing,
> The sunlight bright on the green windowshade,
> And the self articulate, affectionate, and flowing,
> Ease, warmth, light, the utter showing,
> Where in the white bed all things are made. (*IDBR*, 138)

"The actual," Schwartz explains in a drafted piece that praises the "overwhelming actuality" of Eliot's poetry, "is like a moist handshake, damp with nervousness or the body's heat." While the gloved handshake of an ambassador may also be actual "one has encountered less of the reality of the person."[36] This example suggests that physicality is an important component of actuality, but the actuality for which Schwartz yearns is idealized rather than earthly, refined into "ease," "warmth," "light," and abstract Platonic notions of "the mind's knowing" and the self's fluent expression. "Actuality," in this instance, is something closer to the kind of transcendental state in which physical body, mind, and soul cannot be distinguished from each other. Schwartz's wish for "utter showing" is primarily a wish for transparency and complete honesty. The final line envisions the absolute intimacy of love (and lovemaking) in "the white bed" where "all things are made." Like the less alluring, possibly sheetless and certainly more profane "naked" bed, this one represents an original form. But its imagined actuality, as in the rest of the sestet, hardly regards the physical.

Attaining perfect actuality would also mean being able to articulate one's actual thoughts and feelings rather than simply an insipid approximation in speech or writing. It is the "self," not just one's words, that should be "affectionate and flowing," fluent and unconstrained. The sestet of "O City, City," in resorting to abstract terms, betrays the difficulty of achieving the actuality Schwartz so desires. Even in this vision of achieved actuality, he imagines a veil in the form of a "green windowshade," a screen through which the outside world cannot clearly be discerned, however brightly the sunlight falls upon it. Does this suggest that to perceive the actual without impediment might, in fact, be inauthentic?

In "All Clowns are Masked and All Personae," for example, Schwartz notes that "All men are masked, / And we are clowns who think to choose our faces" (*IDBR*, 93). To conceal or disguise oneself may in fact be one's most natural, or actual, state, and may reveal oneself most. However, in "Prothalamion," Schwartz insists that at the point of marriage "None may wear masks or enigmatic clothes." "In this sense," he goes on, "see my shocking nakedness" (105). It may be acceptable to prepare a face to meet most people, but no such disguise can be put on before the person one loves the most. The instances of self-recognition that recur throughout *In Dreams Begin Responsibilities* are shocking because they reveal to the individual how he has been disguised even to himself. Mirrors project reflections that seem close and distant, substantial and ethereal all at once. The mirror itself may be objective, but one can only interpret what it shows subjectively. The gaze, Schwartz postulates in "By Circumstances Fed," converts "every feature / Into its own and unknown nature" (123). That is, we often manage to see things as familiar and strange—uncanny—at the same time. This poem ends with the poet in the drugstore (a favorite city location of Schwartz's) catching sight of his reflection:

I suddenly saw, estranged there,
Beyond all disappointment,
My own face in the mirror. (123)

It is a moment of recognition, and therefore of self-identification, coupled with its opposite, estrangement, a realization that the reflected image is simply that, an image, something outside of oneself that can never be fully known. The artifice of the mirror brings the viewer a greater sense of self-awareness but also a greater sense of alienation because it shows how he is separated even from his own image.[37] Confronted with such a difficulty, how can one affirm or define one's own identity?

The Individual and the International: "Coriolanus and His Mother," "The Commencement Day Address," and "The Ballad of the Children of the Czar"

In "Coriolanus and His Mother" (subtitled "The Dream of One Performance"), in which the poet watches Shakespeare's play alongside the ghosts of Aristotle, Beethoven, Marx, and Freud, a return of the repressed takes place similar to that in the preceding story when the poet, identifying himself with Caius Marcius, finds himself transported out of the audience and onto the stage. There, in the role of "the most belated Shakespearean fool" (*IDBR*, 77), he delivers a series of vaudevillian reflections between the acts (an example, perhaps, of the American poet seeking to reinvent European high culture as popular culture). The whole work is an extended variation on "In Dreams Begin Responsibilities," and the move from cinema to theater largely incidental.

Most importantly, Schwartz continues his investigation into how one can define individuality in relation to one's heritage and society. Although this is a continual concern—with Marx and Freud debating whether Coriolanus is more attached to his biological mother, Volumnia, or his symbolic mother, Rome—the most revelatory passage, in terms of illustrating "international consciousness," comes from "Pleasure," the first of the "Between the Acts" monologues. "The individual requires our focused gaze," Schwartz's persona remarks, but the focus immediately becomes almost untenably broad.

> He is the greatest subject, natural and artificial. Then there is his mother, his wife, his child, all his fathers, all his children. What an enormous crowd it may become! And the audience is already so complex, so full of foreigners. (*IDBR*, 35)

The individual is "natural" because we are each born as separate, individuated beings and "artificial" because personality and identity are, to a large extent, social constructs, established part-consciously and part-unconsciously in response to our particular environments and circumstances. For this reason, we cannot exclude consideration too of all the individual's relations, past and future, each of whom offers new perspectives from which to view the individual. Future generations—the children mentioned here—matter because the present and future alter the past as much as the past alters them. The individual is therefore also the greatest subject because he contains so many other subjects and can be considered from so many different angles. In his isolation he is international. Within the context of "Coriolanus and His Mother," the foreigners in the audience are specifically the four European ghosts; but the implication is that *everyone*, given the "egocentric predicament," is a foreigner to the individual, each with their own alien customs and personal preoccupations.

Schwartz goes on to make explicit some of the hypotheses with which he is grappling.

> "The individual is the only verifiable actuality, the individual, his experience from moment to moment." So said one in French at about the same

time as Lev Davidovich, better known as Trotzky, justly remarked that "The individual—is an abstraction!" He is right and yet you know and so do I...that we cannot regard the warm identity beneath our faces as being no more than an abstraction. (35)[38]

The two views appear to be in opposition, yet Schwartz credits them both. The individual's ever-changing experience from moment to moment is the only means available to him of interpreting his world. He is the only verifiable actuality because he alone can know the truth of his own perceptions. And yet, because individuality is not something concrete that can be clearly defined, proven, or even expressed, it *is* an abstraction. The paradox brings to the fore one of the animating impulses of Schwartz's oeuvre, the conflict between instinct, or sensibility, and the intellect. Intellectually, one has to agree with Trotsky that the self *is* an abstraction. And yet, every living person, however conscious they may be of their individual insignificance as seen from a detached worldwide perspective, feels themselves to be unique, and not simply a generic product of their society. If the individual and, concomitantly, personality are abstractions, they are abstractions without which we cannot live meaningfully.

Schwartz goes on to stress further the paradoxical nature of existence, this time alluding to one of the constituents of Martin Heidegger's concept of *Dasein*: that of "being-in-the-world."[39]

Man is always *in* the world, yes! inconceivable apart from being surrounded by a greater whole than himself. And yet he is at the same time himself and in and by himself and by traveling here and there may separate himself from any particular interior in which he finds himself. There is a thought which will take a considerable amount of chewing and then you will only have to spit it out again. (35)

The flippant conclusion is an attempt not to be paralyzed by the contradictions, while "traveling here and there" brings to mind again Schwartz's fascination with flight: we may never be able to escape our personalities, but by traveling we can change our immediate society and thereby redefine our lives, shifting the contexts and parameters against which they are judged. There may be a sense in which we try to escape not *from* personality, but with the opposite intent—to find out what our personality really is, to prove our individual agency in a context that allows it.

Sensitivity to the burden of personality is central to Schwartz's conception of "international consciousness" because of his desire—to quote Keller—"to transform personal introspection into a broader cultural consciousness."

It was only possible for Schwartz to "break" with the past, Keller argues, "through his efforts to reclaim it in the irreconcilable terms of personal remembrance and future-orientated self-creation."[40] Dr. Duspenser, in Schwartz's story, "The Commencement Day Address," offers a further take on the problem. Like Schwartz in "Pleasure," he suggests that to understand the individual one has to understand all of his forbears: "All men are my fathers!" he jokes.[41] He goes on to consider the discovery of America, outlining two contrary positions. The first attributes progress and discovery primarily to individual agency: "Thus it is said that everything which exists was first an idea in some intellect: the discovery of America was an idea in the mind of Columbus" ("The Commencement Day Address," 118). This view is, for the most part, Bergsonian. Central to it is the recognition that the *potential* for something to happen must exist before such an event can actually occur: Columbus could not have discovered America if he had not been intent upon discovering something, despite the fact that he did not discover what he expected. Equally—and obviously—America needed to exist before it could be discovered.

Duspenser's other argument is essentially Marxist:

History is ruled by the different ways in which goods are made... how, by whom, and for whom... this structure is said to be the prime mover of History. Thus the discovery of America took place because a trade route to the Indies was required. ("The Commencement Day Address," 118)

Duspenser concludes that both versions are right "in a way." The present may be determined by social factors in the past, but this does not preclude the possibility of individuals exerting some kind of influence themselves. The professor's final position is that "History moves towards whatever is supposed, by the heart of man from time to time, to be gold" (120), whether this be something material or a less easily defined kind of fulfillment. The immigration of millions of European settlers at the end of the nineteenth century occurred for just this reason; dissatisfied with their lives in Europe, they sought the promise of wealth and a more fulfilled existence in America.

Typically, Schwartz does not allow the reader to accept Duspenser's proclamations unquestioningly, and by the end his performance has become so histrionic that the campus police have to take him away. But his insistence that we are all "half the serf of the time and place in which [we] live, which is History" (122) is implicit throughout Schwartz's oeuvre (and notably *Genesis*). Within *In Dreams Begin Responsibilities*, it tallies especially with the view expressed in "The Ballad of the Children of the Czar" that "History has no ruth / for the individual" (*IDBR*, 114). Schwartz identified this poem as the first in which he had attempted to articulate "international consciousness." Narrated in unrhymed two-lined trimeter stanzas, the poem's six sections juxtapose the experience of the Czar's children of losing their ball with one of Schwartz's own early experiences of loss—that of knocking a baked potato from his high chair as a two-year old. The scenes initially appear unrelated: the child Schwartz, in Brooklyn, is six thousand miles away from the apparent garden idyll in Moscow that turns out to be anything but idyllic. The switches of focus lend a cinematic effect: the poem cuts from the Czar's children to Schwartz to a view so panoramic that it shows the world from afar "Spinning in its spotlight darkness" (115).

We learn in the poem's second section that it is 1916. The children, referred to throughout simply as "Brother" and "Sister," are the children of Czar Nicholas II and it is less than a year before their father's forced abdication in March 1917.[42] The First World War is raging, Russia has already lost Poland, and Nicholas himself is unsuccessfully leading his country's armies. The children in the garden seem innocently unaware of all this. They are also unaware that it will be a mere two years before their own deaths, alongside their parents, at the hands of a firing squad on July 17, 1918, condemned—as Schwartz would tell Pound no individual ever should be—for their father's crimes.

Given such knowledge, which is never explicitly stated, the "bouncing ball" becomes a kind of time bomb. The children are toying with their own fates. The "bald white" daylight moon hanging in the Western sky, reminding the children of "Papa's face" and the reader of the explosive ball, acquires the ill-auguring significance of an astrological omen. The description, in the fourth section of the ball as "bounding, unbroken" (114) is also ominous, not only indicating that the ball *will* break, but also raising the question of how a ball *can* break, an occurrence more catastrophic than it simply becoming punctured or deflated. The "shattering sun," meanwhile, falls "like swords" (114) upon the children's play, as terrible as the sun in "In Dreams Begin Responsibilities" and evoking the sword of Damocles. The children's play becomes more and more antagonistic as they pinch and kick each other and concludes in screaming and howling as the ball evades their will.

It becomes clear in the second section that, despite the geographical distance, Nicholas II's legacy belongs to Schwartz as well as to the citizens of Russia: "my grandfather coughed in your army" (113).[43] The children in the poem are not only Nicholas's actual children but also, more generally, the Slavic people who owe their origins—and their displacement and suffering—to Czarist Russia. With the death of the literal children, it is the children of the nation who must "carry [their] fathers on [their] back" (114).

Even leaving for America, "To become a king himself" (113), the grandfather cannot negate his origins.

The poem's transatlantic scope is already well-established by the end of the second section. The third draws out more abstract and universal ideas. The paradoxical "I am my father's father" (114) suggests that every child defines his or her father's status. A man only becomes a father when his child is born; the child is therefore responsible for fathering that man's new self. Later in the poem, Schwartz writes, "The past is inevitable," presenting a similar temporal reversal. Inevitability usually anticipates a future: but here it is the future itself that makes the past inevitable, unchangeable, in a way that it would not have been until it had happened.

The rest of the third section enforces the impossibility of escaping the past. Aeneas, carrying his elderly father, Anchises, on his back as he flees from Troy, becomes a prototype of all sons unable fully to escape the claims of family. But he is also, as a forefather of Rome and founder of a new civilization, a prototype of those forced to leave their homelands in search of a new life. Given a heritage in which "Troy is in the nursery, / The rocking horse is on fire" (114), innocence is impossible. As Schwartz announces in the fifth section, "The innocent are overtaken, / They are not innocent" (115). They may be innocent of character, but, like the Czar's children, they will not receive an "innocent" verdict ("not innocent" sinisterly opposing "not guilty"). Given history's ruthlessness, Schwartz suggests, innocence simply cannot survive—and this is one of his reasons for elsewhere advocating self-scrutiny, so that one can discover the ways in which one is "not innocent" and attempt to come to terms with one's heritage.

In the poem's fifth section, Schwartz turns to metaphysical speculation. "The ground on which the ball bounces / Is another bouncing ball" (115). The ball, to borrow Cynthia Ozick's assessment, has swollen "hugely, balefully...into the round earth itself."[44] Will it, too, eventually break—or expend itself (it is currently "unspent")? "The wheeling, whirling world / Makes no will glad" (115): bouncing and spinning as well, its course, like our unavoidable fates, seems distressingly arbitrary and uncontrollable. It is too big for the children's hands and for anybody's hands. The transitions from "wheeling" into "whirling" into "world" and finally into "will," the vowel sounds growing ever shorter, themself enact a hapless ball-like bouncing brought to a stop by "glad"; a similar effect is achieved at the end of the poem in the alliterative bouncing from "will" to "ball" to "uncontrollable" to "wall" and finally to "will" again. The children's ball rolls under the iron gate and evades their will: who knows where the world, a mere "purposeless Thing" that is "chasing itself" will lead us? While the children are fighting over their bouncing ball, apparently civilized nations are simultaneously fighting, just as trivially, perhaps, over their metaphorical ball, the world.

The poem was written in 1937; it is October of this year that is referred to at the start of the final section, with the poet looking back on the past, both personal and international. The international picture in 1937 was as ominous for the Western world as it was for the Czar's children in 1916. The Nazis were in power in Germany and the Second Xino-Japanese War was already underway: there was good reason for supposing the world—a mere star—tragic, even though greater tragedy was to come. In this final section personal and international are drawn together. The child Schwartz's baked potato is his "buttered world" (115). This is a sentimental image, but it recognizes how, for a two-year old, the immediate present—in this case, the task of eating—overwhelms everything: his innocence is evinced by his lack of a wider perspective. However, when the potato falls, pitilessly, purposelessly, like the world itself, the child begins to howl and is thus identified with "Brother," the Tzarevitch, howling in the garden at the loss of his ball. It is hardly surprising, given what has gone before, that the poet should conclude

overtaken by terror

Thinking of my father's fathers
And of my own will. (116)

The poem is largely about the past, but this final word, "will," although it is never used in the poem as a verb, always implies futurity. The poem's final note is one of fear about how improbably the poet will be able to enforce his own will but also, more pertinently, about what kind of heritage his own generation is likely to pass on. What past, he implicitly asks, will be inevitable for future generations?

"The Repetitive Heart"

The "Eleven Poems in Imitation of the Fugue Form," while suggested by the musical arrangement, all also engage fugue's secondary meaning of flight from one's own identity. Immediately following "Coriolanus and his Mother," they advance the book's interrogations of individuation and personality, either expressing a longing to escape the self, or admitting to the impossibility of doing so. Similarly, they seek release from time, or at least try to learn how to live within it. Schwartz's turn from narrative to lyric enables him to draw greater attention to the surface techniques of near—but not exact or systematic—repetition and refrain that distinguish the poems. These work as means of renewal, moving each poem forward while at the same time looking back. Almost all of the poems depict kinds of circular motion occurring within the chronological progression of time: the bouncing of balls; the restlessness of wind; dancing; the whirling of snowflakes; and, most grandiosely, the "great globe reel[ing] in the solar fire / Spinning the trivial and the unique away" (95). Time itself "goes round and round, / Time circles in its idiot defeat" (100); but time is also "perpetually perishing" (104). It moves toward an end, and we are on a "receding road" (104) as we move through it, pursuing our own destinations. Time's circling does not forestall its forward motion; as in the book's title, timeless and time-bound moments are juxtaposed alongside each other.

"All of us always turning away for solace" (91) sets the tone, enumerating the diversions we find to distract ourselves from our essential isolation. Its opening words—"all of us"—are inclusive: they resist the confrontation of self in "the lonely room" through their affirmation of a collective condition and through the refusal of "solace" to succumb to "solitude." But the first and last lines, set apart from the rest of the poem, also enforce a context of separateness, and if the poet is able to hold off "the lonely room" for the time being, it nonetheless returns in the later poem, "Father and Son," when the father warns of the dreams and distractions one pursues "Because one is afraid to be alone, / Each with his own death in the lonely room" (111). "In the Naked Bed, in Plato's Cave," meanwhile, dramatizes exactly such an encounter in a "lonely room." The motif of the "bouncing ball" as a symbol of fate recurs, as we have seen, in "The Ballad of the Children of the Czar," but also as the football in "The Heavy Bear Who Goes with Me." It is unpredictable and uncontrollable, "Bounding, evasive, caught and uncaught, fumbled" (91). We cannot help but follow it, and though it is initially an amusement, it ultimately returns us to the loneliness from which we had originally turned. However hard we try we cannot escape our selves, our fates, or our personalities.

The second of the "Repetitive Heart" poems—"Will you perhaps consent to be" (92)—adopts a more intimate register. Less intent upon establishing a truth applicable to "all of us," it addresses a singular "you" and can be read as a tentative marriage proposal, preparing for the "Prothalamion" that is to come. The beloved is symbolized as a tree: "Will you perhaps consent to be / My many-branchéd, small and dearest tree?" The speaker's mind, figured as a "wild and restless" wind, touches "this single of your flowers, this one only," and yet cannot keep international imaginings out of the exchange, lusting "for Paris, Crete and Pergamus," going off to "Paris and Chicago, / Judaea, San Francisco, the Midi," and imagining a return from Norway. The wind is a symbol of "international consciousness": it is everywhere all the time, all-pervasive. The tree, meanwhile, is rooted, fixed in one place. Read like this, the speaker is asking his beloved to be a permanent, secure support in his otherwise unstable life. The demands he makes are extreme: "Would you perhaps consent to be / The very rack and crucifix of winter[?]" But the speaker does not just see the tree as sacrificial. It has genealogical connotations too. Being small, it may grow. Being "many-branchéd," these may extend. The individual exists by virtue of many branches of a family coming together. Schwartz's tree reveals these origins, and also looks forward to the future and, implicitly, the possibility of having children: the next poem—"All clowns are masked and all *personae*"—exhorts us to "Choose love, for love is full of children" (93). In this way, the tree bears traces of the past but also suggests its transformation into the future. As the next poem concludes, following its consideration of the various genetic traits we inherit and which circumscribe our choices, "the past is immortal, the future inexhaustible!" (93). The world begins again.

"Calmly we walk through this April's day" is the most elegiac of the 11 poems. It asks what restorative capability memory has, partly relying for its tone upon Schwartz's own memory of poems by Yeats and Auden. Schwartz's refrain—"time is the fire in which we burn"—invests time, with implicit recourse to Heraclitus, with both destructive and restorative powers. But it also melds the "conflagration" that Yeats anticipates in the second stanza of "In Memory of Eva Gore-Booth and Con Markiewicz" with his lament that "The innocent and the beautiful / Have no enemy but time."[45] Later, when Schwartz asks of two childhood friends, Bert Spira and Rhoda, "Not where they are now (where are they now?) / But what they were then, both beautiful" (94), he further echoes Yeats, who described Gore-Booth and Markiewicz as "both / Beautiful, one a gazelle." As such, Schwartz admits to idealizing his friends in memory, glorifying the past—as Yeats does—without concern for what they may be like now. He also, once again, summons Auden's "Address for a Prize-Day" at the start of *The Orators*, reversing Auden's parodic opening—"Commemoration. Commemoration. What does it mean? What does it mean? Not what does it mean to them, there, *then*. What does it mean to us, here *now*?"—and recasting it as an earnest "ubi sunt" lamentation: "Where is my father and Eleanor? / Not where are they *now*, dead seven years, / But what they were *then*?" (my emphases).[46] What this suggests is that memory, rather than occurring spontaneously, is constructed by the poet with the aid of poetic references that matter to him. Schwartz's allusions bring him closer to being able to recapture the past, and, even though the poem frets that this might entail misrepresenting the present, it also celebrates anything that helps the memory to "restore again / The smallest color of the smallest day."

How, if at all, the poem asks, can memory bring back those who have been "taken away?" How do death and the "reeling blaze" of time affect our sense of self? The poem's chief anxiety is articulated at the end of the first strophe:

> What will become of you and me
> (This is the school in which we learn...)
> Besides the photo and the memory?
> (...that time is the fire in which we burn.)

Will *anything* become of us? Photo and memory—the first a mere two-dimensional image, the second an abstract entity, vague and inaccurate—do not seem adequate to the commemoration of an individual. And if they can restore vivid impressions for the one who remembers, can they do anything at all for the one who has died?

Schwartz is also intent upon discovering what we might learn from our exposure to time. In the lines just quoted, the parenthetical observation interrupts the emotive impulse: the mind attempts to interpret, to apperceive, what it experiences. The unspecified "school," at this point, seems simply to be the fact of reflecting on the passage of time. Only by acknowledging the particular moment in history (in this case, the year "Nineteen Thirty-Seven"), and by contemplating how so many "great dears" have been lost, can we recognize, experientially rather than theoretically, that we are continually being consumed by time ourselves, and must eventually burn down to nothing. Time, the school, and the fire, which are distinct at the beginning of the poem, are conflated at the end. The refrain, previously sounded across lines, has become a couplet.

> Time is the school in which we learn,
> Time is the fire in which we burn. (95)

If time is at once school *and* fire, its lessons are exciting, painful, and dangerous, threatening to consume us and to destroy former semblances of knowledge. But it is also a source of life and the means by which the past can be transformed into the future and the world can begin again.

The problem of selfhood acquires special urgency in the face of death. The poet struggles to reconcile what changes in an individual over time with what remains the same. "What is the self amid this blaze?" he asks. "What am I now that I was then / Which I shall suffer and act again[?]" (94). The "I" in the present ("now") looks back to the past ("then") and ahead to the future (indicated by "shall"), knowing that he has changed, and that each change alters not just what he is and what he shall be but also what he was. The present changes the past as much as the past changes the present. All the same, the "I," however changed, remains, and will continue to remain, the same "I." The individual is both an abstraction and the only verifiable actuality.

The first six of the "Poems in Imitation of the Fugue Form" are all concerned with the self in relation to others. Poem VI, for example, "Do they whisper behind my back?" further plays upon the motif of the would-be audience member turned reluctant actor. Poems VII and IX, however, "I am to my own heart merely a serf" and "The heavy bear who goes with me," present the self riven by internal conflict. The epigraph to "The heavy bear who goes with me," from Alfred North Whitehead's *Process & Reality*, introduces the problem of physicality: "the withness of the body" (101). Whitehead discusses how the secondary qualities of certain personality traits can be traced back "to their root in physical prehensions expressed by the *'withness* of the body.'"[47] Prehensions are responses to stimuli, regardless of cognition: knee-jerk reactions of a kind. In the context of this poem, they include trembling, bulging, quivering, wincing, involuntary sexual responses, outbursts of violence, and physical hunger. "The withness of the body" is not so much about the existence of such prehensions as their *expression* and the inability to supress them.

The poem enacts a version of the dissociation of sensibility. There is a disjunction between the physical impulse and the considered thought—or, as Eliot puts it in *The Hollow Men*, a shadow that falls "Between the emotion / And the response" and "Between the desire / And the spasm" (Eliot, *CPP*, 85). The actuality of lust and the dream of refined courtship are set against each other, as are id and ego. If the speaker is a kind of Prufrock—whom Schwartz characterizes as "impotent and sensitive"—then the heavy bear is Sweeney, "potent and insensitive" ("T. S. Eliot as the International Hero," 125). A complete separation would be less problematic. Physical lust would hardly matter if it did not corrupt an ideal in the mind or if we were incapable of feeling guilt or shame. If the speaker seeks to define the actuality of his own selfhood, as distinct from the bear, he also attempts—and fails—to deny the bear's actuality. It is an attempt not so much to escape personality as to deny what one's personality really is.

The honey-smeared animal initially seems benign. It is only through the accumulation of clauses—"the central ton of every place," "the hungry beating brutish one" (*IDBR*, 101)—that its dark, inescapable quality is fully realized. The word "heavy" extends the volume's concerns with fateful burden, anticipating charged usages by Berryman and other contemporaries. The overriding pun—connoting that the heavy bear himself is the burden the poet has to bear—is reinforced by some of the poem's further puns and metrical manipulations. The heavily stressed word "goes," for example, here effectively means its opposite, "comes." The bear accompanies the speaker "here and there" and "to every place": no attempt to shake him off will work. In "smear[ing] his face," the bear is not just gorging himself with honey but is also slandering his alter ego and blurring his sense of separate selfhood. "Smear" is used in a similar sense in *Coriolanus*—and we recall that Coriolanus, in Schwartz's description, is "a breathing animal" (*IDBR*, 78).[48] That the bear (the id, despite its egotism) ought to be subordinate to the master he in fact dominates is evident from his characterization as a "crazy factotum." And yet, the bear is created by his master, and is a manifestation of the troubling impulses that he has attempted to repress. Schwartz's description of the bear "distorting my gesture, / A caricature, a swollen shadow, / A stupid clown of the spirit's motive" (101) recalls the return of the repressed that occurs in "In Dreams Begin Responsibilities." The shadow, like the projection on the screen, is swollen and inexact, exaggerated like a caricature. An image of what the speaker had hoped to hide is made visible, and enlarged. On one hand, this shadow can be regarded as an imperfect representation akin to those in Plato's cave; but since no one can escape their own shadow (or personality) there is a sense in which it is also something real and physical in its own right. Schwartz is again challenging clear-cut distinctions between what is actual and what is not. The sounds of the verse themselves at this point are a series of distorted echoes: the awkward assonance of "distorting," "gesture," and "caricature" is met with an alliterative volley of "st" and "c" sounds, the poet trying to recreate the bear's imitative stutter aurally as well as visually.

One of the poem's ironies is that, despite its overt physicality, the speaker finds it impossible to define the bear. He "perplexes"; he remains "opaque," "my private, yet unknown" (a kind of right-hand man, but one who will not leave the speaker in private and one whose very existence seems to reveal a secret). As in all of his poems of actuality, Schwartz yearns for clarity but encounters obstructions: "a word / Would bare my heart and make me clear." Even here, the bear intrudes: the paronomasia of "bare" refuses to let words point only toward their own meanings. This may imply a desire for confession, but the speaker is reluctant to admit that his own actuality may be contingent upon the bear's. The conclusion suggests an even greater dependence than this. A reversal of conventional roles is confirmed as the bear drags the speaker "with him in his mouthing care." The "caricature," the "swollen shadow" has usurped the self it mimics and has become the controlling consciousness—the more real existence.

The absolute entrapment of this situation is partly alleviated by a typically Schwartzian gesture at the end toward the universal: "the hundred million of his kind, / The scrimmage of appetite everywhere" (102). It may be that everyone, everywhere, has their own heavy bear, and if this is not in itself consoling it *is* a further case of an individual's isolation being their means of finding affinity with a world beyond their own. The bear's dominance is also partly offset by the conclusion of the last of the "Poems in Imitation of the Fugue," "Dedication in time." Whereas the bear walked with the speaker when he only wanted to walk with his "very dear," "Dedication in time" ends with the speaker and the beloved "in step, running together, / Our pace equal, our motion one" (104), free from distorting caricatures. The final lines of the sequence, without forgoing the pathos of the clown, anticipate a time when emotion and action will correlate again and when two individuals can move together in sync,

> Walking together on the receding road,
> Like Chaplin and his orphan sister,
> Moving together through time to all good. (104)

It is a muted aspiration, however, the speaker turning to contemporary cinema iconography—the final frame of *Modern Times* (1936)—and finding an image that encapsulates his desire to escape from modern times as much as it, tentatively, suggests a hopeful future.

CHAPTER 3

"The Land of the Old World Failure and the New World Success": *Genesis* and "America! America!"

Ghost Commentators

As early as August 1941, Schwartz wrote to Laughlin announcing, "I am now, I think, the poet of the Atlantic, of the Atlantic migration, which made America" (*DS & JL Letters,* 149). He was, by this stage, well advanced in drafting the long narrative poem, *Genesis,* that he believed would secure his reputation and make him famous. Only the first of its three projected books was published, however, meeting a lukewarm—though by no means wholly negative—reception despite Schwartz's efforts to have it reviewed by critics he knew would be sympathetic. Steeped, as ever, in literary and philosophical reference, and following "Coriolanus and His Mother" in boasting an audience of ghosts to offer Marxist and Freudian analyses of the story proper, *Genesis* was never likely to "obsess the nation" (*DS & JL Letters,* 89) as Schwartz had hoped it might, even had it not been published in the middle of the Second World War. Many admirers of Schwartz's first book found the sprawl and prolixity of *Genesis* aesthetically disappointing too. As Ashbery maintains, however—in a way that brings to mind Catherine Fitzpatrick's argument that Schwartz's best work often represents "a poetry of failure"— "it fails on a lavish scale."[1] If we accept this judgment, the poem may all the same be a more important failure than has yet been acknowledged.

Genesis is the story of Hershey Green, an adolescent insomniac who is "is not remarkable / In the great city [of New York], circa 1930" (*G,* 3) and is thus a broadly representative figure. Hershey describes his parents' and grandparents' immigration and his own New York childhood in what Schwartz described as "Biblical prose," while the ghosts comment on each episode—like a Greek chorus—in blank verse.[2] The story—which is closely based upon Schwartz's own family history and has its origins in a memoir begun in 1931 entitled "Having Snow"—begins with Hershey's paternal grandfather's unsuccessful attempt to desert both the Russian army and his wife, desertions reenacted by his sons when they run away from home and leave for America. Hershey's other grandfather, meanwhile, aggrieved at bad treatment by his boss (who is also his brother-in-law), similarly takes flight, later sending for his wife and daughters. These transatlantic migrations occupy only the first 30 of *Book One*'s 208 pages, but throughout the ensuing descriptions of his parents' unhappy marriage and his own childhood, Hershey continues to dramatize his Atlantic identity, his sense of being conditioned by two separate cultures but properly belonging to neither of them.

Despite the transatlantic canvas of Hershey's story, its international bearing is principally provided by the ghosts. As Schwartz explained in a draft of his preface, they

> can trace and understand the remote causes of action which are hidden from the young man himself. And these causes—historical, social, cultural, and psychological—are the "divinities" of our day, acting upon our free will as fatefully as ever did the gods of the ancient world. (*DS & JL Letters*, 191)

Their role is to provide an etiology of modern life. Among the "divinities" they identify are Europe, America, Israel, "Capitalismus," "Sexhood," the First World War, the "family divinity," and the "school divinity." While Schwartz acknowledges that choices do occur in individual lives, *Genesis*, like many of his earlier lyric poems, regrets that these are limited by uncontrollable circumstances. It is only as a consequence of a series of impulsive decisions (and other factors beyond human influence) made long before his conception that Hershey ends up being born to sparring Jewish parents in early twentieth-century America. He can do little more than negotiate how best to live with what he inherits.

In a slightly earlier defense of his ghost chorus, Schwartz reminded Laughlin, who was skeptical, that "Dante wrote the best poem ever written *by using the dead as voices*" (*DS and JL Letters*, 159, Schwartz's emphasis). In his note "To the Reader," meanwhile, Schwartz cites the Tiresias episode of *The Waste Land* as a more recent precedent for bringing in a character external to the action "to comment and to judge" (viii), also noting Hardy's use, in *The Dynasts*—his panorama of the Napoleonic Wars—of "supernatural spectators of the terrestrial action, certain impersonated abstractions, or Intelligences, called Spirits" (*G*, viii). "Our scope is but to register and watch / By means of this great gift accorded us—," Hardy's Spirit of the Years remarks, disavowing any ability to control the action in a tone that Schwartz's own ghosts emulate in announcing, "We mock with irony and sympathy, / Discuss, explain, listen and give our minds—" (*G*, 6).[3]

More pertinently still, perhaps, Schwartz felt such a device was necessary in a poem intended to reflect the full range of modern international experience:

> This story-succeeded-by-commentary is one of the profoundest most deeply-rooted and most accepted experiences in modern life: The newspaper story-editorial, the play-and-review-of-the-play, the travel film with voice as commentator are all primordial examples of what is going to be an inevitable literary form (inevitable because the life we live forces it upon us). (*DS & JL Letters* 159)

R. P. Blackmur, in the review Schwartz solicited, supports this, describing *Genesis* as "a story of what is sublimated" and maintaining that its "final significance transpires exactly in what the presences of the dead bring from the story into voice."[4] Without the ghosts' exegesis, Hershey's story could be no more than anecdotal narrative. They are far from omniscient, and Hershey learns, as the poem progresses, to interpret many of the episodes for himself. But it is their universalizing perspectives that make it possible to accept the story as containing "some truth about all human beings" (*G*, ix) rather than just a laying bare of his soul.

Genre, Form, Language, and Voice

The universal vision of the ghosts strengthens their own identification of Hershey's story as having an "epic movement" (*G*, 64), a characterization also supported by their interest in modern "divinities"; the preeminence of the journey in Hershey's history; and the mythic aspirations suggested by the title itself. *Genesis* resists absolute generic classification, but this description does help to situate it in relation to long, ambitious poems by elders and contemporaries. Ashbery notes the urge for twentieth-century American poets "to make it big as well as new," placing Schwartz's poem alongside *The Cantos*, *The Waste Land*, and Stevens's "The Comedian as the Letter C."[5] Unmentioned by Ashbery, though also important in this regard, is Crane's *The Bridge*, not least because Schwartz had once been critical of Crane's hubris, suggesting to his biographer, Philip Horton, that Crane "would have been a much better poet if, after writing *White Buildings*, he had worked the symbolist vein in himself… instead of attempting a Whitmanesque myth" (*Letters*, 35). Posterity would pass similar judgment on Schwartz himself.

Ashbery speculates that Schwartz may have intended *Genesis* as a "Brooklyn version of Wordsworth's *The Prelude*," recognizing however that *The Dynasts* was perhaps "a more immediate stylistic precedent" (7). Given Hardy's importance to Auden, it is possible also that his influence upon Schwartz might have been further mediated through the genre-defying example of *The Orators*, a work which, as we have seen, Schwartz had drawn upon profitably in earlier works. Each of these English poems undermines the classical notion of the hero to be found in Homer, Dante, and Milton. *Genesis*, with its prioritization of the experience of an individual self, reaffirms, in the wake of modernism, Hegel's definition of the lyric as "an intensely subjective and personal expression."[6] It is also novelistic in its attention to seemingly trivial details and, at times, self-consciously dramatic. As such, despite the tropes it borrows, it opposes the European genre of classical epic, which has only successfully existed in America in much-adapted versions.[7] It can only be properly understood as a hybrid of lyric, epic, novel, and drama, and this hybridity is appropriate to the work's overt interests in dual identity and intermediateness.

Some of the poem's critics appear to have wished that it were a different kind of poem. Ashbery regrets that its "lyric passages, many of them of great beauty" are diluted by "prose padding."[8] Adam Kirsch, meanwhile, the one present-day champion of *Genesis*, accentuates its narrative and dramatic qualities, going so far as to claim that "Schwartz never really attempted to write great lyric poetry," and citing "The Isolation of Modern Poetry" as evidence of Schwartz's "principled discontent with the idea of lyric poetry that he inherited."[9] Kirsch sees *Genesis* as epitomizing Schwartz's "renunciation of the rich, obscure, musically perfect language of Symbolist poetry" (201). This is to neglect the second part of Schwartz's statement of intent in the preface "To the Reader": "I should also like to think that I am one more of the poets who seek to regain for Poetry the width of reference of prose *without losing what the Symbolists discovered*" (ix, my emphasis). This indicates a desire to redefine lyric poetry, to broaden its scope, and to seek out new possibilities, but not, as Kirsch implies, a rejection of the genre. Putting the problem slightly differently, Schwartz later explains that

> it is natural that [the modern poet] should want to write as directly and clearly as Yeats and Frost at their best… On the other hand, he is bound to be drawn toward an emulation of the marvellous refinements in the

uses and powers of language which have occurred since the symbolists appeared.[10]

Again, Schwartz locates himself between extremes. The poet is likely to want to combine the lyrical and the naturalistic, as Wilson had predicted in *Axel's Castle*. *Genesis* is written in such a spirit of compromise: Schwartz attempts to include lyric verse within a larger scheme.

Formally, rather than generically, the different *modus operandi* are more distinct from each other. The cadenced prose, suggesting the Hebrew Bible of Jewish tradition, is an open form that allows for episodic storytelling and quickly sketched scenes (even if the pace of the narration itself is generally slow). The blank verse, with its primarily English heritage, is stricter, but remains expansive enough to accommodate the ruminative contributions of the ghosts: the form dictates, more or less, the length of each line but not of each section.[11] However, the distinctions between the two forms, though clear, are not rigid. Hershey's prose also contains such usual verse features as enjambment, alliteration, and poetic inversions: "he sneered at it, sneered / With the cynicism of one who suspects all because he knows himself" (62); "his widening wakening gaze" (157); and "a street of suspicion he walked from that day forward" (189). Equally, for all their loftiness, the ghostly interjections are as conversational as they are rhetorical or, in any polished sense, poetic. Their speech is full of phatic phrases such as "Ha! Ha!" (58) and "O God! O God!" (124); they address Hershey informally as "young man" (97) and "New York boy," and regularly implore him to "go on" with his story (124, 163, 170). Many of their meditations fade out with an ellipsis or conclude with a dash, suggesting interruption. Some of them (like the poem itself) start with an ellipsis as well, suggesting thought before speech, and there are numerous ellipses within their speeches too. The consequent lack of fluency is naturalistic and spontaneous, and is at odds with the formal nature of their blank verse.

In his "Note to the Reader," Schwartz insists that he has

> no wish to emulate Swinburne, but rather the "morbid pedestrianism" of such poets as Donne and Hardy, Webster and Wordsworth. The diction of this deliberate flatness—and the heavy accent and the slowness—is an effort to declare the miraculous character of daily life and ordinary speech. (ix)

Despite the precedents that he gives, however, Schwartz also felt that his method was innovative: "a new meter will come of this deliberate flatness," he proposed in his journal on January 31, 1942 (*Portrait*, 25). At his most confident, he bragged to Laughlin that *Genesis* would "start a new school of writing to be called 'Post-Symbolism'" (*DS & JL Letters,* 117), and although he never explicitly defined the tenets of such a school, regaining "for Poetry the width of reference of prose without losing what the Symbolists discovered" (*G,* ix) might be a plausible manifesto. This suggests a keenness to discover, as Schwartz believed Eliot had done, "the hidden, or latent, seed or light of the poetic in prose words; which is to say, in words commonly supposed to be too unpoetic to be used in poetry."[12] For Eliot, "etherised," "tedious argument," and "insidious intent" are such words (Eliot, *CPP,* 13). In *Genesis,* Schwartz goes so far as to include "tactlessness," "indigestion," "prosecution," and "the payment of ten thousand dollars in the proper quarters" (92–93) in a single passage. These prosey words and phrases are granted poetic status by virtue of their context within passages characterized by anaphora and an accumulation of clauses, common features of Schwartz's open versification. Hershey's biblical prose is suited to revealing the poetic quality of prose words, since it is a form that is neither wholly verse nor wholly prose, absorbing features typical of both. The blank verse, meanwhile, accommodates philosophical abstract terms and idiomatic exclamations that in an earlier period might have seemed outside the scope of poetry.

The "new meter" Schwartz sought needed to be free enough to carry a breadth of subject matter but also tight enough to allow for occasional lyric intensity. In his journal he exhorted himself to "seek for the flat five-foot statement which is full of energy and drama…And seek irony, the ironic-colloquial and the ecstatic-exclamatory!" (*Portrait,* 27). Schwartz's conviction that verse can be at once tonally flat and dramatically engaging, simply colloquial and ecstatic is fundamental to his method in *Genesis.* How successfully Schwartz achieves his aim of emulating speech or discursive prose while also achieving a heightened aesthetic or dramatic style can best be illustrated by close analysis of representative passages of blank verse and biblical prose.

One of the first significant events of Hershey's infancy is the death of his uncle, Rupert. This moves the ghosts to extended speculations, of which the following lines are a sample.

"Death. Death. All flesh is grass, no more:
Nature is treacherous as quicksand, Life
May be as quickly torn as tissue paper!
All flesh is mere confetti, falling down
Joyously at the Mardi Gras!"
                                  "Or snow,
The cool flakes quickly stained in city streets—"

"This child
Was rocked by Death, rocked by a man to die,
Uncle, young man of promise, hero,
Such as the famous fiction of the age
Brings forth to be the flower of the page—"

"Next to examples of mortality
As under the tall buildings and long billboards
Of the great city next to the Hudson River
This childhood howls, eats, and misunderstands!"

"We are as water spilt upon the ground.
Stay. Look. Cannot be gathered up again—"
"Twinly the bird flies off, snatching the air:
His wings know well Being's contingency—"

"The death of young men, like the death of Keats,
Terrifies many easy rationalists,
Gnostics and rabbis everywhere—"
          "A light!
The spirit is a light, a sparkling star
So quickly clouded over in the sky!" (73–74)

On the page, this blank verse is more immediately recognizable as poetry than Hershey's narrative, if only for the simple reasons that the lines do not extend to the edge of the page and that there are stanza breaks. There is also a preponderance of alliteration and assonance, notably, in the first stanza, on /f/ sounds and the voiceless /θ/ of "death," and on the short /e/ sound in "death," "flesh," and "confetti." At the end of the passage, the /sp/ and /t/ sounds of the penultimate line are overridden by the fricatives of the last. The first stanza ends with a regular rhyming couplet—an occasional characteristic of the ghosts' verse—while the prosaic description of "tall buildings and long billboards" is rendered poetic by internal rhyme and phrasal mirroring. The passage also typifies the ghosts' penchant for parallelism, a feature associated with ancient Hebrew writing and poetry based in oral traditions that Whitman first introduced into American poetry.

All this, along with the ghosts' attempts to find metaphors and similes that give universal bearing to the individual death, suggests the poem's lyric tendency. The register, despite the exclamations, is generally muted. The first of these lines, with its strongly stressed monosyllables, epitomizes Schwartz's "flat five-foot statement": *Death. Death. All flesh* is *grass*, no *more.*" The caesurae after each utterance of "Death" are pronounced enough to substitute for the weak syllables that would be necessary for a regular pentameter line, and the emphases upon "Death" are made even stronger by the contrast with "Life," strongly stressed at the end of the next line. The tendency of the ghosts to deal in such broad and abstract terms draws attention to their gently pompous gravity.

The suggestion that flesh is as ephemeral as grass nods simultaneously to Isaiah 40: 6, the second line of Eliot's "Difficulties of a Statesman," and, more generally, to Whitman. Many of the other comparisons are also commonplace: it is hardly original to compare the fragility of life to tissue paper or snow, or the spirit to a star. What is unusual, though, is the refusal of the ghosts to settle upon a single summative statement, and the similes are often ambivalent in their connotations. That flesh is mere confetti—an idea seemingly suggested by the previous comparison of Life to tissue paper—initially seems wholly negative. It is surprising, then, when the speaker goes on in the next line to imagine it being thrown "Joyously" at Mardi Gras celebrations, the trochaic first foot heightening this surprise. Confetti also evokes weddings, perhaps reminding us of one of the ghost's earlier suggestions that all brides "ought to be dressed in green," the color of grass and a play on Hershey's surname, so as to suggest "flowers to come" (50)—flowers that, inevitably, will also eventually succumb to "treacherous" Nature.

The description of the spirit as "a light, a sparkling star" has similarly dual connotations. This would seem to be positive, but the line that follows, dwelling upon how easily such a star may be clouded over, challenges such an assumption. The ghosts' proliferation and extension of similes and metaphors also exemplifies their tendency to view every situation dispassionately and from multiple perspectives. Equally, by having them move so quickly from one comparison to another, Schwartz figures their minds in the processes of thinking and forming associations, rather than settling upon already reached conclusions.

Hershey's retrospective narrative engages much more closely with particulars, although he, too, seeks similes and abstract ideas to give universal meaning to his experiences. About three-quarters of the way through the poem, he describes the continued disquietude of the Green household. Jack and Eva Green are in the midst of one of many temporary separations when Jack sends his lawyer to ask Eva to sell the family home.

> All summer long, Eva Green held out, resisted every effort,
>   Made by Jack Green and by his lawyer to persuade her to move from the red-brick house,

But when September came, more money was due on the mortgage and Jack Green promised to come home, if she would move from the house,

And sign the agreement, which permitted him to sell the house at a profit,

And Eva Green consented, although she but half-believed Jack Green's promise to return,

And Jack Green himself did not know what the truth was, for he was full of a tiredness of another evening lady.

And thus on a warm and drizzling day in late September, the family moved from the red-brick house on the Parkway,

Jack Green came for his family to drive them to their new home in his car or machine,

And Hershey cried out because his kitten was being left behind, and both parents promised him that the moving van would bring the kitten,

And then, after driving through the autumn rain, they came to the cheap dark apartment hurriedly chosen by Jack Green,

Who felt that he had already spent too much money. Grandmother met them there, to help them unpack,

And when the moving van came, the kitten was not with the moving men,

And Hershey cried with great bitterness, depressed by the rainy day, and the dark apartment, and the loss of his pet,

And one more deception upon the part of his father and mother. And then after supper,

His father put on his coat, and his mother asked his father where he was going?

And his father said that he might as well stay out the week he had paid for at the hotel where he had been living,

And Eva Green saw and her mother saw and Hershey saw, trembling with disappointment, that he was lying,

But Eva Green kept silent, a self-control unknown to her, inspired by the indestructible hope that silence might help to bring him back,

And Hershey sat in his chair and rooted vainly

That his father would change his mind and come to live with them, and buy him toys,

And be the powerful presence moving Hershey as a king once moved his soldier boys,

And Hershey felt the presence in the darkened air of these relationships, the family divinity,

> The great city, the America in which Jack Green made his way with his
> will, He felt them as the sailor feels the rocking sea under him, vast and
> abysmal, Endless and disappointing! (154–155)

The passage moves from pedantic explanation to greater abstraction as
Hershey contemplates what the events he describes reveal about his family
relationships. The passage's 4 sentences occupy 25 lines, over half of which
begin with "And." The anaphora accentuates the child's perspective and nar-
rative style. Although the Hershey Green who narrates the story is himself
only an adolescent, he often revisits the point of view of his younger self.
This becomes especially apparent in the lines about his abandoned kitten
and the moving van, which illustrate the chronologically episodic nature of
Genesis: this is the first we hear about Hershey having a kitten, and by the
end of the passage it has been forgotten again as he is once more overcome
by the shadow of his parents' marital unhappiness.

This episode's first sentence spans six long lines in which Jack Green's
name recurs four times, Eva Green's twice, and the word "house" three
times. Hershey's habit of referring to his parents by their full names dis-
tances himself from them. Except when in blank verse conversation with the
ghosts, he also refers to himself in the third person, and, while the ghosts
occasionally refer (mockingly) to "Mamma and Papa," Hershey himself
never affects such intimacy. The repetitions emphasize the spondaic meter
of Jack Green's name in particular, two strong stresses that slow the pace of
the verse whenever they occur. Hershey's mother's name is only slightly less
imposing, the second syllable of her first name so lightly stressed that "Eva
Green" becomes almost spondaic too. The repetitions of their full names
makes Hershey's parents seem all the more formidable. Repetition is also
a means of stressing the contrast between the grand-sounding "red-brick
house" (with its three strong consecutive beats) and the "cheap dark apart-
ment" to which the family moves.

Schwartz's reliance on heavy accents is apparent throughout the pas-
sage. Eva Green's defiance and Jack Green's persistence are registered in the
thumping beats of the first two lines:

> All *summer long, Eva Green held out*, / resisted *every effort*,
>   *Made* by *Jack Green* and by his *lawyer* / to per*suade* her to *move* from
> the *red-brick house.*

In the first of these lines there are three consecutive strong stresses followed
by a pronounced caesura that cues in a reassertion of Eva Green's resistance.
There is no narrative need for the subordinate clause except that it further

underlines her refusal to succumb to her husband's will. Similarly, there is no real need to mention Jack Green's lawyer. It is a prosaic detail, but one that strengthens our sense of Jack Green's artillery.

Schwartz's biblical prose can accommodate lighter stresses as well, however. When Hershey tells how, after supper, his father

> put on his coat, and his mother asked his father where he was going?
> And his father said that he might as well stay out the week he had paid for at the hotel where he had been living

the pace of the narrative is much quicker, imitating natural speech, and none of the stresses on the mostly monosyllabic words are heavy. [13] This quick pace sets up a contrast with the more lugubrious line that follows, with its three stresses on the word "saw," mimicking the Green family's gradual realization of Jack's actual intentions: "And Eva Green saw and her mother saw and Hershey saw, trembling with disappointment, that he was lying." The form is adaptable enough to carry a variety of tones, registers, and paces.

Perhaps even more conspicuous than any of the verse features in the two passages just discussed, however, are the quirks of Schwartz's language. Irving Howe has celebrated Schwartz's voice as one that is "at home with the speech of people not quite at home with English speech."[14] Schwartz's prose style, he argues,

> seem[s] to be composed of several speech-layers: the sing-song, slightly pompous intonations of Jewish immigrants educated in night-schools, the self-conscious affectionate mockery of that speech by American-born sons, its abstraction into the jargon of city intellectuals, and finally the whole body of this language flattened into a prose of uneasiness, an anti-rhetoric. (Howe, Foreword, xii)

The idiosyncrasies of Jewish immigrant speech are even more explicitly acknowledged in the story "America! America!" in which Schwartz italicizes terms used colloquially by recent arrivals learning American English. When Shenandoah Fish's mother describes his father as going into the "insurance game," Shenandoah is struck by his mother's "fine memory for the speech other people used."[15] This instance may not strike the twenty-first-century reader as especially unusual, since the term, though still slangy, has become commonplace. Other examples abound, however, among them many that relate more directly to immigrant experience: the term "greenhorn," used of those recently off the ship (and alluded to in the Green family name); "ship sisters"; and "gyp," meaning a swindle, whose first recorded usage by the Oxford English Dictionary (OED) is in a book of criminal slang from 1914 ("America! America!," 12, 26, 31. Schwartz's emphases). At other times, the pitch of Schwartz's writing becomes overtly satirical, such as in "The World Is a Wedding," which repeatedly shows up the excesses of city intellectual jargon. On showing a visiting theater director one of his plays, for example, the central character, Rudyard Bell announces that "in this scene…the ignorance and irony are such that I am supreme among the dramatists who write in the English tongue."[16] He is seemingly unaware that he has implied not a character's ignorance but his own, or that by uttering such a sentence he has exposed his inability to adapt his use of "the English tongue" to any audience less pompous than himself.

If Schwartz's prose is characterized by flatness, unease, and antirhetoric, these traits are arguably even more pronounced in *Genesis*. Such grammatically unconventional statements as "[Albert Green] did not go forward as rapidly to wealth as Jack did" (55) and "Hershey was taken to begin to go to the foreign world each day" (135) exemplify the sing-song intonations and uneasiness with language that Howe identifies. However, such expression establishes itself as the particular idiom of the poem: the oddness is easily overlooked. As assuredly as any of his prose fiction, *Genesis* shows Schwartz to be at home with such awkward speech.

The curious language is a large part of what makes the passages just discussed poetic. The ghosts' description of the "cool flakes [of snow] quickly stained in city streets" evokes a clear enough visual impression of dirty slush, but to describe snowflakes as "cool" is strangely understated and "stained" is a far less obvious choice of word than "melted." The conventional image of the snow is rendered peculiar, even surreal, and yet the image remains naturalistic. Another case of inimitable phrasing is Hershey's euphemistic description of his father as "full of a tiredness of another evening lady." He could hardly be less direct, but this creates a mysterious quality although we are never in any doubt as to what he actually means. Similarly, when Hershey describes Jack Green picking up his family "in his car or his machine," the "or his machine" is redundant except insofar as it suggests that "car" is somehow inadequate as a name for whatever it is that Hershey's father drives.

Genesis is also, conspicuously, a poem for voices. Its emphasis throughout is on language as it is spoken rather than as it is written. Hershey is first introduced simply as "the one who speaks" (3) and the ghosts—who are "bodiless"—can only be discerned by their voices. The first is heard

As from a worn victrola record, needle
Which skims and whirrs, a voice intoned

As of a weak old man with foreign accent,
Ironic, comic, flat and matter of fact,
With alternation measured, artificial,
                            moaned,
And yet with such sympathy, simpatico
                            as if
A guardian angel sang! (4)

The description of this voice reaffirms Schwartz's commitment to "morbid pedestrianism" rather than the floridity of Swinburne. When another voice enters it is "cracked and joyous" (8): the voices are indistinct and muted, yet resonant. It seems likely from Schwartz's description of the first ghost's "foreign accent" that he is Eastern European, foreign to the American Hershey despite his heritage. But nothing more precise than this is offered, vexing the question of how foreignness is to be identified in an international society. That the voices are also "measured" and "artificial" is an implicit acknowledgment that by speaking in verse at all their language cannot be regarded as completely without pretension, and Schwartz's insistence upon their "ironic, comic" tone is a warning not to take their pronouncements as Gospel.

From the outset, *Genesis* is concerned with listening. Hershey variously describes himself as a child who "was always listening" (112), who was "listening and looking always" (126), who "had listened and looked...looked and listened" and who "sat and listened" to his mother "rehearsing" her marriage to her lawyer, a story he has heard many times before (152). It is apt that the first ghostly voice should seem to emanate from a victrola, since it was from his aunt's victrola that Hershey heard the voices of Galli-Curci and Caruso (but also Jolson) as they "Soared, cried and pealed," giving him his first "intuitions of the beauty of formal sound" (117).

Eliot's example is, again, important to Schwartz in this respect. In "T. S. Eliot's Voice and his Voices," Schwartz insists that although Eliot's poems contain many voices the more important point is that they are

> often dominated by a listening to other voices—the voices of other poets, in other centuries and countries; the voices of various human beings of differing classes and stations in society, a diversity of beliefs, values, habits of speech, and views of life. ("T. S. Eliot's Voice and His Voices," 135)

He goes on to argue that the act of listening is as important in Eliot's poetry as the voices themselves, suggesting that in "Portrait of a Lady," for example, "the distinction between listening and speaking is a concrete part of the poem itself" (136): we miss its dramatic force if we ignore the gulf between what the lady says and how the protagonist responds. This is part of a method which Schwartz terms "sibylline (or subliminal) listening" and which "permits all other methods to be used freely and without predetermination": it instigates a kind of receptivity "which opens itself to any and all kinds of material and subject matter" (138). Perhaps the clearest example of Schwartz using such a method occurs in "America! America!" in which Shenandoah develops his understanding of his relationship with his mother by listening to what she says about their neighbors, the Baumanns. But the very premise of *Genesis,* with the ghosts primarily as listeners, is similar too.

Cynthia Ozick has written of the "relentlessly gradual return of aural culture, beginning with the telephone (a farewell to letter-writing), the radio, the motion picture, and the phonograph" and speeded up by the technology of the later twentieth century that has effectively "restored us to the pre-literate status of face-to-face speech."[17] She identifies "the culture of mass literacy" as existing only between 1830 and 1930. Schwartz, writing in the 1930s and 1940s, was acutely conscious of these technological advances, as is evident from his association of "international consciousness" with the radio and from his obsession with cinema. His preoccupation with different voices, and with the acts of telling and of interpretation, is perhaps an acknowledgment that writing of a solely literary nature was no longer adequate to the society in which—and about which—he wrote. His writing is far from being entirely performative. Nonetheless, through its disembodied voices, Schwartz comes closer to suggesting the kind of correspondence that might occur over the telephone (which he regarded, not entirely flippantly, as "one of the most important things in life") than would be read in letters.[18] Schwartz himself was aware of this, explaining to Robert Hivnor, "I find that what I've been doing seems to be based upon the telephone, as 'IDBR' on the movie" (*Letters,* 102). After all, the phone, the movie, the victrola, and the radio all have the ghostly effect of making those who are not physically there seem to be present.

Once all this has been considered, it is surprising that *Genesis* contains so little dialogue. We tend only to hear the voices of Hershey's parents and grandparents indirectly, as reported by Hershey. Their disputes are told, not dramatized. Except in its narrative register, we don't hear much of Hershey's own voice either, and it would be a just criticism of *Genesis* to argue that in his commitment to "morbid pedestrianism" and making Hershey a representative figure, Schwartz neglects to individuate his protagonist's voice: although we acquire a great deal of factual knowledge about him, we come away from the poem with much less of a sense of Hershey as a character than we do of Berryman's Henry in *The Dream Songs* or of Lowell's self in *Life Studies.* Hershey also has as little physical presence as the ghosts, despite recounting such bodily embarrassments as wetting himself and being caught by his father lying on a girl's belly.

Nonetheless, *Genesis*—which precedes *Life Studies* by 16 years—does pioneer poetry as self-representation, and Schwartz shows an acute consciousness of the piece as performance (as does Hershey). The poem's premise allows for a further investigation of the type already undertaken in "Coriolanus and His Mother" and the verse play "Shenandoah" in which the protagonist finds himself simultaneously upon the stage and in the audience, watching his own life as a detached spectator. Hershey describes himself at kindergarten as "already the actor and victim of what a constellation of emotions" (*G*, 101). As victim, he suggests that he has little control over what happens to him, but as actor he acknowledges the degree of self-fashioning in the way he presents himself. Such combined passivity and activity are Hershey's characteristic mode. One of the ghosts remarks that fame and audience begin at home (19), a point repeatedly illustrated by Hershey in describing how he "enacted" (106) writing on his blackboard for visitors and relatives or delighted them with his first metaphor. He also learns, however, to be in the audience at home, much like, later, the "unseen and all-seeing" Lowell of *Life Studies* watches his family's development.[19] An episode in which Hershey listens from the stair as his mother's friend, Mrs. Rinehart, exhorts Eva Green to whip him for revealing to laborers that she had formerly been a Ziegfeld Follies girl shows a distrust of performance. For Mrs. Rinehart, despite the success that popular theater has brought her, there is something shameful about performing professionally. His mother's impromptu performances are most shameful of all for Hershey, not least her denunciation of Jack Green in a roadhouse where she catches him dining with a whore, the episode that brings *Book One* to its climax. All that afternoon, Hershey relates, her "monologue obsessed the afternoon" (203) (and there is perhaps an implicit acknowledgment here that his own narrative is also an obsessed monologue, much more so than it is an actual conversation with the ghosts). Eva Green's oratory, one of the ghosts suggests, is what taught Hershey "to cry aloud [his] life" (207), and it "will abide," making Hershey's "being as a being-in-the-world" a "profoundest theatre" (207). Though Lowell and Berryman's later works more fully realize the dramatic potential inherent in telling one's life, both are indebted to Schwartz's earlier example.

"The Land of the Old World Failure and the New World Success"

For Howe, the only major contribution of the New York milieu to the genres of poetry and fiction was its legitimation of a specifically Jewish American subject matter and tone. Certainly *Genesis*, along with the stories collected in *The World Is a Wedding*, plays its part in establishing the kind of "urban malaise, second-generation complaint, Talmudic dazzle, woeful alienation, and dialectical irony" that is also to be found in the slightly later fiction of Bellow, Norman Mailer, Bernard Malamud, and Philip Roth.[20] But Schwartz's poetry, and *Genesis* specifically, was more noted by fellow poets than Howe's judgment recognizes. Lowell's "To Delmore Schwartz," for example, positioned in "Part Three" of *Life Studies* alongside poems for Ford Madox Ford, George Santayana, and Hart Crane, is perhaps an acknowledgment that without Schwartz (and the others) the sequence that follows could not have been written. Like *Genesis*, *Life Studies* documents a family's collapse against a larger historical backdrop, seeking universal truths in individual experience. In describing his mother's "*Risorgimento* black and gold casket" as being "like Napoleon's at the *Invalides*... ," for example, Lowell makes the same kind of claim for his family's relation to major historical events as Schwartz does when he relates how his grandfather fled the Russian army.[21] Lowell also follows Schwartz's lead, later, in presenting his mother as an American version of Clytemnestra. Both poets present themselves as the children of myth and history.

The "Life Studies" sequence differs from *Genesis*, however, insofar as it does not rely upon the kind of commentary provided by Schwartz's ghosts. The book's three preceding sections—and especially the prose memoir "91 Revere Street" in which Lowell considers his own Jewish ancestry in the character of Mordecai Myers—provide all the context necessary. Berryman's *The Dream Songs*, meanwhile, has Henry's friend who calls him "Mr Bones" fulfill the ghosts' role with more economical humor. Perhaps closer in conception—though different in most other respects—is James Merrill's *The Changing Light at Sandover*, in which identified presences help Merrill and his partner David Jackson to interpret messages received through a Ouija board. Ashbery suggests that, as well as Merrill's epic, Auden's "The Sea and the Mirror" might owe a debt to *Genesis*.[22] "Coriolanus and His Mother" would be a more obvious Schwartz poem to consider in relation to Auden's commentary on *The Tempest*, but it may be that Auden took something from *Genesis* when writing *The Age of Anxiety*.[23] Schwartz thought this long work pretentious and infected by "tourist slanginess," but, like *Genesis*, it pursues religious and philosophical questions from multiple perspectives, sets up characters as psychological case studies representing the malaise of a whole society, and prioritizes the spoken over the written word (albeit in speeches that are more monologic than dialogic).[24] Meanwhile, across their careers, a shared fascination with mirrors, with (as Ashbery observes) catalogue-like lists of concrete and abstract nouns (*The Heavy Bear*, 8), and with modern communication technology like the telephone and the radio further align Schwartz and Auden.

Recognizing an affinity between the two poets helps to explain why Auden took *Genesis* so seriously, even though, on reading a late draft, he discouraged Schwartz from publishing it. Although his criticisms are colored by his own religious preoccupations of that time, they elucidate one of the reasons that *Genesis* falters. The problem, for Auden, is not formal or structural, but Schwartz's inability to establish his religious position. "You have now approached the frontier where the question of religious faith is inescapable," Auden commented,

> the point at which you have become aware that ahead of you lies *either* faith *or* despair, but...you are still confused about what faith is: because the road that has led to this point has been that of aesthetic and ethical consciousness, you still cling to the hope that it crosses the frontier—but it doesn't. (Atlas, 217)

The Prelude comes off aesthetically, Auden argues, because Wordsworth "really manages to believe" that "the poetic imagination and religious revelation are one" (Atlas, 218). Schwartz is "too advanced" to be able to believe this. He is also unwilling to confront his paradoxical insights into the nature of suffering: on one hand, that it has (aesthetic) value, and may therefore be desirable, but, on the other, that it is (ethically) shameful, and that to desire it would be to refuse the pursuit of happiness. Schwartz's psychological and metaphysical speculations, Auden says, are not sufficient substitutes for belief or the honest acknowledgment of faithlessness. These speculations become destructive when they presuppose only human consciousness rather than a religious faith. Nor, in writing about personal memory, will one find significance, value, and belief simply by looking up and remembering enough. This may *lead* one to faith or despair, but it is only at this point that one can really begin to examine one's own life or write from a religious perspective.

To some extent, Auden's reading is overdetermined. As Atlas points out, Schwartz's God is "essentially a poetic device" (Atlas, 220) and the poem does not demand to be read in such theological terms. Auden fails to appreciate, also, that uncertainty is itself a subject for Schwartz. But his central point—that Schwartz needed to decide upon his religious position in order to secure his aesthetic position—is persuasive. Schwartz's agnosticism, however honest, diminishes his authority.

In addition, in questioning Schwartz's approach to writing about personal memory, Auden implies that Hershey's biographical narrative, despite the ghosts' interjections, falls short of the universal bearing toward which it aspires. He is trying to extrapolate wider significance from occurrences that do not readily yield it up. Dudley Fitts, another early critic, felt this too, complaining to Schwartz that he struggled to believe in any of the characters other than Hershey and his father. The "army-deserting grandpa," for example, is diminished for Fitts because "the terribly significant things that happened to him" are told "with an elliptical casualness that robs them of credibility when they are juxtaposed to the minute analysis of comparatively insignificant, if only because less spectacular, things that happen to Hershey."[25] In his overcommitment to "international consciousness," this suggests, in his determination to present *every* occurrence as in some way universal, Schwartz manages to flatten events that really are exceptional.

From the outset the poem is presented as a representative myth not only of early twentieth-century immigrant experience but also of cultural change more generally. But it is also an account of one individual's actual experiences. Schwartz's challenge is to harmonize these two tendencies. Hershey's mother, Eva, is a fallen Eve, while both grandfathers share their names with the original biblical traveler. Such evocative naming allows for little individuation. Their surnames define them as types as well. Noah Newman takes off for America to become a new man, and Noah Green's name prompts numerous puns relating to springtime. (Schwartz may also have remembered Jay Gatsby's belief in the green light at the end of Daisy Buchanan's dock as a symbol of the American Dream.)[26] Many of the episodes narrated appear to have been chosen more because they suggest universal truths or show the individual being made aware of his position in a wider world than because they advance the plot or develop character. For example, the birth of his brother, Roger, is important to Hershey primarily because it reveals to him that he is not, as he was coming to believe, the exclusive subject of his parents' affections. Similarly, when Roger is later ill with scarlet fever, the memory matters less because of any concern Hershey has about his brother's health than because the image of the convalescent Roger waving to him, with their mother, from a high apartment window provides him with a further metonym for separation. Any reader expecting more than the broadest of outlines from these episodes would surely be underwhelmed.

On some occasions, however, Schwartz's practice of making commonplace occurrences emblematic of historical events—as in the analogy with Aeneas in "The Ballad of the Children of the Czar"—illuminates both the local detail and the bigger picture. The habit is not an attempt to claim equal stature for the more negligible episode, but rather a means of suggesting that, for each world-changing act, a source or analogy can be found in quotidian experience. When, for example, Hershey recalls being sent out of the kindergarten classroom for kicking a boy who had kicked him first, he declares: "Exiled, humiliated, persecuted, Coriolanus, Joseph, and Caesar, the child resumes history, each enacts all that has been" (*G*, 101). The aggrandizement of such a trivial mishap gives it a comic tint, but the serious point—that a version of these figures' various rejections by their own people, and their subsequent exiles, is reenacted in microcosm in Hershey's kindergarten and everywhere in daily life—does survive the inflation. The child appropriates the whole history of displacement into his personal feeling of having been cast out. A specifically Jewish context is stressed by the mention of Joseph, but the references to Coriolanus and Caesar as well make the condition less exclusive. And, against the poem's transatlantic backdrop, the episode evokes not just the exile of the Jews from Egypt but also, more concretely, the experience of Hershey's parents' generation as they left Europe and tried to establish themselves in the sometimes hostile new society of America. On the terms that the poem itself establishes, the comparison is not as preposterous as it initially seems; the comparatively insignificant event is just a localized version of the more spectacular one and, arguably, helps make the latter more comprehensible.

All the same, Auden and Fitts's criticisms accentuate—in addition to the religious problem—a further unresolved dilemma for Schwartz: the poem wants us to believe, on the one hand, that each event suggests other events and that nothing is original. But it also insists upon the primacy of individual experience, and, on a number of occasions, Schwartz admits that certain events *are* exceptional. Bismarck and Disraeli, for example, are recognized as individuals who do, atypically, alter the course of history—both international and personal. They are themselves "divinities" of their day, and neither Hershey nor the ghosts really attempts to reconcile this with their merely human agency. Had the Congress of Berlin, over which Bismarck presided, not annulled Russia's victory in the Russo-Turkish war, Noah Green's first attempt at forging a new life by deserting and remarrying might not have been thwarted; his comrades would not have returned home earlier than expected to reveal his plans to the wife he tried to abandon; and, consequently, Hershey would never have been born. As such, individuals are, as one of the ghosts says, the "prey and pin of kings and queens" (14). But they have individual responsibility too. One can blame Bismarck and Disraeli, but Noah Green himself is the one most responsible for his family's future. Neither Hershey, nor Schwartz himself, seems quite able to admit this.

Less politically inflected but also illustrative of the contingency of individual existence is an episode in which, after Noah Newman's death, Leah Newman returns to Europe to visit her family and is given a French bond for her daughter, Eva, by her brother, Benjamin. Eva sells this bond so that she can afford an operation that enables her to become pregnant. "The prosperity of Eastern European capitalism sent the French bond west," Hershey explains. "It went through Paris, the capital of Western culture, / And entered her marriage and entered her womb" (65). The seemingly superfluous reference to Paris is Hershey's attempt to emphasize his Western cultural heritage: he hopes that the circumstances of his conception owed at least something to culture as well as to finance. While some of the ghosts dismiss the episode as a "minor nut," others concur with Hershey that only his grandmother's return trip back across the Atlantic made his birth possible: "Twice, twice! over Atlantic rides and raves," they proclaim, "His thisness tiptoes on Might-Not-Have-Been!" (66).

Whatever difficulties these episodes present for Schwartz in terms of differentiating between unique and universal occurrences, they do illustrate, very clearly, that international and personal history are inextricably intertwined. This is a reticulation that is oversimplified by Kirsch when he argues that the personal is broadly represented for Schwartz by Freud and the international by Marx.[27] Both here and elsewhere, Schwartz tries to force Marx and Freud into a compromise, insisting that personal experience is a part of international experience and that the two are not separable.

Hershey's idiosyncratic name, for example, attests to both the sociohistorical circumstances that surround his birth and the peculiarities of his own family. Absurd mismatches of first name and surname, playing upon Schwartz's own idiosyncratic name, afflict his other protagonists too, most obviously Shenandoah Fish, but also Faber Gottschalk, Cornelius Schmidt, and Bertholde Cannon.[28] Hershey's ancestors, unlike the biblical Noah, whose old world was destroyed entirely, cannot leave theirs behind: they "bring Europe with them, more or less, / The greatest thing in North America!" (33)—and in this context, it is not so much the great and defining artistic achievements of European civilization that they bring as the parochial customs and age-old traditions that jar against the conspicuous modernity of America and betray their Old World heritage. Naming their son, as no true American ever would, after a quintessentially American chocolate brand imprints his non-American heritage upon him, also betraying the particular difficulties his parents (as opposed to other immigrants) had in adapting their lives to their new country. Eva projects a capitalist, consumerist American identity onto her son that marks him as much as his circumcision determines his Jewishness.

Hershey's naming prompts the ghosts to discuss the "joke of individuality," comparing his misfortune at being so named to that of the one man amid a crowd of 70,000 who is "made wet" by a pigeon (70). In the verse play "Shenandoah," which explicitly concerns the naming of a child and the family dispute that ensues, the baby begins to howl at the precise moment that Mrs. Fish decides to name him Shenandoah. In both works, it is emphasized that the child might have been named after its grandfather had it not been for superstition or family objection (it is a Jewish custom that a child should not be named after a living relative). But the idea of the new world exerts as strong an influence as Jewish tradition, acting upon "the foreigner whose foreign-ness / Names his son native." The older Shenandoah Fish, who acts as chorus in the play and often sounds decidedly ghostlike, identifies, among the "world-wide causes" that contribute to his own naming the influences of America, Europe, mortality, and Judaism, whether wholly or only partially believed.[29] He recalls a primitive tradition whereby a child is sometimes named after historical occurrences that provide a context for its birth, concluding that he might as well have been named "The First World War" (*Shenandoah*, 14). As it is, his own name already testifies to a particular historical moment, that of the attempts by European immigrants to become American. But, even more than that, it testifies to his parents' individual response to that moment.

Another way in which Hershey's relatives betray their European background is through their attachment to the idea of kingship. Hershey, for example, "climb[s] the ego's tower, / A prince of the wide world, expecting to be a king!" (*G*, 106). Although one of his proudest moments as a child, is writing the name "WOODROW WILSON" on a toy blackboard (106) (suggesting that he is learning patriotism as well as writing) and although he later imagines himself as "a Giant star and also the President of the United States," heralded by Sousa's "The Stars and Stripes Forever" (181), he also regrets Germany's defeat in the First World War "because it was the end of royalty's hierarchy" (183). "The Ballad of the Children of the Czar" recalls a grandfather leaving "for America / To become a king himself" (*SK*, 4), and in *Genesis*, men like Jack Green bring with them from Europe, "the peasant's sense that land was the most important thing and the owner of land / A king!" (*G*, 78). Commonplace though the metaphor is, the immigrant's notion of kingship is likely to reveal his European heritage in a nation that does not have a king and that defines itself against the very concept of monarchy. What is more, for all his prestige, a king is necessarily a great deal removed from the rest of society, and in any given nation there can only ever be one at a time.

The dream of becoming a king oneself therefore excludes others: it is not a dream of communal success. And with the acquisition of kingly status come the responsibilities and difficulties that a king must face. It is when he is most successful that Jack Green most suffers "the insecurity kings must endure" (146). Hershey explains how all of the immigrants "prospered as a class, although some were failures for the irreducible reasons of persons" (78). Although his own ancestors made their decisions to leave for America individually and impulsively, "troops" of others made the same decisions at around the same time. Whatever hope there may be of a collective American Dream being fulfilled, there is no such possibility of millions of individual and competing dreams also all coming true.

This compounds the immigrant's sense of having a dissociated identity; they are separated not only from long-settled Americans but also from each other as a consequence of competition. This is further suggested in Hershey's description of America as "the land of the refugee and of making a living, the land of the old world failure and the new world success" (78). One does not stop being a refugee when one begins to make a living. Although earning money is likely to improve one's quality of life and self-perception, it does not alter one's status. Equally though, being a refugee does not preclude one from being successful. For many immigrants—mavericks such as Albert and Jack Green—the transatlantic crossing is an opportunity as much as it is a flight. For them too, however, the old world and the new, failure and success, coexist in America. Jack Green's impetuosity, an asset in his various jobs, is disastrous for his family relationships.

It is also implied that unless the immigrants are able to relinquish the values they once held in Europe, the memory of past failure is likely to remain as keen as the joy of any present successes. A man's failures may still live in him even when he has begun to succeed: Noah Newman, for example, never overcomes the grudge he bears against Benjamin Harris, whose provocation prompted his exodus in the first place. "The ideas of failure and success," according to Jacob Cohen in "The World Is a Wedding," are "the two most important ideas in America."[30] Success—specifically financial and social success—is all that can validate the upheaval of the transatlantic voyage, but in order to achieve it one must also risk failure and risk separating oneself from one's peers. In twentieth-century America, to be part of a prospering class is little consolation for the individual who is a failure.

The "Idea" of America: Misimagining and Displacement in Genesis and "America! America!"

The monarchical fantasies of Hershey Green's family sit uneasily alongside their investment in the American Dream, but both are aspirational illusions that are far removed from the way their lives really are. *Genesis* is replete with such moments of misimagining. Noah Green divorces his wife and flees the Czar's army because he is dissatisfied on account of his life not resembling "the images of adolescence" (8). Leah Harris initially resists the courtship of Noah Newman because he "did not at all embody the ideas of romance she had seen in the novels she loved"; he, meanwhile, never stops regarding her as "the difficult prize, ... the image of his first glimpse" (21). And later, Jack and Albert Green fall out because Albert manages to injure Jack's "idea of himself" (55) as self-reliant. The poem's opening scene has Hershey himself mistaking the light of an electric street lamp for snow—prompting him to remark "'How each view may be false!'" (4)—while his own name is testament to his mother's mistaken expectation of his character: he is named after her neighbor's son, Harold, whose nickname is Hershey and who is the "the image of what she wanted her child to be" (69).

The poem's recurrent attention to idealized images and ideas incites one of the ghosts to remark, "How images may dominate a life!" (21). It also suggests how each act of individual imagining may contribute toward the creation of a myth on a larger scale. Schwartz's most explicit suggestion that the American Dream is about attachment to images comes in the story "America! America!" in which Shenandoah Fish listens to his mother talking about friends of hers, the Baumanns. The Baumanns's circle of friends, disappointed in their expectations but unable to admit that they are, invest themselves in images of "the wonders of America." They are awed by planes, elevators, and the new subway.

> When the toilet-bowl flushed like Niagara, when a suburban homeowner killed his wife and children, and when a Jew was made a member of Theodore Roosevelt's cabinet, the excited exclamation was:
> "America! America!"
> The expectations of these human beings who had come in their youth to the new world had not been fulfilled in the least. [31]

Sanitary progress finds its image in one of America's most spectacular natural phenomena; the murder story is pure gossip, presumably made a topic for open discussion by a Hearst newspaper; and, for the Jewish immigrant, the political success of one of their people is both a stage toward more general acceptance by society as a whole and a promise that they could succeed similarly. Schwartz makes the reader skeptical about this possibility, however, pointing out that these people "had above all expected to be rich, and they had come [to America] with a very different image of what their new life was to be" (22). What is remarkable is that despite their own lack of personal fulfillment, these immigrants are able to find something "more marvellous than fulfilment" (22) in the wonders, technological and social, of the new society, making these into the images which they "view as" the new world.

Considered rationally, this is mere self-deception, but devoting themselves to such images is what enables these people to endure.

In *Genesis*, Hershey makes clear that America, at the turn of the century, was far from being just a new and successful world, but Mrs. Baumann in "America! America!" is blinkered by her images of the new world and cannot understand why her sons are unable, or disinclined, to make a living. "In America everyone or almost everyone was successful. [She] had seen too many fools make out well to believe otherwise" (24). It is beyond her imagination to think that they too might be fools, or that they might have a different conception to her of what it is to be successful. Mrs. Baumann's husband prospers as an insurance broker, but as the story progresses it becomes apparent that this success is relatively limited and that his only clients are other immigrants: he does not try to "acquire new customers" (14), and relies upon affability and loyalty to old world customs rather than the business acumen and ruthlessness that characterize the true late-nineteenth-century American tycoons. Shenandoah remembers that Baumann resembled the first J. P. Morgan in photographs (13), but that is where the similarity ends. Baumann clings to his European and, by implication, old-fashioned ways, drinking his tea "in the Russian style," for example, "from a glass, not a cup: a cup was utterly out of the question" (13). His pedantic tone, as much as the custom itself, shows how reluctant Baumann is to adapt to the new country's ways, and, in common with the Greens, he is fixated on monarchy, eagerly discussing "the private lives of the kings and queens of Europe" (13). He is, perhaps, a more refined version of Bellow's Father Herzog, who had also been a gentleman in Russia but who had failed in his various jobs since arriving in Canada, and who is remembered by his son as "a father, a sacred being, a king."[32] The Baumanns's son Sidney, is a far from sympathetic character, but he is perceptive in comparing his father to much richer men and pointing out missed opportunities. Among a people who value success so highly, it is not enough that Baumann himself feels successful if that view is not shared by the world at large or even by his own family. His Russian-style tea-drinking and his royal gossip make him anachronistic, an old world failure; and, above all, it alienates his sons who hold very different values.

Alienation, for Schwartz, sometimes means, generally, "a state of estrangement in feeling or affection" (OED 1. a), but it also indicates, more specifically, the Marxist concept of *Entäusserung*. Although this has been variously interpreted, and has, in some contexts, been translated as "externalization" rather than "alienation," the term covers each facet of what, for Marx, is the inevitable consequence of the ownership of private property: the sinking of the worker himself "to the level of a commodity," and his separation from the product of his work, from the experience of working, from himself, and from all others.[33] The worker not only loses the object of his labor, the product he has worked to create, but also ends up in bondage to it.[34] In this respect, capital might be regarded as another of Schwartz's "divinities" of the day, controlling the lives of those who ought, instead, to be controlling it.

Characters such as Hershey and Shenandoah can only feel helplessness in the face of such a situation. At the beginning of "America! America!," for example, Shenandoah perceives a "great change" in the people he used to know. "The depression had occurred to these human beings" (10): they have become the passive subjects of a force beyond individual control and, by referring to them as "human beings" rather than "people," regarding them not as individuals but as a species, Schwartz exposes the facelessness of Shenandoah's one-time acquaintances, denying them any trait to which the reader, or Shenandoah himself, might be able to relate. They are "ashamed of what they had made or what had been made of their lives" (10). The main implication here is that, however unavoidable a force the Depression may have been, they have failed to strive against it and make the best of difficult circumstances: it is this of which they are most ashamed. Shenandoah himself epitomizes such resignation. Despite the economic crisis, he is content to spend his mornings in dressing gown and pyjamas listening to his mother's gossip, and although he does begin to feel uneasy about this he does nothing to change it.

Shenandoah's sense of estrangement from his peers is acute, but his sense of separation from his own family and other immigrant families, such as the Baumanns, is even more so. Listening to his mother, he "felt that in every sense he was removed from them by thousands of miles, or by a generation, or by the Atlantic Ocean" (19). The separation is both temporal and physical. There is a generation between himself and Mr. and Mrs. Baumann, and the Atlantic Ocean metaphor is more than just that because the most crucial difference between his experience of America and that of his parents' generation is that they really did cross the Atlantic Ocean to seek a new life. We learn in the story's first sentence that Shenandoah has just returned from Paris: so he too has crossed the Atlantic, but for him the journey was not an upheaval. Living for a time in Paris is a rite of passage for the young American writer in the 1930s, and Fish expects to go back. The monumental aura of travel has diminished, and his visit to Paris even implies a degree of defiance: his parents risked everything to leave Europe and one of his first independent acts is to go back there. Nonetheless, later in the story Shenandoah recognizes that, despite his contrary ideals, it would be false to judge his elders from his privileged position because "nothing in his own experience was comparable to the great displacement of body and mind which their coming to America must have been" (27). His own sense of displacement, while real enough, is more metaphorical than literal.

In *Genesis*, Hershey, like Shenandoah, has to accept that if there is a separation between himself and his parents there is also "an unbreakable unity" ("America! America!," 32). The link between the first-generation immigrant's separation from their fatherland and the children of these immigrants from their parents is spelt out by one of the *Genesis* ghosts, who suggests to Hershey that in telling his story he is trying to escape, cathartically, the overdetermining influence of his parents and thus to enact a symbolic transatlantic migration of his own:

> Let then these lives so drive
> Your future life that you become, in truth,
> A colonist, by th'Atlantic voyage
> Of this long night taken away from them! (*G*, 94)

Hershey's response is emphatic. "I cannot go / Away! The mind is my own place, my world" (94), he cries, echoing Milton's Satan who, despite his claim that the mind itself "Can make a heaven of hell, a hell of heaven" can do nothing to change his own nature.[35] The allusion aligns Hershey with Satan, the rebellious subject, reacting against the ultimate father figure, God. The Atlantic is not quite the gulf of chaos through which Satan fell, but simply by inviting this as a frame of reference, Schwartz emphasizes the ocean's immensity. Against this, however, the mind being its own place renders specific geographical location irrelevant and epitomizes the ultimate internationality toward which Schwartz so often aspires.

The ghost's suggestion that Hershey is a "colonist" is provocative. Unlike the immigrant, who does not continue to live under the government of his homeland, the colonist remains a subject of his own nation. Given the context of *Genesis*, the choice of word might seem careless. It is appropriate, however, that the poem should occasionally gesture toward the first crossings of Puritan colonists, crossings that the modern immigrants repeat ("each enacts all that has been" [*G*, 101]). America's colonial past is alluded to on a number of occasions, sometimes explicitly, such as when one of the ghosts observes, in contemplation of America's role in the First World War, how "The colony becomes a major nation—" (78), and sometimes through association, such as when Hershey describes his mother and aunt feeling uneasy as children "when confronted with native Americans" (32), imagining them in the same situation as the first colonists. Is it possible for a colonist, or a colonist's descendants, ever to become a true native? In terms of Hershey's hypothetical exodus from his parents, the colonist's experience is perhaps also a truer analogy than that of the immigrant, since the child's character remains conditioned by his parents' even after he has become an adult. It suggests, too, the faint hope that Hershey might one day also be able to declare independence.

By evoking America's colonization, Schwartz also suggests a perhaps surprising affinity between himself and the first Puritan settlers in America. Although he was a modern writer extraordinarily different in temperament and ideals to them, his anxious questioning of how far the modern divinities ("historical, social, cultural, and psychological") determine one's fate indicates a similar obsession with questions of predestination and American exceptionalist ideology. Schwartz's insistence on the international nature of modern life would seem to go against any belief that America was in some respect exceptional, or that any one individual exerted influence alone. Once again, however, Schwartz's sense of the individual turns out to be heightened, rather than contradicted, by his sense of the international. The questions of who might be the chosen, successful ones in a modern, international, and increasingly secular society, and of what examples might be drawn by the general population from the individual whose life is taken to be representative, are pressing concerns of *Genesis* and his stories in particular. And these concerns become even more acute when considered within the contexts of the modern metropolis and the Second World War.

CHAPTER 4

"An Innocent Bystander": The City, *Vaudeville for a Princess,* and Schwartz's Postwar Cultural Criticism

The "World-City": Schwartz and Spengler

Schwartz was only 12 when, in 1926, he read a review of Oswald Spengler's *The Decline of the West*, which he soon went on to read for himself. The book had recently been translated into English and its influence on the aspiring writer was to be profound. Spengler's challenges to the idea of straightforward linear progress in history, and his attempts to understand "world-history, the *world-as-history*," rather than history told simply from a Western-centric perspective, may have informed Schwartz's conception of "international consciousness" to as great an extent as did Eliot's "historical sense" (no matter that, in practice, Schwartz's perspective remained Western-centric).[1] Even more importantly, however, the German historian's theories of the cyclical growth and decline of cultures and civilizations, and his conviction that "Western civilization had reached autumn," proved a creative provocation.[2] Schwartz's efforts not so much to dispute Spengler as to regard such processes in a more optimistic light are held back by the generally bleak prognoses of *In Dreams Begin Responsibilities*, *Genesis*, and *The World Is a Wedding*, but ultimately lead, via his transitional volume *Vaudeville for a Princess and Other Poems*, to his advocacy, in the mid-1950s, of faith in American actuality over and above the American Dream.

This might seem a surprising outcome when considered against the contexts of the "immense alienation of metropolitan life" ("America! America!," 16) and the tragedy of the Second World War, even despite the United States' comparative postwar stability over Europe. It is not, however without logic. The discovery of America, Schwartz recalls, immediately suggested "the possibility that Spengler might be wrong" ("Memoirs of a Metropolitan Child, Memoirs of a Giant Fan," 133). For Saul Bellow—admitting, as Schwartz does not, that part of his anxiety arose from Spengler's characterization of the Jews as part of an archaic civilization, the "Magians," superseded by the superior "Faustians"—America represented a potential further stage in Spengler's cycle. An American Jew, rather than a German or French Jew, Bellow saw his situation as different, his "boyish hunch" being that "America, the enlightened source of a liberal order, might be a new venture in civilization, leaving the Faustians in the rear."[3] In *Book II* of *Genesis*—drafted but unpublished—Hershey Green has a similar idea in devising an ideal state, "The True Republic," that he believes will disprove Spengler.[4] But he is never able to define this vision: it is no more than a dream. And although Schwartz suggests in a 1954 journal entry that only "The daring of the dream / Which the half-wakened / enact" can alleviate Spengler's philosophy by which "In the autumn of the city / There can be no more a Keats, a Mozart" (*Portrait*, 471), such a dream needs first to have a basis in actuality, no matter how inhospitable that actuality might sometimes seem.

Schwartz's hard won struggle to accept American actuality is enacted in poems and stories that explicitly address the nature of metropolitan experience. It is also on prominent display throughout *Vaudeville for a Princess*, which veers between societal engagement and withdrawal. Schwartz's eventual embrace of American actuality, however, is complicated by the insight continually suggested in his works that dream and actuality are never wholly distinct from each other. This difficulty is particularly evident in those poems and stories that suggest the impossibility of comprehending the modern city as anything other than simultaneously a physical entity *and* a mental concept.

For Spengler (who shared no expectations of America as a potential site for progress), it is the emergence of "world-cities"—cities "that have absorbed into themselves the whole content of history"—that, above all, foretells the gradual decline of a civilization (Spengler, 25). He speculates that "the rise of New York to the position of world-city during the Civil War of 1861–5 may perhaps prove to have been the most pregnant event of the nineteenth century" insofar as it seemed to mark "the end of organic growth and the beginning of an inorganic and therefore unrestrained process of agglomerations" (248). "World-city" and "province," he argues, are "the two basic ideas of every civilization"; and Western civilization had reached a point at which

> in place of a world, there is a *city*, a *point*, in which the whole life of broad regions is collecting while the rest dries up. In place of a type-true people,

born of and grown on the soil, there is a new sort of nomad, cohering unstably in fluid masses, the parasitical city dweller, traditionless, utterly matter-of-fact, religionless, clever, unfruitful, deeply contemptuous of the countryman...The world-city means cosmopolitanism in place of "home"...To the world-city belongs not a folk but a mob. (25, Spengler's emphasis)

Such an analysis concords with Schwartz's fears about his generation's lack of a universal world picture, not to mention his consciousness of immigrants as nomads, sacrificing their own traditions in an attempt to be accepted in the new international megalopolis.

For Schwartz, it is this loss of tradition that most exacerbates the individual's alienation. One of the reasons for his having to work to acquire a (literary) tradition is that the more ritualistic Jewish customs he inherited did not seem appropriate to the context of the United States. But the very nature of the city itself further widens the rift between the individual and his or her society. It is too populous and atomistic to allow for any overall sense of community—except for an imagined one. A drafted passage from *Genesis* stresses how New York City is a conglomeration of disparate local communities, its unity a mental construct. It is

> a sum compounded by the mind,
> A vast abstraction, like a sick monarch
>   who
> Rules without reason like an untrue god
> . . .
> It is a sum of living neighbourhoods;
> Each neighbourhood defines itself this way:
> Is felt as being from Downtown removed
> A certain distance,
>   subway, car, and bus
> Count the relationship and no-one walks,
> For walking distance *is* the neighbourhood—[5]

The "sick monarch" and "untrue god" similes suggest that the authority the city wields is more emblematic than actual, granted by submissive residents rather than deserved in its own right. The view Schwartz expresses here affirms the principles of "international consciousness": each region can only be understood in relation to all others and to the city's center.

"The overwhelming presence of the great city," as an idea as much as an actuality, is most explicitly discussed in a passage from "The World Is a Wedding." Jacob Cohen tries to understand his position, and that of his friends, within a city that seems to have no place for them.

> "In New York," he said to himself, … "there are at least six million human beings and during holidays there are more than that number. But, in a way, these numbers hardly exist because they cannot be perceived (we all have four or five friends, more or less). No human being can take in such aggregation: all that we know is that there is always more and more. This is the moreness of which we are aware, no matter what we look upon. This moreness is the true being of the great city, so that, in a way, this city hardly exists. It certainly does not exist as does our family, our friends and our neighbourhood." ("The World Is a Wedding," 50)

If the city in its totality hardly exists to each individual, then it follows that each individual hardly exists to the millions of others who, along with him, make the city what it is. The consequence is the anonymity that is such anathema to Schwartz, making intimate relationships impossible and causing a lack of total knowledge that prevents the individual from achieving "international consciousness." Parts of the city, and some of its inhabitants, can be perceived, but not the entirety. As a result, the city, despite its indisputable concrete existence, may be reduced to little more than an abstraction.[6]

Cohen's speculations provide the germ of the poem "America, America!" (in which Schwartz also proclaims his Atlantic identity), but this poem— "the song of the natural city self in the 20th century"—is more celebratory. It acknowledges, but refuses to dwell upon, the alienation of the individual among vast crowds: "It is true but only partly true that a city is a 'tyranny of numbers,'" Schwartz writes. The poem's ending suggests not an affirmation of self but an Emersonian transcendence of self: in contemplating the lighted windows that, impressionistically, are reduced to squares and checks, and in thinking about the city's many hidden lives, one's selfhood diminishes, lost in a collective "city consciousness / Which sees and says: more: more and more: always more." Such a state is only possible, however, as a consequence of intense contemplation of the actual, substantial city. And, in the recurring echo—"more: more and more: always more"—the second syllable of Schwartz's own name, Delmore, can be heard. The repetition evokes the presence of the individual, and his resistance to becoming completely anonymous, even when subsumed by something greater than himself.

Elsewhere, in "The Mind Is an Ancient and Famous Capital"—the first of three extracts taken from the unfinished "The Studies of Narcissus" and included in *Summer Knowledge*—Schwartz follows Freud, in *Civilization and Its Discontents*, in suggesting that the mind itself might be its own city,

> a city like London,
> Smoky and populous: it is a capital
> Like Rome, ruined and eternal,
> Marked by the monuments which no one
> Now remembers. (*SK*, 226)[7]

The mind depicted here seems a communal one, carrying within it relics not just of one's personal past but also of the pasts of every member of every previous generation. Such relics may have fallen into disrepair, and no one—consciously—remembers them, but they still affect the way in which the mind, or city, develops in the present. Schwartz brings together in this conceit all the connotations of the "historical sense" and of "international consciousness," a conviction that every moment is determined by everything that has ever happened anywhere in the world. Rather than seeing the city as a symbol of the mind—which is how Emerson saw "Nature"—he internalizes the entire external world and its history. But one effect of this is essentially to turn the city into an abstraction.

"I Will Always Stammer, Since He Spoke": Influence *in* Vaudeville for a Princess

In 1940, Schwartz wrote to Robert Hivnor, "It's the city-state, I think, the Athens and Florence, which generates great art with great social power; and probably that's because the national state tends to spread out its energy, while the city-state contracts and unifies it" (*Letters*, 103). The problem of creating art with social power, and of doing so in a vast "world-city," vexed Schwartz throughout his career. One of the overriding questions with which he grapples—particularly in *Vaudeville for a Princess*—is what obligation the poet has to write about political and societal matters.

According to Allen Tate, writing in 1951, he has none whatsoever:

> To suggest that poets tell men in crisis what to do, to insist that *as poets* they acknowledge themselves legislators of the social order, is to ask them to shirk their specific responsibility, which is quite simply the reality of man's experience, not what his experience ought to be, in any age.[8]

The poet, for Tate, should be responsible only to his own conscience, and he abdicates some of that responsibility if he uses his status to speak on a political platform. This is not to deny that poetry might, sometimes, acquire social or political agency, but this must not be its raison d'etre. Against such New Critical orthodoxy, the tendency of the *Partisan Review* circle toward a kind of proto-New Historicist social criticism nurtured a sense that the poet—and certainly the intellectual—ought to adopt an explicit public role. Schwartz was drawn to both positions and the conflict is played out most starkly in *Vaudeville for a Princess*, written in the immediate aftermath of the Second World War.

The book's three sections broadly represent different degrees of societal engagement. The prose "bagatelles" of the first section can be taken as a public performance, an approximation of an actual vaudeville show upon the page, although the section's densely allusive lyric poems are more inward looking. The second section, "The True, the Good, and the Beautiful"—with its eight dramatic monologues orated by an isolated philosopher-king figure—sets the public and the private more emphatically against each other. Meanwhile, the 40 sonnets of the final section—"The Early Morning Light"—adopt a more intimate tone. While no resolution is reached, the poems themselves often suggest that distinctions between public and private voices may be little more than superficial.

Plato's ideal philosopher-king, as described in *The Republic*, exemplifies the contemplative, withdrawn position for Schwartz. However, there is a paradox insofar as such a philosopher's isolated life is intended, ultimately, to enable him to acquire the kind of wisdom that will benefit society as a whole. He can never, therefore, be entirely disengaged. Schwartz's regular references to popular culture, epitomized by his reveries of "riding up Fifth Avenue under great snowstorms of ticker-tape, in a beautiful open limousine, cheered by admiring throngs" (*V*, 10), suggest that he was as interested in those things that Plato might have dismissed as mere appearances— particular examples of beautiful things rather than beauty itself—as he was in understanding the concepts of truth, goodness, and beauty as universal essences, things in and of themselves that exist in an ideal state. In this respect, Schwartz's vacillations between an interior world of contemplation and an external world of surface impressions reflect not just an attraction to both worlds, but also an ongoing and unresolved philosophical debate.

The book's political concerns are also unresolved. The anxious poems of "The True, the Good, and the Beautiful" in particular are informed by Schwartz's attempts to justify his role as an intellectual and writer at a time of war. The hesitant tone of "The True, the Good, and the Beautiful" suggests that Schwartz was not as confident in his position as he sometimes appeared to be in private correspondence. Because, as a nonparticipant, he only experienced the war indirectly, much of his wartime poetry is characterized by what he described in 1958 as "the guilt of the innocent bystander" ("The Present State of Poetry," 48). He never went so far as Adorno did in 1951 in claiming that it was barbarous to write poetry after Auschwitz—and the symbolism of some of his later poetry does suggest a greater effort to comprehend the inhumanity of the holocaust than is immediately obvious—but he was no less troubled by the question of how lyric poetry might truthfully engage with a society that was confronted by far more pressing humanitarian concerns than purely aesthetic art forms could adequately address.[9] Even in poems that seem far removed from the international crisis its indirect influence is felt, encapsulated by what Schwartz described in the story "New Year's Eve" as "a post-Munich sensibility: complete hopelessness of perception and feeling" ("New Year's Eve," 113).[10] *Vaudeville for a Princess*, uneven though its aesthetic quality certainly is, represents a necessary stage in Schwartz's attempts to recover hope and to reinvigorate perception and feeling.

On publication, the critical consensus was that the collection's irreverent prose passages were more memorable than its verse, and that only "Starlight like Intuition Pierced the Twelve" stood comparison with the best lyrics from *In Dreams Begin Responsibilities*.[11] Schwartz himself admitted to Stevens that he was "not particularly pleased with it" (*Letters*, 255), and only three of its poems were retained for *Summer Knowledge: Selected Poems*. The book was savaged in October 1951 by Hugh Kenner for its "divers uncertainties of tone" and its tendency to recall "the gestures—but not the techniques—of *Prufrock* and *Portrait of a Lady*."[12] Much of its tonal strangeness is created by Schwartz's ambivalent appropriation of lines and phrases not just from Eliot but also from Shakespeare, Christopher Marlowe, and Sir Edward Dyer. Several of the poems take their titles or first lines from well-known Elizabethan lyrics, while the book's many epigraphs—from *The Symposium*, Swift, Joyce, and Fitzgerald—steep it further in other writers' words. The effect is different from the allusive texture of *In Dreams Begin Responsibilities* because the borrowings are generally more overt and direct. Except in the obviously satirical prose passages, it is hard to know whether to read them as homage or send-up.

Although the first section seems the most performative, and therefore public, its indulgence in, on one hand, the comically absurd, and, on the other, the purely literary can be taken as a means of delaying a necessary confrontation with the most pressing of societal concerns—the war. Taking his cue, in the book's opening poem, from Pascal's aphorism that "True eloquence mocks eloquence" (*V*, 3), Schwartz sets about subverting high culture and reinventing it as various kinds of popular culture. He identifies himself, at the beginning of the section, with the comic actor Danny

Kaye: it should be no surprise, then, that he also identifies himself in this first poem—via the word "snickers" and the "meticulous" / "ridiculous" rhyme—with Prufrock, who is "not Prince Hamlet" but "Almost, at times, the Fool" (Eliot, *CPP*, 16).[13]

Many of the pieces appear to lampoon Eliot in particular, but, as Bruce Bawer has remarked, they do so in such a way that Schwartz proves himself "still a disciple in spite of himself."[14] The prose bagatelle "Fun With the Famous, Stunned by the Stars," for example, concludes with Schwartz and a drinking companion "reciting to each other just like a barber shop quartet" lines from "Mr Eliot's Sunday Morning Service": "'In the beginning was the word,'/ Superfetation of τὸ ἕν—" (33). Schwartz just as gleefully travesties—and Americanizes—*Hamlet, Othello,* and *Don Giovanni* in pieces which, Bawer suggests, "play off Eliot's highbrow prose style."[15] Hamlet looks like he "has slept for three nights in a railroad coach" and Gertrude sings him songs entitled "My Old Kentucky Womb" and "Carry Me Back to Old Virginity" (15), while Shakespeare himself is described as a "brilliant country boy" who wrote Broadway hits (46).

There is little sense, however, of Schwartz really attempting to undermine Shakespeare, or even Eliot. The tone is more resigned than genuinely satirical, as though Schwartz was accepting the impossibility of emulating Shakespeare or Eliot and resorting instead to mockery that is as directed toward himself as it is toward either of them. It is perhaps also the case that, by debunking the idea of any work of art being so valuable and timeless that it is beyond mockery, Schwartz finds reassurance at a time when he feared civilization to be in decline. Decimating the work of one's idols oneself might help one to prepare one for worse. But his defacements are also, strangely, acts of preservation, ensuring—in case there was ever any doubt—that readers do not forget Shakespeare or Eliot's originals.

The poems that mimic Elizabethan works, meanwhile, do not turn out to be the parodies that they initially look like becoming. They are, instead, rewritings without satirical design, uneasy acts of homage, though their emphases are generally quite different to those of the originals. If the prose pieces are the comic acts on the vaudeville programme, then these are the songs performed straight, cover versions of a sort. None of them bears comparison with the poem to which it responds, but Schwartz's poems of this kind are not all without virtue. The most assured of them, "The Winter Twilight, Glowing Black and Gold," fruitfully draws upon Shakespeare's sonnet 73, its blazing Christmas trees fusing the leafless, or nearly leafless, trees of Shakespeare's first quatrain with the glowing fire of his third, and the "bare ruin'd choirs" of Shakespeare's poem countered by the "hurrahing" of Schwartz's Easter choir (*V,* 67).[16] Schwartz's sonnet moves away from its source in its fractured sestet, revisiting a childhood memory of offering a girl an apple that is also recounted in "Prothalamion" and *Genesis*. In describing his "swollen heart" as "Now boxed in the learning and music of art," however, Schwartz makes reference to the boxlike form of the sonnet and again evokes the choirs (and perhaps also the boxy choir stalls) of sonnet 73. The line suggests the poet's frustration at no longer being able to express himself without the artifice of form or without having to draw upon lessons learned from previous masters.

Its debt to Shakespeare aside, "The Winter Twilight, Glowing Black and Gold" is important within Schwartz's oeuvre because it is one of his most succinct expressions of the positive spin that he manages to put on Spengler's philosophy of history, presenting annihilation followed by restoration, death followed by rebirth. The burning of Christmas trees symbolizes the end of winter, an act of incineration that anticipates spring and Easter, the time of resurrection. And the poem itself essentially destroys one poem in order to create a new one.

Of all the poems in *Vaudeville for a Princess*, "Starlight Like Intuition Pierced the Twelve" has justly received most acclaim. Although it was written in 1943, presumably some time earlier than most of the volume's other poems, its position at the end of the first section (and, later, as the last poem in *Summer Knowledge*) means that it can be taken, to some extent, as a reflection upon the poems that precede it. It is primarily, Schwartz explained, a dramatization of "attitudes which accept Christianity as a reality while at the same time dismissing the question of literal belief as, at most, irrelevant" (*Letters*, 367). But it is also a poem of witness, preparing for the more protracted interrogation of how events that one has not experienced for oneself may yet permanently affect one's life. It can be read, as well, as a poem about the stymieing effects of overinfluence and—pursuing Schwartz's earlier fixation—the difficulties of perception. Christ's disciples are rendered impotent by their Savior's excessively good, excessively forgiving, and excessively eloquent example. Coming after poems crammed with short-circuited allusion, it is hard not to read such lines as "'And I will always stammer, since he spoke,' / One, who had been most eloquent, said, stammering" (*V*, 49) ("stammering" here appropriately disrupting the rhythm) as anything other than self-referential.

Schwartz is obsessively conscious of his precursors, both recent and more distant, and anxiety about overinfluence is written into "Starlight Like Intuition Pierced the Twelve" throughout, beginning with its title. Starlight is self-generating: it comes from no other source than a star itself. It is like intuition—"spiritual perception or immediate knowledge" (OED, 4), immediate sense apprehension (OED, 5), or, more generally, "direct or immediate insight" (OED, 6)—because intuition similarly comes from no obvious source. Intuition is the antithesis of reasoned thought and logical deduction. It is thus an ideal for a poet who, from the beginning, albeit with some unease, had valued intuitive knowledge over book learning. It is also, however, threatening for whoever is unable to access it themselves. Starlight "pierced" the twelve: it inspired, but also wounded them. Piercing, in a poem that features wound-bearing disciples, evokes the nailing of Christ to the cross. Allied to starlight, however, it could also suggest the Star of Bethlehem, pointing needlelike to the place of Christ's birth. Symbolically, the Magi, in following the star, could be seen as following their intuition. Such opposing inferences are characteristic of a poem in which Christ's goodness is described as both "awe" and "abyss" (V, 48). The disciples are privileged to have witnessed the starlight, but it only sets into relief their own shortcomings, prompting despair. To one who has seen what is truly awesome, "the sea and sky no more are marvellous" (47), and surprise is incomprehensible.

When the poem was first published, in *Kenyon Review* in 1944, its title was the same as its first line: "The starlight's intuitions pierced the twelve." The change is seemingly minor, but as in other Schwartz poems the slight shift from title to first line creates subtle effects. Starlight and intuition go from being general in the revised title to specific in the first line: "*The* starlight" and "*intuitions*," plural, implying that there are such things as individual intuitions that combine to make up one singular and more abstract "intuition" much as individual rays combine to create an overall impression of starlight. These intuitions also go from *resembling* the starlight to *belonging to* it: but they do not belong to the disciples who cannot generate their own intuitions but can only experience, or perceive, them passively.

The disciples' proclamations make clear the various ways in which Christ's influence has paralyzed them. Less directly, however, the poem also suggests a kind of contagion through its aural effects—the *abcbdefe* rhyme scheme, the recurrence of the word "it" at the end of each but the final stanza, and an abundance of internal rhyme, half rhyme, and assonance. Allied with the prominence given to the moon in the first stanza, these overabundant echoes could be taken as reflecting sublunary influence rather than simply expressing musicality for its own sake. The moon takes its light from the sun. What beauty it has, then, is a reflection of a greater beauty that cannot be looked at directly. It thus functions in a similar way to the screens and mirrors in some of Schwartz's other works. To the disciples, the moon's beauty is "useless" because it is inauthentic. They feel similarly toward Christ. His goodness is God's goodness at one remove. And yet even this is too much for them.

Schwartz acknowledged that his writing of this poem was informed by reading Arnold, Hardy, Valéry, and Stevens, as well as an annotated Victorian copy of the *New Testament*, but, in contrast to other poems in *Vaudeville for a Princess*, none of these influences becomes suffocating. Schwartz notably does not acknowledge Eliot, whose Anglo-Catholic faith the poem appears to oppose. Eliot's presence is still felt, however, partly through this opposition and partly through echoes that are subtler than elsewhere. The tone of the disciples' speech, for example, recalls passages from *Ash-Wednesday*. "Though all may be forgiven, never quite healed / The wound I bear as witness, standing by" (*V*, 47) one disciple exclaims, his cadences and sentence structure hinting at such lines as Eliot's "For what is done, not to be done again / May the judgement not be too heavy upon us" (Eliot, *CPP*, 90). Even in the frustrated cry, "No matter what we do, he looks at it!" (47), and its variations, there is a slight, but discernible, echo of "The Love Song of J. Alfred Prufrock": "I am no prophet—and here's no great matter" (Eliot, *CPP*, 15). And when Schwartz has the ninth disciple ask, "Who now will ever sit / At ease in Zion at the Easter feast?" (*V*, 49) he is both alluding to Amos 6.1 (which he also summons in "On a Sentence by Pascal") and evoking the discontent of Eliot's Magi, who return to their Kingdoms after witnessing Christ's birth and find that they are "no longer at ease here, in the old dispensation" (Eliot, *CPP*, 104).

For Morton Seiff, Schwartz's Jewishness provides a context in which to read the poem. No Jewish poet, he remarks, can afford to surrender to Eliot's Anglo-Catholic aesthetic "without fear of obliterating his own identity."[17] "Starlight Like Intuition Pierced the Twelve," he argues, is a poem of "guilt-burden," revealing Schwartz's "sensitivity to a remote 'crime' [Christ's crucifixion] which is doubtfully ascribed to the Jews by legend and staunchly denied by reliable historians."[18] Such a perspective on the poem cannot be dismissed, and is strengthened by the poem's indirect references to the crucifixion. All the same, it only relates directly to the seventh stanza in which the eighth and ninth disciples lament that though "He gave forgiveness to us," "The crime which was will be; and the least touch / Revives the memory" (*V*, 49). Even here, the lines can be read in a more general context without any loss: the poem resonates beyond any specifically Jewish reading. Given that Christ forgave *all* sins, there is no need to dwell upon one specific instance, particularly one that is questionable. The fact of forgiveness itself, though ostensibly a gift, is a burden because it comes with a sense of indebtedness that denies one's own independence. This is the case regardless of the gravity of the crime forgiven.

More importantly, "Starlight Like Intuition Pierced the Twelve" engages with the questions Schwartz addresses in his essay on Hardy, in which he argues that Hardy was a poet whose sensibility was essentially Christian despite his inability to believe in a Christian God. There is an analogy with the young poet who has become disillusioned with his former master. Schwartz's loss of faith in Eliot is clear from his criticism of *Four Quartets*, in which, he argues, "one hears a man *trying* to be modest, sincere [and] frank...rather than the modesty, sincerity, or frankness as such."[19] The disciple's belief that his master has started, in effect, to parody himself, is a gauge of the distance that has developed between them, and throughout *Vaudeville for a Princess,* Schwartz is increasingly conscious that the style he borrowed from Eliot has started to forestall rather than aid his development. This helps to account for Schwartz's greater antagonism toward Eliot in the volume, but does not conceal that his attachment appears all the stronger at the moment of renunciation—a renunciation that is never, in fact, completed.

One of the ways in which Schwartz attempts to dissociate himself from Eliot is by increasingly drawing upon influences from outside literary and philosophical spheres. But Eliot himself engaged with the popular culture of jazz, the music hall, and vaudeville; Schwartz's gestures toward an emerging cult of celebrity are simply a more overt manifestation of the same impulse.[20] Schwartz's excursions into the world of popular culture also sit uneasily with the more solipsistic tendencies of his poetry; and this tension is rendered even more starkly in *Vaudeville for a Princess*'s middle section, a sequence of poems that also attempt to justify the poet's continued detachment when faced with the societal upheaval caused by war.

"The True, the Good, and the Beautiful": Societal Engagement and Withdrawal

In "The True, the Good, and the Beautiful," the mind and self are "in Civil War" (*V*, 7) throughout (to borrow a phrase from Schwartz's rewriting of Sir Edward Dyer's "My Mynde to me a Kingdome is" in the previous section). The speaker attempts to justify his position as "a *privileged character*" (Schwartz's italics) who has been "excused / From the war" (53). He insists upon the value of contemplative study even at such a time of crisis, claiming that he has dedicated himself "to poetry, / The true, the good, and the beautiful" (53). Schwartz had justified his own refusal to become involved in the politics of the Second World War on similar grounds. "Since surgeons are not asked to throw overboard their activities in wartime," he argued to Dwight MacDonald—who was particularly infuriated by Schwartz's noncommittal stance—"those who are doctors of the spirit ought to continue their professional engagements also" (*Letters*, 133). And to William Carlos

Williams he maintained, "I am a kind of dentist as you are a doctor, and it is an honorable calling" (189). As teacher, poet, and intellectual, Schwartz regarded himself as a defender of his nation's cultural health.

His speaker's position is derived from the view expressed by Socrates in *The Republic*:

> Unless philosophers become kings in their cities,...or those now called kings and potentates legitimately and sufficiently come to love wisdom; unless political power and philosophy coincide in the same person...there can be no surcease from evil...for cities nor...for the human race....[T] here is no other way to attain happiness, public or private.[21]

According to Socrates, only philosophers have the capability to be ideal rulers because only they can see the beautiful itself rather than simply beautiful things, and the just itself rather than simply just things. They see *through* and *beyond* things, rather than looking *at* them. They are lovers of wisdom, of absolute and incontrovertible knowledge, rather than of judgment or opinion, which are contingent.[22] Those who cannot see "what is most true"—those, that is, who are not philosophers—cannot "establish conventional notions...about things beautiful and just and good" and they equally cannot "guard and preserve what has been established."[23] For this reason, Socrates suggests, they are not fit to rule.

In claiming that to have a legitimate philosopher-king as ruler is the only way "to attain happiness, *public or private*," Socrates states the paradox that the philosopher's detachment from society is in fact for the good of society, for individuals and for communities alike. The problem for Schwartz's speaker—though it is one that he does not himself acknowledge—is that he also regards himself as a poet, a perpetrator of images, and poets were excluded from *The Republic* for precisely the reason that they dealt with illusions. In the speaker's case, he is more attracted to the diversions of mid-twentieth-century society—Tin Pan Alley, Hollywood, and Luna Parks—than he cares to admit elsewhere, and this raises the question of how much of a philosopher, a lover of pure wisdom, he really is. How prepared is he to accept the self-enforced isolation that his position appears to demand. There is real bitterness in his complaint that he has been cut off "from the normal pleasures of the citizen" as a consequence of studying "the art which in / America wins silence like a wall" (*V*, 55).

The poems appear, at first, to be public addresses and thus to engage directly with societal concerns. Five of them begin "Dear Citizens," hinting at socialist sentiment. The address "Dear" also invites the possibility of the poems being read as letters rather than speeches. The seemingly public purpose of the poems is undermined, however, when it is "the silence," rather than any citizen, that responds. The dialogues take place in the mind rather than any real public arena. Through the silence's reproaches and his own tentative remarks and questions, the speaker's self-doubt becomes apparent. But the interest of the poems lies not in their flimsy attempts to justify being a poet, student, and teacher (the terms become almost interchangeable) while "other boys" are "slumped like sacks on desperate shores" (V, 55), but rather in the way in which they reveal survivor's guilt. As an innocent bystander in "a world in which an innocent bystander is continually faced by an overwhelming and inexhaustible threat," and in which "there is often a feeling that to be an innocent bystander is in itself one form of guilt" ("The Present State of Poetry," 48), Schwartz's speaker is in a similar position to the disciple in "Starlight Like Intuition Pierced the Twelve" who regrets the "never quite healed" wound he bears "as witness, standing by" (V, 47). And although Schwartz never states it directly, this kind of guilt might be intensified for the noncombatant American Jew, safe from the threat suffered by all European Jews.

The speaker's doubts are of various kinds. First, he questions the success of his philosophical endeavor. What truth, if any, has he been able to attain? "What starlight have I glimpsed for all my guilt?" (V, 53). Coming immediately after "Starlight Like Intuition Pierced the Twelve," with its dramatization of the sacrifices undergone by those who *have* witnessed starlight, it is possible to discern some resistance to achieving such a goal. This may be one reason why Schwartz's speaker is more committed, instead, to studying the softer, less piercing "morning light" (53). The poem that follows concludes with a call to celebrate the fact that "Plato's starlight glitters amid the shocking wars" (54): amid the horror, evidence of universal truth, goodness and beauty remain. But this is immediately dismissed, by the silence at the start of the third poem, as "empty rhetoric" (55), and further undermined two poems later in "Some Present Things Are Causes of True Fear" by the appeal to his citizens not to be embittered "because the beau ideal once glittered for us" (57) (and implicitly glitters no more). Finally, in the section's last poem, "The Past's Great Power Overpowers Every Hour," starlight is at once associated with obscenity and senselessness, but also with the blaze of truth, goodness, and beauty (63). By this point, one can't help wondering whether "the true, the good, and the beautiful" ought to be spoken with an ironic sneer, but the evidence of the 40 sonnets that follow under the heading "The Early Morning Light," and the poetry that he would write afterwards, suggests that Schwartz—if not his speaker—did not abandon hope in these Platonic ideals, even if he could not rationalize why they were so important to him.[24]

The speaker also doubts whether his efforts are in any way beneficial, asking, "What have I done which is a little good?" (*V*, 53). Perhaps he *is* devoted to art merely for its own sake, and not for the good of society—a possibility that is obliquely suggested in his description of poetry as "old as the rocks" (53), alluding to Walter Pater's description of the *Mona Lisa* in *The Renaissance*, the central text of Aestheticism.[25] The society presented in the sequence is one for which the speaker appears to have considerable contempt, one that he would want to change. Although "Some Present Things Are Causes of True Fear" begins with a call *not* to jeer, it is hard to read such lines as "Come, let us praise the noble lies which were / To justify the millions dead in war" (56) as anything other than jeering. Initially, they seem grossly to simplify the causes of the Second World War, and to contribute to the uncomfortably snide tone of the sequence in general. On further consideration, however, it becomes apparent that the speaker's attitude toward his nation and its leaders is more complex. One notes, for example, that the silence has already dismissed the speaker's own commitment to poetry as "a noble lie" (54): he is perhaps as bad, then, as the politicians for whom he has so little respect, and over whom, despite being a would-be philosopher-king, he has no influence. However, the lines *can* also be taken in earnest: men, regrettably, *are* able to commit atrocities for reasons that are "noble as Jesus Christ" (56).

For all the poem's extravagant tonal shifts and ambiguities, there is little doubt that the speaker's call to "praise the life in which we live" (56) is sincerely meant. He sets the benefits of modern life against the atrocity of the war; and although describing the radio as "poet laureate / To Heinz, Palmolive, Swift, and Chevrolet" (57) sounds cynical, it equally underlines just how much choice is available to the modern American citizen. In one respect, despite the international horror, life has never been better. "Who could want more?" (57) the speaker asks at the end of the poem. This is a bold stance, but it is undermined by the rhetorical question that precedes it: "Do we not have, in fine, depression and war / Certain each generation?" (57). This is a variation on the oft-stated Schwartz conviction that history is forever reenacted. The answer may be "yes," but the question remains naïve insofar as it ignores the unprecedented scale of the Second World War and fails to take into account those aspects that distinguish it from previous conflicts: the use of technology to facilitate genocide, for example, or the nature of the precarious alliance of Britain and the United States with the Soviet Union. As political analysis, it is insubstantial, even if the poem's tonal uncertainties prove to be a vivid reflection of how difficult it is for the lyric poet to engage with an uninterested public.

The final poems in the sequence have more to say about poetry and the role of the poet than they do about politics. "Disorder Overtakes Us All Day Long" too glibly asserts, "These politicians have an easy time, / They can say anything, they have no shame" (*V*, 60), but the comparison that follows—of the poet to someone struggling to complete a puzzle while "Making the huge assumption that there is / A lucid picture which these fragments fit'"(60)—is an important comment about how Schwartz conceived of his art. In his search for a unifying principle other than religion, Schwartz becomes increasingly reliant, in *Vaudeville for a Princess* and his later poetry, on the idea simply of hope—not just in the American Dream, but also in the actuality of American life. However, he is ever aware that this, like religion, might simply be illusory. The critical point, almost amounting to a manifesto, comes at the end of "Disorder Overtakes Us All Day Long." What if, the speaker wonders, there *is* no unifying picture, and poets just "handled foolishly essential chaos?" The answer is that this hardly matters: "What but with patient hope to try again?" (61). Whether hope is real or not, foolish or well-founded, it is necessary. Schwartz (or his speaker) comes very close here to endorsing Stevens's philosophy that we cannot really believe in anything unless we can recognize it to be a fiction.[26] Such an attitude also accounts for why it is inadequate to see only the destructiveness of the war and not to see also the potential for peace, or Plato's glittering starlight.

To sustain such a belief in hope, however, is difficult. The final poem in the sequence concludes by asking, "What is our hope, except to tell the truth?" (*V*, 63) but what the truth itself might be is so unclear by this point that the issue remains unresolved. The penultimate poem, "Most Things at Second Hand through Gloves We Touch," harking back to the perceptual difficulties laid bare in *In Dreams Begin Responsibilities*, appears to celebrate truth-telling through its assertion that if we can "lay bare our hearts" and "take away the masks which hide us" (62), we need not be estranged from each other. However, the speaker then goes on to say, "We know our lives are lived by lies" (62). Perhaps to admit this is to begin to resolve the problem. The poem ends, however, with outright theatrical posturing—affectedness, inauthenticity—as an "arch-Shakespearean radical" recites how "*The true, the good, / And the beautiful have been struck down / Because of what they are*" (62, Schwartz's italics). The question of what the truth may be is further complicated due to the fact that here, in the given context, what the actor says really does appear to be the case. If the question remains unresolved, the conclusion of the sequence does at least suggest why a philosopher-king—someone who will dedicate himself to discovering what the truth is—might be necessary for a society that seeks to sustain itself through hope.

The question of the overbearing burden of hope also dominates several of the sonnets that follow. They are less urgent in tone than the poems that go before, but in picking up on many of Schwartz's preoccupations from the first two sections—including his indebtedness to Elizabethan poets such as Sidney—they provide the book with thematic unity. In "He Does to Others What He Wants Them to Do to Him," Schwartz contends that

> it is false and true to hope at all
> For gratitude and love. Yet who can cope
> With hope, no matter what cynicism shows (81)

Hope may be true, false, or, paradoxically, both, and while it may be a means of salvation, it can also be hard to bear, whether disappointed or fulfilled. Another sonnet, "Demons and Angels Sing Ever in the West," proposes that "the present moment always is untrue!" and that "light brings back old hope's ingenious lies" (95). "Cartoons of Coming Shows Unseen Before," meanwhile, finds the poet at the movies, "sad about being sad," but able to lose himself for a while in versions of the American Dream—"boy meets girl," "poor young man may win the boss' daughter"—until the newsreel interrupts to show Churchill and Roosevelt nudging each other and playing "Mah-jong or pat-a-cake with history" (97). Like many of the earlier poems, this trivializes the particular politics of the moment in a way that is more clumsy than considered. However, it further illustrates Schwartz's persistent sense that the circumstances of most people's lives are predetermined by the random decisions of a powerful few. In the final poem in *Vaudeville for a Princess*, entitled "Why Do You Write an Endless History?," the poet gives a frank answer to the question of why he so frequently looks in his heart and revisits past events. "'I think'," he explains,

> "I wish to understand
> The causes of each great and small event
>
> Chosen, or like thrown dice, an accident
> . . .
> For, as the light renews each incident,
> My friends are free of guilt or I am free
> Of self-accused responsibility." (106)

In other words, revisiting these scenes makes it apparent that no individual—not the poet himself, nor his friends—can be held wholly accountable for what has happened. In every instance there are numerous unavoidable factors that condition the decisions that individuals make. Elsewhere in Schwartz's oeuvre, the relative lack of control that individuals have over their own destinies is a cause for alarm and dismay. Here, however, it is consolatory, releasing the individual from responsibility. Be that as it may, it can never be a total release: realizing that one is never wholly responsible for any given occurrence does not free one of all responsibility, as the writer of "In Dreams Begin Responsibilities" well knew. Nonetheless, this marks a development in Schwartz's thinking on the subject, and one that demands further consideration in light of Schwartz's private political views and in comparison with Dwight MacDonald's rather different idea of responsibility.

The Responsibility of Peoples

As early as September 8, 1939, Schwartz wrote to Robert Hivnor of "the necessity that you keep yourself going and living as a writer, no matter what demands the new war and the entelechy of revolution make upon you" (*Letters*, 75). While there may be good sense in this essentially Platonic position—don't let yourself be distracted by the particular instance but attempt to appreciate, instead, the universals—Schwartz was not able to ignore what was happening to his world. Contemporaries such as MacDonald voiced outspoken disapproval of America's involvement in the war, and Lowell was imprisoned as a conscientious objector, while Randall Jarrell trained pilots, and Karl Shapiro and Anthony Hecht served in the Pacific and Europe respectively, addressing their experiences in their poetry. Schwartz, meanwhile, had avoided being drafted on account of various factors—a "'glandular' malady," Theodore Spencer's endorsement of his teaching post at Harvard, and the pretense that he still had to support his estranged wife, Gertrude Buckman (*Letters*, 171)—and insisted that he maintained no political or ideological standpoint. To maintain no position is, however, to maintain a very conspicuous position—one of passive resistance, a refusal to let the overwhelming changes occurring all around alter the way one lives one's life. It is a position that MacDonald in particular took it upon himself to challenge.

"The initial assumption," Schwartz explained to MacDonald in a letter of October 5, 1942,

> is that no political position is possible for intellectuals at present. Second, the intellectuals must, as a necessary myth, conceive of themselves as a class, or rather a club, or at any rate, a group which, by the very nature of their profession, have a vested interest in truth, an interest which must be defended more than ever in wartime. (*Letters*, 133)

This is more or less the argument of the speaker of "The True, the Good, and the Beautiful" when he says that he is a student of the morning light. Schwartz implies throughout his letter that intellectuals alone are capable of searching for some objective standard from which it is possible to analyze and judge the war. But it is his self-identification here as intellectual, as distinct from poet, that weakens his authority. By defining himself in this way he denies himself the argument that Tate would later put so persuasively.

Schwartz took criticism of intellectuals in wartime personally. In August 1943, he responded to an essay—"A Fault of Learning"—that William Carlos Williams had submitted to *Partisan Review*. The elder poet had "castigat[ed] intellectuals for attacking Stalinism at a time when Russia was [America's] military ally" (*Letters*, 188). Schwartz's instinct to question this stance may have been sound, but rather than address this specific issue, he sets about defending himself as an academic, first of all challenging Williams's implication that intellectuals, because some of them are prepared to question some of the tenets of democracy, "prepare the way for totalitarianism" (187). This "is strange," Schwartz maintains, "in view of what Hitler as a practical man did about intellectuals. It reminds me of the point of view that attributes the rise of Hitlerism to Wagner and Nietzsche" (187). How could a thinker or composer, he implies, inspire a regime that would attempt to obliterate culture?

Schwartz was not, primarily, a political writer. As he himself recognized, "political insight does not coincide with literary genius."[27] Furthermore, he adds, if literature does engage with politics, and has serious political meanings, "this is not at all the same kind of knowledge of political reality which is necessary at the ballot-box or when France has just been occupied and conquered by Germany" ("The Fabulous Example of André Gide," 249). In the same way, even if the literary pieces published in *Partisan Review* are politically engaged or inflected, that cannot be the primary basis on which they are judged. All the same, it is almost impossible to conceive of a literature that is not political in any way, and Schwartz's generally leftist attitudes and unease at America's role in the war tend to be apparent in his writing even when they are not explicitly stated.

The war itself accentuates questions of the individual's relation to society and of how to define nationhood. MacDonald, for all his disagreement with Schwartz about his particular stance, grapples, in a group of essays later collected as *The Responsibility of Peoples and Other Essays in Political Criticism*, with many of the difficulties that Schwartz had already begun to address in his fiction and poetry. MacDonald objects above all to the contemporary tendency to think "of peoples as responsible and individuals as irresponsible."[28] MacDonald explains: "If the German people are not 'responsible' for 'their' nation's war crimes," he argues, "the world becomes a complicated and terrifying place, in which un-understood social forces move men puppet-like to perform terrible acts, and in which guilt is at once universal and meaningless. Unhappily, the world is in fact such a place."[29] A nation is, to use Benedict Anderson's term, an "imagined community."[30] Nations are no less real for that, but as largely abstract social constructs, decisions can only be made on their behalf by individuals who can be regarded as representatives.

MacDonald's "un-understood social forces" sound very much like the social, cultural, historical, and psychological "divinities" that Schwartz identifies in *Genesis*. For all their differences, both men agree that individuals are subject to conditions over which they have no control and which are not their fault. MacDonald goes so far as to maintain that even in the smallest and most integrated of communities—"like the ancient Greek city state"— the individual's wants will always be at odds with those of society in general; in the "industrial-bureaucratic societies" of the United States, USSR, and most of Europe, even the possibility of struggle is suppressed: the individual "has about the same chance of determining his own fate as a hog dangling by one foot from the conveyer belt of a Chicago packing plant."[31] Another point on which Schwartz and MacDonald are in agreement is that one of the challenges in modern life is learning how to exercise whatever free will one might have within such constraints, and how to do so responsibly.

At times, such an effort seems especially futile. MacDonald cites the unignorable example of the atomic bomb. Whatever moral responsibility can be attributed "rests with those scientists who developed it and those political and military leaders who employed it." Because the American people as a whole had no say in developing or using it, and because most of them were ignorant of what was being planned and had no way of stopping it, "the Bomb becomes the most dramatic illustration to date of the fallacy of 'The Responsibility of Peoples'."[32] And yet, MacDonald goes on, because of the impersonality of the social order, and of the way in which war itself proceeds, any individual's attempt at rebellion will be ineffectual. Those who refuse to cooperate are replaced: "their rebellion will mean that they are simply thrust aside, without changing anything."[33] It is at this point that MacDonald most forthrightly spells out his conviction. Individuals, he goes on, can nonetheless refuse to play a part in such a mechanism. Even if their individual actions do nothing immediately to curb the progression of international events, they can still follow their consciences, and if enough individuals act in this way it could be for the good of mankind. Only by reversing the tendency "to think of peoples as responsible and individuals as irresponsible," he insists, can the "present decline to barbarism" be halted.

His proposition is inflected by the idealism of Emerson's conception of "Man Thinking": "The more each individual thinks and behaves as a whole Man (hence responsibly) rather than as a specialized part of some nation or profession (hence irresponsibly), the better hope for the future." [34] In practical terms, however, as MacDonald himself would later confess, this is hardly a realistic solution. From the perspective of 1953, he concedes that the hope he had held out for a "third camp" to arise and, through peaceful revolution, overthrow the Nazis, seems like willful self-deception. "The only historically real alternatives in 1939," he laments, "were to back Hitler's armies, to back the Allies' armies, or to do nothing. But none of these alternatives promised any great benefit for mankind, and the one that finally triumphed has led simply to the replacing of the Nazi threat by the Communist threat."[35] It is a bleak assessment, and an oversimplified one—could he really maintain that a Nazi rather than an Allied victory would have made no significant difference to United States or world politics?—but it does not invalidate MacDonald's stance on personal, rather than collective responsibility; fully accepting one's own obligations may still be the only means by which to live one's own life meaningfully. However, MacDonald acknowledges, this is extraordinarily difficult to do.

One gets a sense of Schwartz's overall agreement with MacDonald on this issue when he writes to Gertrude Buckman in November 1943 about his projected conclusion to *Genesis*. The ghosts (who now include Hershey's father) present the boy with a choice: "If he forgives his parents and accepts his own guilt, then he can live. If he refuses the responsibility for what he is, then he must die, because that is a denial of the freedom of the will and the possibility of human goodness" (*Letters*, 200). The choice is to be left, he says, without resolution: readers will have to decide for themselves whether Hershey is strong enough to accept such responsibility. Schwartz's implication here is that if one concludes that everything is impersonal and predetermined one might as well stop trying to live responsibly. The *possibility* of human goodness, if not its actual fulfillment, is perhaps as much as we can hope for.

"Our Country and Our Culture": Schwartz's Postwar Criticism

These questions were not resolved with the conclusion of the war. Much of Schwartz's postwar criticism asks where the individual stands in relation to his nation at a time of recovery and the emergence of the liberal society, but also of renewed fear as tensions between the Soviet Union and the United States intensified, the Korean War broke out, and the possibility of nuclear conflict grew. Increasingly, he advocates a belief in the actuality of American life rather than the chimera presented by the American Dream—a perhaps surprising turn given the deepening turmoil of his personal life as the 1950s progressed and his sensitivity, as we have seen, to the necessary symbiosis of dream and actuality.

"The present which confronts us in 1952 was inconceivable in 1935," Schwartz remarks in a symposium piece published in *Partisan Review*. It is not, in and of itself, the fact that this present is different that perturbs him, but rather that he is unable to establish its relation to what was still the relatively recent past. There has been "a complete breach with the social consciousness which preoccupied intellectuals then."[36] So dramatic were the changes that postwar novelists had a hard time competing "with the sensational reality of the Second World War, the atomic bomb, and world-wide revolution": reality eclipsed the fantastical.[37] But it is still through the imaginative arts that Schwartz is best able to trace the changes in social attitude that define the new actuality. With reference to the realization that the Allied victory did nothing to relieve a sense of foreboding, that wealth and social status, which should have been fulfilling, brought only disillusionment and despair, and that Hitler's defeat intensified rather than diminished racial discrimination ("by bringing a greater consciousness and self-consciousness of it"), Schwartz nonetheless finds reassurance in the evidence that Americans have at last become "mature enough to want the confrontation of reality which tragedy provides" ("The Grapes of Crisis," 383–384). Belief in the American Dream in its traditional manifestation, which Schwartz now associates with childishness, is no longer adequate to the contemporary situation. Utopian fantasies might have sufficed in the Depression years, Schwartz explains, but in the face of civilization's own capability for self-destruction, and without any imminent likelihood of resolution, "it is a genuine relief and blessing to be able to contemplate images of the worst that may happen" (384). A consequence of this is that it advances "the conditions under which a serious literature can thrive," creating "the possibility of a genuine tragic art" that would be characterized by courage and intelligence (384).

It is not a universal condition, however, and when it comes to film, Schwartz is in turn impressed by surprisingly serious performances by big stars and dismayed by Hollywood's habit of trying "to please everybody by providing everything."[38] The performances of Bing Crosby and Grace Kelly in "The Country Girl"—two of America's most feted stars offering "a genuine and sustained portrayal of fear and trembling and the sickness unto death"—are typical, for Schwartz, of Hollwood's newly uncompromising attitude toward reality.[39] No less stark is "The Bridges at Toko-Ri," in which "the blaze of visual meaning obliterates the story and dims all individuality," the camera showing "freedom as subjugation,...strength as weakness."[40]

Elsewhere, Schwartz's film reviews give him prompts for further social and cultural criticism. The 1955 film "The Blackboard Jungle" provokes him to contest the attitude that the disaffection of some of America's youth is an indictment of the nation's social attitudes. Blaming delinquency on the liberal society—"democracy, liberation, mass culture, universal education, industrialism, agnosticism, human nature, psychoanalysis and the New Deal"—is an abnegation of responsibility on the part of adults analogous to claiming that "Proust was the cause of the fall of France."[41] Meanwhile, he relates the revival of the Western in the mid-1950s to anxiety about the threat of nuclear war, arguing that when "survival, happiness and the quality of life depend on uncontrollable and hidden powers," and when people seem "helpless in the face of history," nothing "could be more attractive than an epoch in the past when a gun was enough to keep a man alive and a horse sufficed to ride to destiny."[42]

Schwartz regarded cinematic adaptations of novels as, at their best, "comparable to reading a critical essay about a great work of fiction...the entire process can be regarded as an extension of the art of translation."[43] This attitude is in line with his view that the continual interpretation of everything one encounters is one of the most deeply rooted experiences in modern life. He does not see cinema as a threat to the reading of books, though he also stresses that the reader "inhabits the interior of another being in a way which no other art makes possible" ("Novels and the News," 390). Schwartz is more cautious, however, about the relatively new phenomenon of television, largely on the grounds that it gives rise to an existential dilemma. The filmgoer who starts to watch films on TV instead of on the big screen, he argues, loses "what must be called, for lack of a better phrase, that portion of his 'escape from freedom' which he found when he saw a motion picture on the screen."[44] When characters in Schwartz's stories go to the cinema it is almost always to escape from the discontent of daily life: the movies are a "refuge," a "sanctuary," and part of the reason for this is that as soon as one is immersed in a film one is "done with the anxiety of choice."[45] For the TV viewer, however, "the escape from the continual daily pressure of freedom and choice not only has been annulled, but the alternatives of choice have increased" ("Some Movie Reviews," 467). This potentially causes increased anxiety and even stasis rather than respite from the responsibility to make a decision.

A late essay, "Survey of Our National Phenomena," unpublished in his lifetime, offers a summative account of how Schwartz felt popular culture could help to define the unstable entity of nation. National phenomena are often arbitrary. They can be international: Princess Margaret's romance with Group Captain Peter Townsend, Schwartz observes, received a great deal of public attention in the United States. They can be things, or crazes, such as *Scrabble*, an extraordinary success in the 1950s. Sometimes a national phenomenon "is a person of genuine genius or eminence," but "he is often, however, a mediocrity and sometimes the status is thrust upon him for freakish, bizarre, eccentric, questionable, or lawless behavior."[46] In some cases—Lindbergh is the example Schwartz gives—a national phenomenon can be "a swift, indisputable demonstration that the American Dream [is] still alive, that the courage, initiative, and self-reliance of the solitary individual might still accomplish new wonders" (107). Most of the time, however, it is hard to determine what causes any one person or thing to become a national phenomenon. Schwartz draws three tentative conclusions that throw light upon his lifelong preoccupation with the relation of the individual to his society. "For one thing," he explains, "the mere existence of a national phenomenon indicates a degree of national homogeneity," no matter how varied each individual's attitude to it may be. A national phenomenon is also "often the most spontaneous manifestation of the democratic process, because it is an expression of the public's moods and aspirations, hopes and fears." And finally, national phenomena make "the individual aware of the entire public, helps him to know he is part of that public, and shows him what he has in common with others and how he differs from them," an awareness that leads, ultimately, to self-knowledge (112). By providing a focal point, the likes of Marilyn Monroe, Bing Crosby, Adlai Stevenson, and Lindbergh manage to unify otherwise disparate individuals.

Schwartz did not look favorably upon the phenomenon of the Beat Generation (whom he nicknamed "The San Francisco Howlers"), accusing them, in his 1958 lecture on "The Present State of Poetry," of being "imaginary rebels" and failing to take account of the relative liberality of American society in international terms. He accuses them of failing to distinguish between John Crowe Ransom and the *Kenyon Review* critics and Soviet totalitarianism.[47] A wisecrack as wicked as any of Randall Jarrell's, this may grossly oversimplify the endeavors of the Beats, but it also leads to a statement—the central point of the lecture—that Schwartz sets forth in absolute earnestness. American literature, he says, both classical and more recent, has typically and predominantly criticized American life, whether in comparison with European culture or "from the exalted point of view of the American Dream." This is a criticism that Schwartz indulged in much of his own pre-Cold War writing. For the creative writer in the second half of the twentieth century, however, writing in full consciousness of the atomic threat, "the spectre of the totalitarian state," and the desperation of the war's aftermath in Europe, such an approach becomes inadequate. Not even the most detached or isolated of poets could ignore the gravity of the international situation, and Schwartz's response is to reiterate—but in public, and without admitting that America might in any way continue to depend upon Europe—what he had proposed to Laughlin 15 years earlier: "America, not Europe, is now the sanctuary of culture." This being the case, "civilization's very existence depends upon America, the actuality of American life, and not the ideals of the American Dream." Schwartz's "international consciousness" here enables him to make an argument for US exceptionalism: the unique benefits of life in America are set into relief by worldwide events. Once again admitting that the embrace of actuality may not preclude aspirational hoping, Schwartz sums up his point by maintaining that, "To criticize the actuality upon which all hope depends thus becomes a criticism of hope itself. No matter what may be wrong with American life, it is nothing compared to the police state, barbarism, and annihilation" ("The Present State of Poetry," 46). This conviction that one should celebrate rather than criticize helps to account for the change of focus in much of Schwartz's later poetry.

CHAPTER 5

Summer Knowledge: "Infinite Belief in Infinite Hope"

"A Fabulous Discovery of America": Schwartz and American History

In his introduction to *Last & Lost Poems*, Robert Phillips responds to Berryman's lament that Schwartz's "lovely work" did not improve by implying that to use such baldly qualitative language (albeit in an elegy, not an evaluative essay or review) is critically lazy. "His poetry did not, in fact, 'improve,'" writes Philips. "It became different. Few readers have been willing to examine these differences, to find merit in the later work" (*LL*, "Foreword," xiii). Phillips is not wrong to draw attention to Schwartz's "enormous stylistic change of direction" (xv), but this should not conceal a real continuity between early and later works. There are thematic and even stylistic similarities, to the extent that Douglas Dunn can read a poem such as "Seurat's Sunday Afternoon along the Seine" as "a summation of virtually everything Schwartz had been endeavouring to express from the very beginning."[1]

Even though Schwartz's essay on "The Present State of Poetry" seems to dismiss the American Dream in favor of both "the actuality of American life" and a "clear and explicit consciousness of the international span of experience," his late poems can nonetheless be read, collectively, as the culmination of his investigations into the subject. Although many of them seem, at first, to be straightforward, if effusive, nature poems, with little reference to the contemporary world, their repeated meditations on the importance, and nature, of hope implicitly link them to Schwartz's wider concerns about the world in which he lived. In positing a vision in which death always heralds rebirth, and in which "It is always darkness before delight!" (*LL*, 3), Schwartz endorses a hope for America that he longed to embrace in the decades after the Second World War. Taken alongside essays and stories of the same period, those demanding a celebration of the actuality of American life rather than just an idealized version of it, Schwartz's poems acquire social resonances that may not be apparent on a first reading.

They also remain "internationally conscious," partly because they resist attachment to any single place. It is impossible to locate their landscapes, many of which are, in fact, more like dreamscapes, nebulous and indefinable. "Darkling Summer, Ominous Dusk, Rumorous Rain," for example, ostensibly describes a late summer sunset against a damp backdrop. Atlas dismisses the poem's "haphazard, euphonious, virtually incomprehensible effusions" (Atlas, 326), but Phillips argues that it "accurately recreates a sensuous experience" (*LL*, "Introduction," xiv). Phillips's argument stands up better when one approaches the scene as a dreamscape, recognizing that a lack of total clarity is inherent to the experience expressed: lines describing "a filming gown / Of grey and clouding weakness" and a "clouding vagueness" that fogs the windowpane, for example, attest to elements that muffle rather than elucidate, and "the land's great sea" suggests a complete inversion of usual distinctions (*SK*, 149). The poem may depict truly enough the descent of misty cloud on a summer's evening, but it is truer still, in a metaphorical sense, to the haziness of a semiconscious mind grasping for entities that seem perpetually to merge into each other.

The dream logic of such poems releases them from association with any fixed locale, making them more universal than they might otherwise appear. The poems also repeatedly question notions of beginning and ending: they are skeptical about the possibility of locating the origin of any given event in a specific moment, but fascinated with the idea of perpetual resurrection (as symbolized, in particular, by the phoenix and the ever-changing reflections of light on flowing water). Drawing out Schwartz's conviction that all experience is relative or comparative, the poems remain deeply concerned with how the individual can define himself in relation to those around him. They tend to place greater emphasis on the individual's relationship with his environment than with his peers or family history, and in this respect they differ from Schwartz's earlier lyrics and from *Genesis*. However, their moments of transcendence, in which the individual loses any sense of himself as an individual and is subsumed by his wider environment, are similar; and the poems' interrogations of the relationship between the beholder and what is beheld recall Emerson's rhapsody about becoming nothing but seeing all.[2] At such moments, the poet temporarily overcomes the "egocentric predicament."

The discovery of America is an important trope in some of these poems, illustrating as it does the good that can arise from error. The number of published poems that make explicit reference to Columbus and other pioneering figures of American history are relatively few, but in poems such as "The True-Blue American" and "Kilroy's Carnival," the discoverer of America is seen as epitomizing "infinite belief in infinite hope" (*SK*, 163): he is presented as delusional, but also as achieving something far greater than he could understand, establishing a tradition within which

> every tragedy has a happy ending, and any error may be
> A fabulous discovery of America, of the opulence hidden in the dark
> depths and glittering heights of reality ("Once and For All," *SK*, 222)

The "Lincoln" passage from *Genesis*, the only one reprinted in *Summer Knowledge*, is Schwartz's most overt engagement with American history in the latter book. It is arguably extracted because it is better able to stand alone outside its context within the longer poem than other passages, and perhaps also because what Schwartz says about Lincoln—that he was a "manic-depressive" "Hamlet-type" and yet a "national hero"—has some resonance when considered in relation to his own "Summer Knowledge" poems. Lincoln, Schwartz writes,

> spoke
> More than he knew and all that he had felt
> Between outrageous joy and black despair (*SK*, 237)

This is essentially the spectrum that Schwartz himself covers in poems that celebrate intuitive knowledge over book learning and instinct over studied allusion (although Schwartz never wholly abandons either of these). They are poems that purport to speak more than they know.

In some respects, "Lincoln" jars in its position as the penultimate poem in *Summer Knowledge*, following poems that are stylistically more expansive and which are predominantly governed by a single voice (including the dramatic monologues spoken by Abraham, Sarah, and Jacob, with which it is most closely linked). It is unlikely that a reader not already familiar with *Genesis* would realize that the stanzas are spoken by ghosts, rather than a single agitated thinker trying to account for Lincoln's success. However, the choice of passage (Schwartz refers to it in his "Author's Note" as a poem in its own right) matters because it indicates, more overtly than other poems, that American history continued to fascinate Schwartz. His journals and unpublished drafts from the 1950s reveal that he was writing a great deal about the topic. These drafts propose alternative dates to 1492 and 1776 for the beginning of US history, among them 1607 (the founding of the Virginia colony) and 1815 (the end of the second Anglo-American War and the point at which the principle of populating the entire continent as one unified nation was confirmed). They also set Aaron Burr against Lincoln as a representative of American national character: Schwartz sees Jefferson's vice-president—who notoriously killed Alexander Hamilton in a duel—as a precursor to the likes of P. T. Barnum, J. P. Morgan, and John D. Rockefeller.[3]

Inconclusive in themselves, the existence of these unfinished, unpublished drafts indicates that the poems published in the second half of *Summer Knowledge* are only a sample of what Schwartz was working on at the time. Atlas explains that Schwartz relied entirely upon his friend, Elizabeth Reardon, to assemble the poems in the book on his behalf: "He never even glanced at her selections" (Atlas, 350). Be this as it may, there is coherence and unity between the poems chosen, and they do represent what Schwartz describes in his "Author's Note" as "the point of view which is signified by the title of the volume." This does not mean, however, that they entirely ignore the social and historical points of view that are more explicitly addressed in the unpublished poems. In their meditations upon time, flux, and continual resurrections and discoveries, Schwartz's "Summer Knowledge" poems bear the weight of American history.

Style

Any defense of Schwartz's late poems must address their style. Phillips endorses Dunn's view that this is characterized by "energy and delight," terms that Dunn himself borrows from Humboldt's list of "sacred words" in Bellow's novel (Phillips, xiv; Dunn, xi; Bellow, *Humboldt's Gift*, 7). It is not difficult to find passages to support this judgment. In "The Fulfillment," for example, the speaker finds himself disorientated (possibly in a dream, and possibly after death, although his companion insists that this hardly matters) in a place where

> all things existed purely in the action of joy—
> Like light, like all kinds of light, all in the domination
> of celebration existed only as the structures of joy! (*SK*, 150)

There is no lack of "energy and delight" in the insistent repetitions of "joy" and "light" here, in the internal echoes, and in the exclamatory clamor. However, the apparent idyll is undermined by the realization that occurs in the next stanza.

> It was then that we saw what was lost as we knew where
>   we had been
> (Or knew where we had been as we saw all that was lost!)
> And knew for the first time the richness and poverty
> Of what we had been before and were no more (150)[4]

Although this is even-handed in acknowledging the poverty, as well as the richness, of what is lost when one finally achieves fulfillment, its tone of regret remains strong. This time the repetitions sound enervated rather than energetic, monosyllabic and backward-looking rather than reveling in action and immediacy. There may be instances of "energy and delight" in the poem, but these are counterbalanced by a more somber, reflective tone, and this is true of Schwartz's late poems in general. Many of them gain poignancy precisely because they cannot sustain the ecstasies for which Schwartz strives, and cannot conceal the strain inherent in promoting such a vision.

Dunn's celebration of the poems for their "energy and delight" is also problematic as a critical assessment because it defines poems that often deal with abstractions in equally abstract terms. His point that "critical discretion is over-willing to withhold its approval from a poem like ['Seurat's Sunday Afternoon along the Seine'] which rhapsodises itself out of any recognised form" (Dunn, xviii) does not overcome the fact that any reader's evaluation of how energetic and delightful the poems are, will have more to do with personal taste than with the technical or aesthetic qualities of the poems themselves. It is for this reason that the contemporary reviews of Anthony Hecht and John Hollander, which do attend to the poems' composition as well as to their more general effects, are especially important. Like Dunn, both Jewish American poet-critics have caveats, but both also recognize that, far from indicating a loss of formal control, Schwartz's later poetry is technically daring and innovative.

Remarking on the "sudden breaks and new starts" that characterize Schwartz's development, Hecht celebrates "the courage of such radical innovation." [5] By crediting Schwartz with conscious innovation—of the kind Tate had praised at the outset of his career—rather than lamenting a falling off of technical ability, Hecht resists the general tendency to attribute Schwartz's new style to his troubled personal circumstances. He appreciates that the move away from a detached, ironic style occurs because such a style could no longer serve what Schwartz needed to say rather than because he was no longer capable of writing tightly.

The late poems, Hecht notes,

> are freer, metrically and emotionally, than the earlier ones...the polarities of the early poems, always linked in a nagging, bitter, or ironic marriage, have been divorced and are trying to work out their own lives as discrete and separate attitudes.[6]

Such freedom, for Phillips, suggests the influence of Whitman, as do the poems' "accumulations of details and syntactical repetitions" (*LL*, "Introduction," xv). The lines, like Whitman's, are long, and many of the poems contain expansive and ebullient passages that project a more overtly democratic vision than is apparent in much of the earlier work. Hollander, however, suggests that Schwartz's development cannot be understood simply in terms of a shift from one master to another. The late poems, he says,

> are not really written in lines in the sense that the earlier poems are; the long lines and verse paragraphs stem not so much from Whitman or from psalmody via Christopher Smart as from the impulse to produce incantations and spells. At its most successful there is a hypnotic quality about the music of this new poetry, resulting from the manipulation of faintly heard interior rhymes, syntactical parallels, and more phonological patterns.[7]

This is not to say that inspiration alone accounts for these poems: it requires an artisan to manipulate sounds in this fashion. A consequence of Schwartz's method, for Hollander, is that relatively few individual lines are memorable: instead, the poems seem to "fuse into one another, to gloss and amplify each other," although Hollander does insist that "Seurat's Sunday Afternoon along the Seine," "Narcissus," and "Once and for All" are "outstanding as self-contained performances" (Hollander, "Poetry Chronicle," 368). Hollander ends his review by hoping that Schwartz will turn his attention "back to the outer world again" (368); but his esteem for what Schwartz achieves in his "Summer Knowledge" poems is never in doubt.

How can we define Schwartz's relation to Whitman? At its best, the movement of Schwartz's alliterative, assonantal, and internally rhymed verse imitates the effects it describes. This is less commonly the case in Whitman, for whom anaphora and repetition cumulatively give weight to bold declarative statements of the kind that Schwartz is usually too skeptical or self-questioning to make without qualification. In "Crossing Brooklyn Ferry," a poem of clear sonority for someone claiming to be "a poet of the Hudson River," Whitman describes the effect of sunlight upon water.[8] Describing a halo of light—"the fine centrifugal spokes of light round the shape of my head in the sunlit water"[9]—he associates sunlight with inspiration. Although Whitman admits to greater self-doubt in this poem than he does elsewhere, presenting himself as "disintegrated" and admitting that "The dark threw its patches down upon me also" (Whitman, 136, 138), it remains an assured statement of his affinity with all people, especially those who have not yet been born who will cross Brooklyn Ferry in the future. It concludes with the poet apostrophizing the river, the light, and Manhattan, instructing nature, conferring his blessing but also imposing his own order:

> Receive the summer sky, you water, and faithfully hold it till all downcast eyes have time to take it from you!
>   Diverge, fine spokes of light, from the shape of my head, or any one's head, in the sunlit water! (Whitman, 140)

The poet does not simply respond to nature but expects it—and, indeed, the city—to shape itself around him.

Schwartz's "May's Truth and May's Falsehood" also describes the effect of sunlight glittering on rippling water, but his overall effects are quite different. With less emphasis than Whitman upon the self as active participant in the scene depicted, Schwartz attempts to convey an indescribable impression in words, and does so by seeking an aural equivalent for the kind of motion he discerns in the light:

> The litter and ripple of the river was excited by the advent and descent of light upon its slow flowing:
>   The river was opulence, radiance, sparkle and shine, a rippling radiance dancing light's dances (*SK*, 213)

The light, this suggests, is what actually makes the river ripple, and it acts similarly upon other, seemingly fixed, features of the landscape as well: "the dark statues of the trees," a few lines earlier, are described as "flowing," and "every solid thing / Moved as in bloom" (213). The way in which the short /I/ sounds in "litter," "ripple," and "river" gives way to the long /aI/ sounds in "excited," "light," and "shine" suggests a state of flux, of things continuously changing, but maintaining a clear relation to their earlier state under the influence of time. The /I/ sound is not entirely subsumed: it recurs in the adjective "rippling," as Schwartz reprises the noun "ripple" in a different form. Similarly, the participle "dancing" precedes the noun "dances," the words enacting a kind of dance of their own. The exact repetition of "radiance" further draws out the shared /ns/ sounds in "dancing" and "dances," as well as chiming, sibilantly, with "descent."

These motions continue in the lines that follow:

> And the birds flew, soared, darted, perched, perched and whistled, dipped or ascended
>   Like a ballet of black flutes, an erratic and scattered metamorphosis of the villages of stillness into the variety of flying (*SK*, 213)

Here the repetition of "perched" demands a pause, a momentary cessation of all the movement before it begins again, while "dipped or ascended" looks back to the earlier "advent and descent." The connotations of some of Schwartz's words enhance the sense of protean form that is already suggested in the sounds. "Advent" and "descent" are not opposites, but as Schwartz uses it, "advent" takes on the meaning of "ascent" in addition to its primary meaning of arrival.[10] This consequently blurs the word's Christian connotations, conflating advent and ascension, Christ's coming and his final return to heaven, suggesting the kind of timelessness that Schwartz insists—in this poem and in others—exists alongside our daily experience of transience. "Litter" is evocative in a slightly different way, suggesting a bed of reeds, a birth, and all the debris carried by the river, but also—because of its proximity to radiance—"glitter." Schwartz draws out associations from words that are sometimes at odds with their primary meanings: his subtle ability to "manipulate undertones of language," a trait Ashbery particularly admires in his earlier poetry, remains evident in these later works.[11]

In answer to any objection that the lines are formless, it can be said that light—although it defines the forms of whatever it may fall upon—also lacks any form of its own; it is therefore appropriate that it should be described in nebulous lines, particularly as, in this case, it falls upon water, whose form is unfixed too and which, here, is in continual motion. As in earlier poems such as "In the Slight Ripple, the Mind Perceives the Heart" (*SK*, 39), Schwartz is trying to perceive what is imperceptible in itself and which can only be known by its influence upon the things it surrounds. It is one of the most important concerns that he takes up from Stevens, whose poetry, especially in *Harmonium*, is full of such ambiguous motions, and which regularly suggests how "fluttering things" (like love) might have a "distinct shade."[12]

The beholder in Schwartz's poem is as excited by the "advent and descent" of light as the river itself is. As in the city poems, a kind of pathetic fallacy is at play whereby what is beheld reflects back the viewer's own feelings even while it affects those feelings. It is difficult and painful for Schwartz's viewer to "believe in the reality of winter" (*SK*, 213); he would seem not to have "a mind of winter," and is therefore not immune to the misery that comes from thinking of a desolate winter landscape.[13] He is only able to console himself from the thought of May's green and gold giving way to "holly, ivy, barberry bush and icicle" (or, in Spenglerian terms, of civilization's summer ceding to winter) by detaching himself from the particulars of the immediate scene he views and thinking of universal truths—by thinking "of how all arise and aspire to the nature of fire," and of "how all things must suffer and die in growth and birth, / To be reborn, again and again and again"(*SK*, 214). This move away from the landscape is mirrored in the concluding sentence. This is given its own stanza and set apart from the rest of the poem by the fact that it occupies five whole lines. It is perhaps best described as a poetic paragraph, since it can properly be described as neither a single line, nor many; but it is not prose either. Like Whitman, Schwartz seeks to apply a particular experience to a universal vision. But the movement of his poem is quite unlike that of "Crossing Brooklyn Ferry": he withdraws from the scene at the end, rather than addressing it directly, as Whitman does. He is also much more interested in how the mind perceives and responds to a landscape than Whitman, whose notion of self is informed by a much closer sense of relation to the landscape he inhabits.

In common with the modernist poets he admired, Schwartz remained ambivalent about Whitman. Though the nineteenth-century poet increasingly mattered to Schwartz, both stylistically and as a poet of democracy, some of this influence is diluted by Schwartz's inability, even in poems that seem hopeful, to overcome his sense of alienation. Perhaps the most telling of Schwartz's occasional journal jottings on Whitman are those that question his vision of a unified nation. "Whitman was in love with experience to the point of morbid infatuation," Schwartz noted on May 19, 1955. "He tried to force his genuine experience to be a kind of witness and proof of his idea of experience" (*Portrait*, 488). This suggests that Schwartz perceived a disconnection between Whitman's actual experience and his doctrinal proclamations about it. Probing this further in an undated draft for a piece of fiction, Schwartz imagines *The New York Daily News'* advice columnist referring to Whitman in support of his contention that most people feel ashamed of being alone. "No one in America has ever been quite as lonely as the poet of democratic friendship," the columnist writes, "one and all united, now and forever—with evil as with good, death as well as life—Walt Whitman: the poet of complete health was also the paralytic of the last twenty five years of his life."[14] Schwartz, in reflecting on the difference between his own unhappiness at the time and the usually affirmative beliefs he was setting forth in his verse, might have considered this a point of identification. His belief in the disparity between Whitman's experience and the philosophy he projects in his poetry is also, however, a reason why he could never embrace Whitman's vision fully.

Schwartz's tendency toward euphony, half rhyme, and internal echoes, though of greater structural importance in the "Summer Knowledge" poems (because of their abandonment of more traditional metrics), is also discernible in his very earliest poems and cannot, therefore, be attributed solely to Whitman's influence. The new style does not constitute an absolute break from Eliot either. Schwartz did not much admire Eliot's plays, but he was aware that Eliot was experimenting in them with a new kind of meter. The choruses of *Murder in the Cathedral*, he notes, depart from "the habitual iambic norm."[15] Schwartz's praise of Eliot's succession of accented syllables in these choruses suggests one of his own techniques. Although Schwartz's repetitions are never as insistent as Eliot's in lines such as "O late late late, late is the time, late too late, and rotten the year / Evil the wind, and bitter the sea, and grey the sky, grey grey grey" (Eliot, *CPP*, 243) or "O dark dark dark. They all go into the dark" from "East Coker" (Eliot, *CPP*, 180), there are many instances of him seeking to emulate such a metrical effect. A voice in "During December's Death" commands the speaker: "*Wait: wait: wait as if you had always waited*" (*SK*, 217; Schwartz's italics), while, in another poem, Schwartz describes a landscape as "Wet, white, ice, wooden, dulled and dead, brittle or frozen" (212), 4 stressed syllables beginning a 13-syllable line of which 8 are emphatically stressed. Eliot's chorus also shares late Schwartz's concern with the passing of the seasons, singing of how "golden October" declines into "sombre November" and how the new year waits (Eliot, *CPP*, 239). For Schwartz—also influenced in this regard by Stevens and by Spengler—the seasons epitomize nature's continual cycle of birth, fruition, death, and rebirth, the cause of all the hope he can muster in his "Summer Knowledge" poems.

"The Phoenix Is the Meaning of the Fruit": The Principles of "Summer Knowledge"

Schwartz's longer lines and euphonic principle of composition may be the first features of his late verse to strike a reader, but they are inextricably bound up with a particular worldview that could not adequately be expressed in any other way. "At a Solemn Musick," the first poem in the "Summer Knowledge" section of *Summer Knowledge*, can be taken as a statement of intent, introducing almost every question, figuration, and technique to recur in the poems that follow. These can be read as variations upon a common concern: like the resurrected phoenix—their dominant symbol—they are at once the same but different, and each of them continues to explore the poet's sense of selfhood and his relationship to the world around him, albeit in ways quite different to the early poetry.

"At a Solemn Musick" takes its title from a poem of Milton's, probably written in 1633. Milton's poem longs for a renewal of "That undisturbed song of pure concent" formerly heard in nature until "disproportioned sin / Jarred against nature's chime."[16] It also celebrates unity and harmony, and the "Blest pair of sirens," "Voice and Verse," whose music is a pledge of "heaven's joys."[17] Schwartz's poem likewise invokes the music of the spheres.[18]

> Let the musicians begin,
> Let every instrument awaken and instruct us
> In love's willing river and love's dear discipline:
> We wait, silent, in consent and in the penance
> Of patience, awaiting the serene exaltation
> Which is the liberation and conclusion of expiation. (*SK*, 147)

Where much of Schwartz's earlier poetry dwelt upon the heavy burden of guilt, his poetry of the 1950s increasingly seeks occasions for forgiveness and redemption. It celebrates the possibilities of love, usually quite abstractly, in a quasi-religious way (almost like Dante at the end of the *Paradiso*), rather than to refer to love for a particular person.[19] The shared suffixes of some of the words in the first stanza of "At a Solemn Musick" invite a reader to consider more closely their semantic similarities: "penance" cannot be achieved without "patience"; true "expiation" is a cause for "exaltation"—though, lest such rejoicing become overexultant, it is tempered by being "serene." Love, exaltation, and expiation in the first stanza, are separated from the italicized "lust and emulation" rejected by the chief musician in the second. Love is imagined as a river and associated with the natural world, while lust is like "barbarous kings," a comparison that evokes Tereus, "the barbarous king" (Eliot, *CPP*, 64) whose rape of Philomel is presented in *The Waste Land*, and perhaps also the "barbarous kings" in Pound's "Lament of the Frontier Guard."[20] Love triumphs over this, and the poem's final chant celebrates its omnipresence in a direct address.

> *Before the morning was, you were:*
> *Before the snow shone,*
> *And the light sang, and the stone,*

Abiding, rode the fullness or endured the emptiness,
You were: you were alone. (*SK*, 148; Schwartz's italics)

There is a strain in these lines, however: "*you were alone*" seems to be saying "you (that is, love) alone existed, and nothing else did." Is it possible, however, to conceive of love without an object—something, or someone, to love, and to be loved? It is hard to take "alone" without overtones of isolation that undermine the communal feeling of the "entire choir" chanting in unison. It is almost as though one has overheard the poet talking to himself, recalling himself to his own alienation even at the point at which he seems most to transcend personal concerns. Such tensions serve to undercut the apparent optimism of many of Schwartz's late poems.

Harold Bloom's inclusion of "At a Solemn Musick" in his anthology of *American Religious Poems* invites an association of the poem with the Emersonian theology, distinct from any of the "devotional creeds of the Old World," that worships "the God within; solitude; [and] the best and oldest part of the self, which goes back before creation."[21] There is nothing to suggest that Schwartz's liturgy takes place in an actual church or temple. There is no reason, in fact, to suppose that the poem describes an actual performance at all: its terms are speculative, hypothetical. None of its recurring verbs—"let," "may," and "shall"—indicates a definite occurrence. The logic of Schwartz's "Summer Knowledge" poems is often at odds with that of the external world. They are poems of the mind, universal insofar as they try to reach beyond the particulars of the world as we experience it.

Schwartz's late poetry is no less allusive than his early work. Beginning a poem with the word "let" may seem like another Eliotic gesture, but "At a Solemn Musick" has a greater affinity to Shakespeare's "Let the Bird of Loudest Lay" (often referred to as "The Phoenix and the Turtle"), George Herbert's "Antiphon," and Smart's *Jubilate Agno*.[22] Schwartz's "chief musician" reprises the role of Shakespeare's "priest in surplice white," while Shakespeare's poem also informs the chief musician's gnomic utterance that

"*The phoenix is the meaning of the fruit,*
Until the dream is knowledge and knowledge is a dream" (*SK*, 147;
Schwartz's italics)

The phoenix and ripe fruit are Schwartz's dominant symbols in the "Summer Knowledge" poems for fulfillment followed by decay and regeneration. The earlier declaration, by all the players, that

"*The river of the morning, the morning of the river*
Flow out of the splendor of the tenderness of surrender" (147; Schwartz's
italics)

also highlights two dominant preoccupations—the continual recurrence of morning and the ever-changing nature of the river, defined by its motion—that are present throughout the poems. In both cases, the use of chiasmus indicates the symbiotic relationships between knowledge and dream, morning and the river, and simultaneously emphasizes similarity and difference.

The poem titled "Summer Knowledge" suggests that such knowledge—the kind that Socrates distinguishes from mere opinion in *The Republic*—cannot be derived solely from felt experience. It eludes precise definition and this is one reason why it cannot be set forth in an already established poetic form: the composition, like the knowledge itself, needs to be instinctual—although this is not to deny that the verse is consciously crafted. This is also a reason why Schwartz needs to try out a number of different definitions, many of them outlining what "summer knowledge" is not, rather than what it is. It "is not the winter's truth," nor is it "May knowledge." It "is not picture knowledge, nor is it the knowledge of lore and learning." Instead, it "is green knowledge," "bird knowledge and the knowing that trees possess when / The sap ascends to the leaf and the flower and the fruit" (*SK*, 157). As the poem gains momentum from its accretion of definitions, the definitions themselves become more confident. "Summer Knowledge," Schwartz asserts toward the end, "is the knowledge of death as birth, / Of death as the soil of all abounding flowering flaring rebirth" (*SK*, 158). The poem concludes, like "May's Truth and May's Falsehood," with the verse collapsing into a kind of prose, although its more traditionally poetic nature is reasserted through the poem's one true end-rhyme.

> For, in a way, summer knowledge is not knowledge at all: it is
> second nature, first nature fulfilled, a new birth
> and a new death for rebirth, soaring and rising out
> of the flames of turning October, burning November,
> the towering and falling fires, growing more and
> more vivid and tall
> In the consummation and annihilation of the blaze of fall. (*SK*, 158)

Although Schwartz charts the progression of time as we experience it, summer giving way to October which then gives way to November, he presents consummation and annihilation as occurring simultaneously rather than consecutively. This reaffirms the idea of death *as* birth, or rebirth—an idea that is also suggested by the fact that the fires tower and fall at the same time. To apply this kind of thinking to Spengler's model of history, Schwartz is suggesting that if civilization is in decline it might, simultaneously, be reviving.

In his late period, Schwartz's belief in death as birth, and of the moment of death or decay as also marking a point of ultimate fulfillment, is conveyed in two potent symbols—the phoenix and ripe fruit. One of his most deceptively simple poems, "'I Am Cherry Alive,' the Little Girl Sang" (whose title suggests that the girl in question feels optimally alive, ripe with youth) concludes with the girl singing "I am red, I am gold, I am green, I am blue, / I will always be me, I will always be new!" (*SK*, 161). She celebrates that state in which one retains individuality but is also continually changed or renewed and which Schwartz associates with the phoenix—the mythical bird, itself brightly colored, that burns after death and is then reincarnated from its own ashes.

One of the subsections of the "Summer Knowledge" part of *Selected Poems* is titled "The Deceptive Present, The Phoenix Year." The present is deceptive because, as "May's Truth and May's Falsehood" puts it, the "super-exuberant vitality" of summer makes it "difficult" and "painful" to "believe in the reality of winter" (*SK*, 213), while in the poem that shares its title with the section heading, it is suggested that to live only in the moment—and in the poem's stark world of winter—would not only be unremittingly bleak but also be a falsification of experience. To have knowledge of summer, however, and to see the potential for birth—and rebirth—in this desolate scene is akin to intuitive hopefulness. The speaker of "May's Truth and May's Falsehood" finds consolation in recognizing that winter (like sleep) is also part of nature's vitality, a necessary part of the continuous cycle without which the very idea of summer is unfeasible. Summer, for Schwartz, is inconceivable without winter and therefore winter is a part of summer. Life is inconceivable without death and therefore death is a part of life. It is in this respect that Schwartz can write in another poem, "The First Morning of the Second World," of the "illusion of death" (as opposed to the "reality of the agony of dying") (*SK*, 156), and it is in this respect also that he can offer his definition of "summer knowledge" as "knowledge of death as birth" (158). Whitman—for whom "to die is different from what any one supposed, and luckier"[23]—informs Schwartz's sensibility and philosophy here, as does Stevens, for whom "death is the mother of beauty."[24]

The condition of the phoenix, then, figures nature's cycle of life, death, and rebirth, a cycle that Schwartz's late poems emphatically assert is to be celebrated. In a gesture that grants nature its own will, "May's Truth and May's Falsehood" concludes by imagining the

> *desire* of the bud and the flower and the fruit the tree and the vine to be devoured and to be phoenix in nature, fulfilled in the phoenix sensuality of blood and of wine, or stilled in the mud near the root under the

ground once more awaiting the sun's domination, the sun's great roar and fire. (*SK*, 214, my italics)

Such a cycle not only exists but is the intense wish of every living thing. Implicit here is the recognition that it is in burning, ending its life, that the specific identity of the phoenix *as a phoenix*—not just any bird—is fulfilled.

In "The Kingdom of Poetry," Schwartz announces that "Poetry resurrects the past from the sepulchre, like Lazarus" (another figure who recurs in the late poems, with obvious resonance), and goes on to claim that "poetry invented the unicorn, the centaur and the phoenix" (*SK*, 188): they are not, then, natural phenomena, and this suggests a belief that it is poetry alone that is able to effect the rebirths upon which Schwartz dwells. Schwartz's use of the phoenix symbol evokes many of its previous poetic incarnations, notably in works by Shakespeare, Donne, and Milton.[25] Of these, the phoenix simile in Milton's *Samson Agonistes* especially suggests why the phoenix might have mattered so much to Schwartz as a symbol in the 1950s. Milton's semichorus describes the return of Samson's strength and virtue:

So virtue given for lost,
Depressed, and overthrown, as seemed,
Like that self-begotten bird
In the Arabian woods embossed,
That no second knows nor third,
And lay erewhile a holocaust,
From out her ashy womb now teemed,
Revives, reflourishes, then vigorous most
When most unactive deemed,
And though her body die, her fame survives,
A secular bird ages of lives.[26]

Milton's use of the word "holocaust" here is imbued with wholly new significance for any post–Second World War reader. Schwartz may rarely directly address the mass genocide that constituted the darkest passage of twentieth-century history, but his poetry often makes reference to burning and to ash, and the holocaust is perhaps implicit in every reference he makes to the phoenix. He writes of the Jew surviving "the annihilating fury of history" ("The Vocation of the Poet," 23) at the same time as the phoenix becomes his dominant symbol. The conclusion of "Summer Knowledge" suggests that such annihilation could also be a consummation; and that if, as Schwartz had earlier written, "Time is the fire in which we burn" (*SK*, 67), then something might yet be salvaged from that burning.[27]

The moment of the phoenix's combustion is, additionally, analogous to optimum ripeness, when fruit is at its best but also imminently likely to decay. In referring so often to ripe fruit, Schwartz takes his immediate cue from Stevens, whose early poetry is full of "good, fat, guzzly fruit."[28] Stevens is as important an influence upon Schwartz's late poetry as Eliot and Yeats are upon his earlier works: his questioning of what beauty there could be in an unchanging heaven, for example, is one of the prompts that helps Schwartz to accept an actual, not an idealized, world. "Is there no change of death in paradise?" the elder poet asks in "Sunday Morning":

> Does ripe fruit never fall? Or do the boughs
> Hang always heavy in that perfect sky[?]

If so, what beauty, or what purpose, can there be in having fruit at all?

> Why set the pear upon those river-banks
> Or spice the shores with odors of the plum?

At the heart of Stevens's philosophy is the belief that "Death is the mother of beauty": a world, even a heaven, without change could only be sterile.[29] In "Le Monocle de Mon Oncle," Stevens also strives for an acceptance of earthly things, proposing,

> The honey of heaven may or may not come,
> But that of earth both comes and goes at once.[30]

This is concordant with Schwartz's insistence that consummation and annihilation may occur simultaneously. Love, Stevens further speculates, "comes, it blooms, it bears its fruit and dies."[31] There is no way to preserve love at its stage of blooming, but Stevens reconciles himself to this in his awareness that this is precisely what makes it beautiful.

Similarly, Schwartz often suggests the inevitability of fruit rotting. At his most desolate, in the 1962 poem beginning "Remember midsummer," he describes pears hanging "yellowed and over-ripe, sodden brown in erratic places, all bunched and dangling, / Like a small choir of bagpipes, silent and waiting," and sees in their decay a mockery of "hopes and ambitions" that have been long abandoned (*LL*, 13). The "cherry alive" girl is more accepting in her song. She admits that "The peach has a pit" (*SK*, 161): it is not perfect.

The pit, however, is also the seed from which the peach grew: "the pit has a peach." The stony, inedible part of the fruit is what sustains the edible flesh. The girl goes on to admit that

> both may be wrong when I sing my song,
> But I don't tell the grown-ups: because it is sad,
> And I want them to laugh just like I do
> Because they grew up and forgot what they knew (161)

Both ways of viewing the peach may be wrong. One's actual experience of eating a ripe peach may be so absorbing that one can completely disregard the fact that it has a pit at all, whereas if one focuses solely on the pit after the flesh has been eaten it is easy to forget that this, in due course, could be used to grow a new peach tree. Both may be wrong in the same way that May may be false in "May's Truth and May's Falsehood." There is the question, on the one hand, of one's immediate experience, but also of one's knowledge of how things change over the course of time. Characteristically, Schwartz adopts a position in which he accepts two apparently opposing positions are both valid at the same time.

Like Stevens, Schwartz relates the full bloom and ripeness of fruit to being in love. In "The First Morning of the Second World," Schwartz—drawing upon Whitehead's discussion of "the withness of the body," previously used as the epigraph for "The Heavy Bear Who Goes with Me"—declares:

> Withness is ripeness,
> Ripeness is withness,
> To be is to be in love
> Love is the fullness of being. (*SK*, 154)

This is one of many allusions in the "Summer Knowledge" poems to Edgar's speech to Gloucester in Act V Scene ii of *King Lear*: "Men must endure / Their going hence even as their coming hither, / Ripeness is all," lines which evoke birth and death, ending and beginning, and which support Schwartz's belief in seeking the fulfillment of one's nature.[32] "Gold Morning, Sweet Prince," which is specifically a tribute to Shakespeare, modulates *Ripeness is all* (Schwartz's italics) into "Love / Is all" and, with further Shakespearean echoes (this time of *The Tempest*), Schwartz goes on to state how

> our little life, green, ripe, or rotten, is what it is
> Because of love accepted, rejected, refused and jilted, faded, raided,
> neglected or betrayed. (*SK*, 174)

One must do whatever one can to enable love to ripen, but love's more negative aspects also make us who we are.[33]

An important facet of Schwartz's "Summer Knowledge" is the realization that ripeness cannot be achieved in isolation: one cannot think only of oneself. Once again, the use of a chiasmus in "The First Morning of The Second World" indicates the necessary reciprocity in any fulfilled relationship. It would be easy enough to argue that "Summer Knowledge" is really just a new, all-embracing way of looking at the world. However, Schwartz insists that it is actually transformative. At the climax of "The First Morning of the Second World," for example, when the poet recognizes *both* the autonomy of the self *and* its dependence upon others, Schwartz writes:

> Suddenly it was the awe and moment when Adam first looked upon another self, a self like his own self, yet an absolute other and newness, being the beginning of being and love and loving and being loved (*SK*, 155)

The second world, created by this realization, may resemble an earlier world but it is, in fact, entirely new. The paradox is that the moment of Adam's first understanding of a world outside himself is both unrepeatable, because the world is always changing, and yet continually reenacted, because each moment renders the world new again and makes necessary another such realization. Although not evoked explicitly in this poem, the phoenix symbol still hovers around these lines—in its continual resurrections, the phoenix is forever making "another self, a self like its own self, yet an absolute other and newness." As has been noted in previous chapters, Schwartz makes much, elsewhere, of how history and myth are forever reenacted, but this is not to deny that individual experience is also unique, absolutely other and new. "The First Morning of the Second World" also, through its considerations of Adam, ripeness, and knowledge, evokes the forbidden apple, and attempts to recover a kind of knowledge that is purely instinct whilst celebrating the reality of an imperfect world in which ripe fruit does continuously fall.

"Seurat's Sunday Afternoon along the Seine"

In his review of *Summer Knowledge*, Hecht warns that "there is very little visual interest" in Schwartz's work, adding that "there are probably more abstract nouns and adjectives per page in the book than in the work of almost any other modern writer in English."[34] This is not offered wholly as a criticism; Hecht sees it as an interesting countertendency to the dominant belief that poems should contain lots of images. However, although there *is* a great deal of abstraction in Schwartz's late poems, it is not entirely accurate to say that they also lack visual interest. The "sunflower-lanterned" (*SK*, 216) summer afternoon described in "The Mounting Summer, Brilliant and Ominous," for example, turns the sunflowers into sources of light in a way that suggests much more than that they are merely bright and yellow. In "The Deceptive Present, The Phoenix Year," Schwartz's description of a poplar as rising "Like a slender throat" requires us to revisualize the tree as a human body, while his description of apple blossom as "surf... delicately foaming" (212) transports us to the seashore. His further presentation of trees in winter as "Silent soldiers, a vigil of woods" whose

> hidden feelings
> Scrawled and became
> Scores of black vines,
> Barbed wire sharp against the ice-white sky (212)

evokes, as much as winter's desolation, Margaret Bourke-White's first harrowing photographs of Buchenwald—further suggesting that these poems are obliquely engaged with the fate of the Jews and international history.

The poem that most clearly engages with the world of visual art is "Seurat's Sunday Afternoon along the Seine." It is unique in Schwartz's oeuvre as an ekphrastic poem, but it also epitomizes many of the tendencies in his late poetry.[35] Like the earlier "Far Rockaway," which also presents an artist-figure observing "Sunday people" (190) at play, the poem addresses the relation of the artist to the world he depicts. In both poems, the artist takes in the scene he beholds fully but does not participate in it. In the Seurat poem, "The one who beholds them, beholding the gold and green / Of summer's Sunday is himself unseen" (190). Seurat, says Schwartz, is "fanatical" (194), and the poem invites the reader to seek analogies throughout between the painter's method and that of the poet. Even though the unusual length of Schwartz's poem seems to imitate the vastness of Seurat's canvas, it is impossible to read the poem in the same way as one looks at a painting, taking in the whole impression first and then honing in on the finer details. Because poems are traditionally written in lines, and progress chronologically—as well as physically, across the page, down it, and then over it—one cannot take in the whole effect at once as one can with paintings.[36] Schwartz, however, seeks to emulate, within the limitations of his own craft, what Seurat achieves through his.

As Atlas notes, the poem draws heavily upon Meyer Schapiro's lecture on Seurat. Although this was not published until 1958, Schwartz had heard it many years earlier (Atlas, 257). Aside from the numerous direct borrowings that are so important in Schwartz's poem, Schapiro's discussion of Seurat's technique must have prompted Schwartz into a greater awareness of his own method. Schapiro begins with a defense of Seurat's pointillism. It is this technique, he claims, that gives rise to the "marvelous delicacy of tone, the uncountable variations within a narrow range, the vibrancy and soft luster" of Seurat's canvasses, and it is inconceivable that these effects could have been achieved through any other means. What is even more distinctive, for Schapiro, is the way in which Seurat's paintings build up "continuous form" from discrete units: he describes the emergence of "solid masses" from "an endless scattering of fine points" as "a mystery of the coming-into-being for the eye."[37] He is claiming that Seurat's canvases do much more than just create a pleasant visual impression: they require contemplation and prompt a new consideration of perception. Seurat's dots belong to an "artificial micro-pattern" that "serves the painter as a means of ordering, proportioning and nuancing sensation beyond the familiar qualities of the objects that the colors evoke" (Schapiro, 102).

In Schwartz's work, the euphony compensates for the visual delicacy of Seurat's painting, but he, too, is concerned with far more than creating pleasing impressions: his poem is a meditation upon perception and the relation of the viewer to the artwork he or she observes. Seurat's "artificial micro-pattern" is replicated in Schwartz's poem through the variations in the way that sounds—and sometimes whole words or phrases—recur with slightly different emphasis each time, and also in the particular scenes within the painting to which Schwartz returns.

There is also the fact that Schwartz's "continuous form" is built up from discrete units—words, lines, and verse paragraphs—which, taken alone, may have their own interest but may also give a skewed perspective of the whole work, appearing to be little more than "artificial micro-patterns." Richard A. Johnson, for example, objects to the lines

If you look long enough at anything
It will become extremely interesting;
If you look very long at anything
It will become rich, manifold, fascinating (*SK*, 191)

on the grounds that this "is not…a very interesting way of saying it."[38] Taken outside the context of the whole poem, he is right. However, the inclusion of these lines is justified, partly because they are an apt summation of a verse paragraph that delineates the various points of visual interest in the painting, segueing into a paragraph that takes a more universal view, and partly because they show how the poem is not afraid to accommodate the mundane alongside the exuberant—much as Seurat is able to invest a picture of normal people simply standing or sitting by a river with a radiant aura. More importantly, the lines are consistent with the whole poem's fascination with ways of looking. After all, "Seurat's Sunday Afternoon along the Seine" begins by asking "What are they looking at?" and goes on to contemplate the people looking at the river (or at least in its direction), the painter looking at the people, the viewer/poet looking at the painting, and even the painting itself looking back at the viewer: at one point Schwartz describes Seurat's dots as "eyes" (190). The poem, then, demands to be taken as a whole. Its overall effect is distorted when individual lines are extracted rather than seen as constituent parts of a larger project. The same would be true of the painting: a small enough segment would reveal little more than a formless amalgamation of colorful dots.

This relation of the individual component to the greater whole recollects, again, the principles of "international consciousness." Schapiro remarks, "One can enjoy in the *Grande Jatte* many pictures each of which is a world in itself" (Schapiro, 103). Schwartz takes this idea further in a passage that recalls the obsession with lineage that is so prominent in *Genesis*. Each of Seurat's many pictures, Schwartz says,

> is a world itself, a world in itself (and as a living child links generations,
>   reconciles the estranged and aged so that a grand child is a second
>   birth, and the rebirth of the irrational, of those who are forlorn,
>   resigned or implacable),
> Each little picture links the large and small, grouping the big
> Objects, connecting them with each little dot, seed or black grain
> Which are as patterns, a marvelous network and tapestry. (194)

This way of looking at the painting—and, indeed, at life itself—prioritizes each individual component but only insofar as it contributes to, or mirrors, a much larger vision of unity and a sense of order that cannot be discerned by looking only at the components themselves. Again, this works not only as an analogy for the method of "Seurat's Sunday Afternoon along the Seine," but also for Schwartz's late poetry in general. Some of the individual poems may seem slight in themselves, but taken together they constitute a complete—though sometimes contradictory—philosophy or ideology. The sense of overall cohesion that Schwartz gleans from Seurat's pictures within the painting is heightened a few lines later when the poet withdraws further from the details of the painting—a technique reminiscent of the panning in and out of poems such as "The Ballad of the Children of the Czar"—and announces, "Each micro pattern is the dreamed of or imagined macrocosmos" (195). Schwartz's cosmological language here suggests that Seurat may be depicting truths that apply beyond our immediate experience of the world. Such universal application (in every sense) represents the furthest extents of "international consciousness."

Perhaps Schwartz's most important borrowing from Schapiro is his depiction of Seurat as an alchemist. Schapiro, in accounting for Seurat's use of minute dots as compositional units, quotes Rimbaud's *Alchemy of the Word*, in which the French poet explains: "I regulated the form and the movement of each consonant" (Schapiro, 102). This, Schapiro says, "was to inspire in the poets of Seurat's generation a similar search for the smallest units of poetic effect" (102). Schwartz does not necessarily go to this extreme, but he, too, weighs up his consonants, conscious of how each word contributes to the larger scheme. Schapiro goes on to maintain that "Seurat practices an alchemy no more exacting than that of his great forbears, though strange in the age of Impressionist spontaneity" (103). This is as if to say that Seurat's effects are almost all reliant upon meticulous, studied technique in an era that values careful craft less than capturing a sense of immediacy. Schwartz, equally—however effusive he may seem—is not really an impressionistic writer. His free verse is as patterned and as technically accomplished as any of his more conventionally formal poems.

Schwartz develops Schapiro's alchemical references by insisting upon the golden quality of the light in *La Grande Jatte*. Seurat, he writes,

> is at once painter, poet, artist, and alchemist:
> The alchemist points his magic wand to describe and hold the
>   Sunday's gold
> ...
> —His marvellous little marbles, beads or molecules
> Begin as points which the alchemy's magic transforms
> Into diamonds of blossoming radiance (*SK*, 192–193)

The process by which alchemy turns the mundane into the wonderful can be seen as akin to the transformative ability of the phoenix; and the magical (yet scientific) practice evokes not only Rimbaud but also Donne. In this context, when Schwartz writes again of "time's great fire" (194) it acquires a quite specific sense, evoking the furnace in which base metal might be melted down and purified. This fire, aided by the alchemist himself, "turns / Whatever is into another thing, continually altering and changing all identity" (194). It is a process to which all things are subjected, but which yields the most valuable results in the hands of an artist who knows which materials he can use and how he can use them.

Schwartz's dedication of "Seurat's Sunday Afternoon along the Seine" to Schapiro and his wife, Lillian, is an acknowledgment of the debt he owes to his art historian friend. There is also, however, another possible—and intriguing—source for the poem. In March 1952, Schwartz accepted Frank O'Hara's "On Looking at *La Grande Jatte* the Czar Wept Anew" for publication in *Partisan Review*.[39] O'Hara's poem imagines the czar looking at Seurat's painting and wanting to escape into it, joining Seurat's Parisians by the river. In the poem's second section, the czar, suddenly recalling Seurat's painting at an informal dinner party, impulsively steps, quite literally, inside a mirror (64) (or so we are to imagine, as the poem takes a surreal turn). There is a strong sense of disorientation, both here and at the start of the third section. Did he mean to step into the painting instead, and does he somehow end up in it anyway, despite the fact that, at the start of the third section, he sends a telegram from the "Ice Palace?" The czar's alienation is underlined by his inability to communicate with his "muzhiks," who are unable to read: sending them a telegram, then, is pointless. The czar himself finds it equally difficult to find meaning in the trees that surround him, presumably those that appear in Seurat's painting. Because of the czar's personality and status, and because he does not know how to appreciate the artwork, he can only bring winter to Seurat's idyllic scene rather than inhabit it as a means of prolonging summer: in the poem's final lines he is figured as a "stranger" trapped in a frozen scene (63). This is a projection of alienation that it is easy to imagine Schwartz appreciating.

O'Hara—who had playfully alluded to "In Dreams Begin Responsibilities" in "Memorial Day, 1950"[40]—clearly engages here with Schwartz's "The Ballad of the Children of the Czar." The prominence of snow and of the mirror also suggests that O'Hara was well aware of the symbols that characterize much of the verse in *In Dreams Begin Responsibilities*. Schwartz's awareness of O'Hara, apart from his publication of "On Looking at *La Grande Jatte*, the Czar Wept Anew," is harder to gauge. His only reference to O'Hara in his journals (from April 22, 1957) shows little more than that he intended to read the younger poet, along with others (*Portrait*, 572). The affinities between "Seurat's Sunday Afternoon along the Seine" and "On Looking at *La Grande Jatte* the Czar Wept Anew" are strong enough to suggest, however, that Schwartz owed a veiled debt to a poet whose encounter with the same painting had also prompted a consideration of the relationship between the viewer and the painting he regards.[41]

Both poems acknowledge the sense of escapism that a work of art can provoke, but also the poignancy of not being able to sustain such a sense of escape, or to make it actual. Schwartz's poem concludes by stepping away from the painting in which it has been so thoroughly absorbed. First of all, Schwartz acknowledges that by looking at the painting in a gallery he has also been performing an act of homage to the city in which he lives and where he has been able to see the painting. This is a gesture that would seem to equate him looking at the painting in New York with the Parisians looking at the Seine.

> —Here we have stopped, here we have given our hearts
> To the real city, the vivid city, the city in which we dwell
> And which we ignore or disregard most of the luminous day! (*SK*, 196)

But if this is a wholly positive attitude, the lines that follow indicate how brief the experience has been. They bear the revelation that

> Seurat's *Sunday Afternoon along the Seine* has gone away,
> Has gone to Chicago: near Lake Michigan,
> All of his flowers shine in monumental stillness fulfilled. (196)[42]

Both Schwartz and O'Hara's poems end on a similar note of regret for the fact that it is impossible for the viewer actually to inhabit the painting. Schwartz—although he cites Flaubert to affirm the sense of immediacy that the painting maintains ("*Ils sont dans le vrai!*")—imagines, in his final lines, Kafka saying:

> "Flaubert was right: *Ils sont dans le vrai!*
> Without forbears, without marriage, without heirs,
> Yet with a wild longing for forbears, marriage and heirs:
> They all stretch out their hands to me: but they are too far away!"
> (196)[43]

This is as if to say that, yes, the painting maintains its immediacy; but it still has to go away. Its vision is true, because it is fully accessible to all, visually and imaginatively; but it is also false, illusory, because there is no physical way of entering into its world. Schwartz's response to Seurat's painting of summer is not unlike his attitude to summer itself in a poem such as "May's Truth and May's Falsehood": it is true and false at the same time. The desperation of Schwartz's final line echoes the inability of O'Hara's czar to take his muzhiks by the hand; and it infects a poem that had celebrated all that a great work of art *can* achieve with a tone of sadness at its limitations.

Conclusion

In Dream Song 282, Berryman reflects on past conversations with dead friends ("Richard & Randall.../ & Delmore") about the relation of European culture to that of America. All three, along with others of their generation, shared a self-conscious sense of modernity, set in relief by a determination to establish what Berryman here describes as "our meaning to the Old World, theirs to us." In attempting to understand what relation modern American life might have to age-old Western philosophies, and how "ancient thought" might endure in "new forms," Schwartz, like his contemporaries, was questioning the role of the poet—and, indeed, the critic—in twentieth-century American society.[1]

This is a problem that he never resolved. If his "Summer Knowledge" poems suggest a final commitment to detached lyricism, many of the poems posthumously published in *Last & Lost Poems*—including "Love and Marilyn Monroe," which Ashbery published as poetry editor of *Partisan Review* in 1976, repaying Schwartz the favor of publishing his own "The Picture of Little J. A. in a Prospect of Flowers" in 1951—continue to comment upon the state of America. Eliot's assessment of the varying demands that criticism has historically made upon poetry, in *The Use of Poetry and the Use of Criticism*, highlights the difficulties incumbent upon the poet whose lyric impulse is constrained by a sense of social obligation. Schwartz, with his Jewish heritage, felt such difficulties more than most. "The important moment for the appearance of criticism," Eliot speculates, "seems to be the time when poetry ceases to be the expression of a whole people."[2] This is when it becomes more necessary to ask exactly what poetry is and what its uses are: these are no longer self-evident. Eliot concludes that the tendency of modern criticism is "to expect too much, rather than too little, of poetry."[3] For Dr. Johnson, "poetry was still poetry, and not another thing," but since Johnson's time more and more "expectations and demands" have been made upon it, culminating in a modern age whose critics seem "to demand of poetry not that it shall be well written but that it shall be 'representative of its age.'"[4] For Eliot, the modern critic's challenge is to distinguish between "what is permanent or eternal in poetry" and the sociological and other purposes that poetry may have been made to serve but which are not, in fact, its essence. It follows that the modern poet must equally be aware of such distinctions in his own work, perceiving, however, that not to be representative enough could be just as fatal to posterity as not reaching enough for the eternal.

Schwartz was, without doubt, a representative poet—representative both of Jewish American intellectual experience in the mid-twentieth century and of the generation of poets shaped by, but desperate to move beyond, Eliotic modernism. Kenneth Koch, in "A Momentary Longing to Hear Sad Advice from One Long Dead," affectionately presents his former teacher as knowingly belonging to a particular historical milieu—America in the "late Forties"—obsessed with the zeitgeisty question of whether or not Walt Kelly, creator of the long-running Pogo cartoons, had read Joyce.[5] Howe, meanwhile—who advocates reading all of the period's Jewish American writers specifically as regional writers—notes how, "For one or two poets, the influence of New York meant becoming aware of the cultural pathos resident in the idea of being a Jew (not always distinguishable from the idea of Delmore Schwartz)."[6] At times, Schwartz certainly courted such an image and, arguably, he produced his most lasting work—*In Dreams Begin Responsibilities* and the stories of *The World Is a Wedding*—while conforming to the type established by the *Partisan Review* circle.

But he also sought for the "permanent and eternal" and was torn, throughout his career, between writing a poetry of conscious social engagement and pursuing the doctrine of "art for art's sake"—which, Eliot points out, is not in any case as purely aesthetic as it claims to be but is rather an extension of Arnold's view that poetry is "a capital substitute for religion."[7] Schwartz's dilemma manifests itself in the Atlantic dialectics of his dual impulses toward the overtly lyrical (the aesthetic) and the "morbidly pedestrian" (the social), toward high culture and popular culture, and toward the individual and the universal. At its best, his poetry admits these binaries, holding them, engagingly, in counterpoise. At other times, however, it gives way to indecision, Schwartz's conflict of purpose apparent but unsettled.

Such difficulties are exemplified in "The Would-Be Hungarian." This 1955 poem—prompted by an anecdote told him many years earlier by Berryman's first wife, Eileen Simpson—is memorable insofar as it ironizes the hopes that had driven Schwartz's own Eastern European ancestors to emigrate, reversing them in the titular character's desperation to forsake his Americanness and be Hungarian.[8] It captures a moment of social history at which, in a certain locality, a minority community can become a majority. As an interrogation of American identity, however, it struggles to negotiate between the specific instance recounted and the envoy's vast claim that the boy's experience of alienation is emblematic of what everyone in America feels. The poem strains as Schwartz attempts to make it more than a diverting anecdote:

> Behold how this poor boy, who wished so passionately to be
> Hungarian
> Suffered and knew the fate of being American.
>> Whether on Ellis Island, Plymouth Rock,
>> Or in the secret places of the mind and heart
>> This is America—as poetry and hope
>> This is the fame, the game and the names of our fate:
>> This we must suffer or must celebrate. (*SK*, 164–165)

The move from particular incident to general statement is familiar from *Genesis*, with which this poem, despite its brevity, has formal and tonal affinities. However, whereas the dramatic context of *Genesis* enables us to set the ghosts' generalizations against each other, and to question them, these lines admit no such skepticism. Their tone is earnest and didactic, especially in contrast with the wry long-lined narrative that precedes them. This does not mean that they are assured. The preponderance of internal rhymes and nebulous substantives conceals the fact that there is little analysis of what is actually being stated. As a consequence, the piece suffers, both as social analysis and as a poem.

The less socially engaged "Summer Knowledge" poems are more probing in their search for universal truths. They succeed better as works of decorative art, which is what, Eliot suggests, the earliest English critics considered poetry to be.[9] Even when unresolved, however, the processes by which Schwartz arrives at beliefs, doubts them, reasserts them, abandons them, and replaces them survives in the poems themselves. Despite the uncertainties of "The Would-Be Hungarian," for example, its final line is an important statement of Schwartz's ideology. Its implication initially seems to be that the child should celebrate who he is, rather than hopelessly wishing to be somebody else. However, one has to know oneself and one's fate before any such celebration is possible. The "or" is therefore misleading. One can only decide to celebrate one's fate when one has first endured the suffering. This is a reason why Schwartz, in the spirit of another of his child-subjects, the "true-blue American" (*SK*, 163) Jeremiah Dickson, so often chooses both—to suffer *and* to celebrate.

By the later 1950s, when he was trying to become reconciled to the actuality of modern American life but understood that the American Dream might be part of that actuality, accepting every available option became a fundamental principle. Schwartz's final position is that the poet must be neither solely a commentator on his culture and times, nor a Platonic philosopher-king figure, but both. This is clear enough from one of his final poems, "Apollo Musagete, Poetry, and the Leader of the Muses" that talks of how the poet "must be a nymphomaniacal whore yet preserve his virginity," be "Chaste yet a gigolo," and "The Czar yet Figaro" (*LL*, 55). The poet must be able to sustain such contradictions, to live in the world as he experiences it, yet also to live in a world of his own creation.

If this is hedge-betting of the kind that Auden criticized in *Genesis*, it is nonetheless a distinct and definite stance in its own right. Berryman, more charitably than Auden, sees Schwartz not as indecisive but as intellectually restless. Schwartz's refusal to settle upon a single definitive worldview or poetic form is indicative, in the view Berryman gives in Dream Song 282, of a "labile" soul: one that is prone to lapsing or displacement (OED, 1, 3), but also, perhaps, to the kind of transformation that might adapt "Old World" culture to a modern sensibility. Schwartz's lability indicates (as Berryman goes on) his restless pursuit of "insights" and his unwillingness to stop pondering the questions that had occupied him in his youth.[10] Whether seen in a positive or negative light, as evidence of a mind too intelligent to accept anything without questioning or of one too distrusting ever to believe in anything, such tentativeness is one of Schwartz's defining characteristics. If it eventually counted against him, the fact remains that, in 1938, when *In Dreams Begin Responsibilities* was published, the directions that American poetry might take after Eliot, Pound, Stevens, and Williams (all of whom were to keep writing for many more years) were not clear. Schwartz experimented with a number of possibilities, some of which were taken up and further developed by middle generation and younger New York school contemporaries. He did not, like Pound's disciple, Charles Olson—a poet who seems never to have caught Schwartz's attention—commit to a polemical position. Where Olson used Black Mountain College and his manifesto on "Projective Verse" to define a specific audience, to school followers in a Poundian tradition, and to establish a particular agenda ("the getting rid of the lyrical interference of the individual as ego, of the 'subject' and his soul": an aim Schwartz might, but for his lyric attachment, have found attractive in principle though he would have believed it unachievable), Schwartz gradually moved away from, without ever quite escaping, his own circle and mentors—the New York Intellectuals and Eliot—all the time trying to assimilate a number of different influences and to test the hybrid categories of prosaic lyricism and Romantic Modernism.

Though he admired Pound and Williams, Schwartz's closer affinities are emphatically with Eliot and, especially in his later work, Stevens. His severest critics—among them Kenner and Marjorie Perloff—have tended to be ardent advocates of the Pound line.[11] His most sympathetic readers, meanwhile, have tended to be other poets. Stevens himself did Schwartz the honor of alluding to "The Ballad of the Children of the Czar" in "An Ordinary Evening in New Haven," lines on being unable to "evade / The will of necessity, the will of wills—" clearly evoking the ball that evades the children's will in Schwartz's poem.[12] And, as was seen in chapter 3, Auden may also have borrowed from Schwartz—who had, in turn, borrowed from Auden.

For Paul Muldoon, it is Auden with whom Schwartz should be most associated. Laughlin had, after all, publicized Schwartz as "the American Auden" before Auden himself arrived in America.[13] Later, in wishing to be regarded as a "minor Atlantic Goethe," Auden also challenged Schwartz (albeit mock humbly) to his self-appointed Atlantic laureateship.[14] That Auden has, undoubtedly, been the more influential, wider-reaching poet, should not diminish Schwartz's contribution to the still-ongoing debate that Muldoon re-examines in "7, Middagh Street" about whether or not poetry can make anything happen—and, if so, what. "Louis" (MacNeice), the speaker of the final section of Muldoon's poem, puts Schwartz in the company of Crane and Yeats as well as Auden, and evokes the principles of "international consciousness" as he discusses how the slightest individual action might have worldwide implications. Imagining Auden losing "his faith / in human nature" in the same movie theater from which "Delmore was ushered" in his most celebrated story, Muldoon's MacNeice reflects that "the displacement of soap-suds in a basin / may have some repercussion // for a distant ship."[15] The poem's associative movements—from Auden to Schwartz and from Schwartz to the German neighborhood's "*Schwartzbrot*," which in turn evokes Hitler's "*Sieg / im Poland*"—play out the kind of string of coincidence that can lead to far-off repercussions. Muldoon revels in the comic pathos of Schwartz's story, but also accepts the seriousness of its title, with its understanding that some are prepared to die for, or may be killed in the name of, a dream:

In dreams begin responsibilities:
it was on account of just such an allegory

that Lorca
was riddled with bullets[16]

This leads to a further affirmation, not only of poetry's potential to make things happen, but also of its obligation to do so.

Though Schwartz is only a supporting actor in the extensive cast of "7, Middagh Street," Muldoon's poem does him the service of bringing him back into a discussion from which, for some time since his death, he had been excluded. Joan Didion, by including lines from "Calmly we move through this April's Day" as an epigraph in *The Year of Magical Thinking*, similarly reinstates Schwartz as a live presence, in this case within a study of grief.[17] It may yet prove that, by overlooking him, critics have not only slighted Schwartz's own reputation but have also only partially represented the writers with whom he was associated and those whom he influenced. Schwartz, for example, is the most consistently overlooked of Ashbery's many diverse influences. Mutlu Konuk Blasing has noted that "Ashbery's cityscapes," with their tall buildings, "often recall Auden's."[18] They do. But, as Ashbery himself observes, tall buildings are also one of Schwartz's recurring motifs. It seems likely, given Ashbery's acknowledged admiration for both Auden and Schwartz, that his own high buildings are derived from both of them. Schwartz's own poetry illustrates that a poet's works will often owe debts to a multitude of mentors. Whether or not Schwartz eventually comes to be regarded—as Ashbery believes he should be—as a major poet, he certainly deserves renewed attention as an animating figure for both exact contemporaries and the generation that followed. His poetry reveals, and fights against, the titanic influence of Eliot, but it is also at once representative of its age and innovative in its own right, containing much that is permanent and eternal.

Notes

Introduction

1. Delmore Schwartz, *Last & Lost Poems*, ed. Robert Phillips (New York: Vanguard Press, 1979), 4. The poem is dated 1954, but it gathers preoccupations from over a decade earlier.
2. Walt Whitman, "Preface 1855—*Leaves of* Grass, First Edition," in *Leaves of Grass and Other Writings*, ed. Michael Moon (New York: W. W. Norton, 2002), 616.
3. James Atlas, *Delmore Schwartz: The Life of an American Poet* (New York: Farrar, Straus and Giroux, 1976). The rock star Lou Reed, a former student, dedicated the song "European Son," on the album *The Velvet Underground & Nico*, to Schwartz.
4. Delmore Schwartz, *Genesis* (New York: New Directions, 1943), 5.
5. Delmore Schwartz, "America! America!" in *In Dreams Begin Responsibilities and Other Stories*, 20.
6. Delmore Schwartz, "The Fiction of Ernest Hemingway: Moral Historian of the American Dream" (1955), in *Selected Essays of Delmore Schwartz*, 271.
7. Schwartz, "The Fiction of Ernest Hemingway," 272.
8. Howe, "Foreword to Atlas, ed.," in *In Dreams Begin Responsibilities, and Other Stories,* vii; Alfred Kazin, *New York Jew* (London: Secker and Warburg, 1978), 25.
9. Cited in *DS & JL Letters*, 47.
10. Atlas, *Delmore Schwartz,* 154. Eliot regretted that he was unable to bring out a British edition of Schwartz's poems.
11. Atlas, *Delmore Schwartz,* 129. Wallace Stevens, *Letters of Wallace Stevens,* ed. Holly Stevens (New York: Knopf, 1981), December 27, 1940, 382.
12. John Berryman, *The Dream Songs* (London: Faber, 1990) (149), 168.
13. Delmore Schwartz, "Views of a Second Violinist" (1949), in *Selected Essays of Delmore Schwartz*, 25.
14. He was also film editor of *The New Republic* between 1955 and 1957.
15. Howe, "Foreword," x.

16. William Phillips, *A Partisan View: Five Decades of the Politics of Literature* (New Brunswick, NJ: Transaction Publishers, 1983), 75.

17. Lionel Trilling, "The Function of the Little Magazines," in *The Liberal Imagination: Essays on Literature and Society* (Oxford: Oxford University Press, 1951), 95.

18. Atlas, *Delmore Schwartz*, 141.

19. Benjamin Schreier, "Jew Historicism: Delmore Schwartz and Over-determination," *Prooftexts*, 27, no. 3 (2007), 514.

20. Berryman, *The Dream Songs* (147), 166.

21. David Lehman, "Delmore, Delmore: A Mournful Cheer," in *The Line Forms Here* (Ann Arbor: University of Michigan Press, 1991), 74.

22. Saul Bellow, *Humboldt's Gift* (London: Penguin, 1976), 1, 2, 11.

23. Bellow, *Humboldt's Gift*, 6.

24. Berryman, *The Dream Songs* (155, 151, 150), 174, 170, 169.

25. Robert Lowell, *Collected Poems*, ed. Frank Bidart and David Gewanter (London: Faber, 2003), 533.

26. Dwight MacDonald, "Delmore Schwartz (1913–1966)," in *Selected Essays of Delmore Schwartz*, xx; Karl Shapiro, "The Death of Randall Jarrell," in *Creative Glut: Selected Essays of Karl Shapiro*, ed. Robert Phillips (Oxford: Oxford Publicity Partnership, 2004), 176.

27. Shapiro, "The Death of Randall Jarrell," 176.

28. Kazin, *New York Jew*, 24.

29. Catherine Fitzpatrick, disentangling the confusion courted by Schwartz's contemporaries in taking his life and work to be coextensive, argues that "Schwartz was a writer whose greatest literary successes came in his treatments of failure." Fitzpatrick's argument calls to mind Denis Donoghue's conviction that there is a specifically American style of failure, and that "much American literature achieves its vitality by a conscientious labor to transform the mere state of failure into the artistic success of forms and pageants." See Catherine Fitzpatrick, "Life, Work, Failure: Delmore Schwartz," *Cambridge Quarterly* 42, no. 2 (2013): 112, and Denis Donoghue, "The American Style of Failure," *The Sewanee Review* 82, no. 3 (Summer 1974): 408.

30. Berryman, *The Dream Songs* (150), 169.

31. John Ashbery "In Discussion with Al Filreis, 26 March 2002," *Pennsound*. http://writing.upenn.edu/pennsound/x/Ashbery.php.

32. Charles Simic, "All Gone Into the Dark," *London Review of Books*, September 9, 2010, 12.

33. Kazin, *New York Jew*, 25.

34. Anthony Hecht, "The Anguish of the Spirit and the Letter," *Hudson Review* 12, no. 4 (Winter 1959–1960): 595.

35. "The Art of Poetry No. 16," *Paris Review* 53 (Winter 1972). http://www.theparisreview.org/interviews/4052/the-art-of-poetry-no-16-john-berryman; Berryman, *The Dream Songs* (156), 175.

36. Ashbery, *The Heavy Bear: Delmore Schwartz's Life Versus His Poetry: A Lecture Delivered at the Sixty-Seventh General Meeting of the English Literary Society*

of Japan on 21st May 1995 (Tokyo: English Literary Society of Japan, 1996), 3. Among the others that Ashbery appears to have had in mind are John Wheelwright, Paul Goodman, David Schubert, and early Randall Jarrell.

37. Ashbery, *The Heavy Bear,* 23.
38. *LL*, "Introduction," xiv.
39. There have been just three book-length studies of Schwartz's writing—Richard McDougall's *Delmore Schwartz* (1974), Robert Deutsch's *The Poetry of Delmore Schwartz* (published posthumously in 2003, some 20 years after Deutsch's death), and Edward Ford's *A Re-evaluation of the Works of American Writer Delmore Schwartz, 1913–1966* (2003). McDougall and Deutsch offer chronological readings of the major works, though these are sometimes cursory and each underplays the thematic and stylistic unity of Schwartz's writing. Ford's indiscriminating paean, meanwhile, is undermined by the author's overidentification of himself with his subject.

1 "The Greatest Thing in North America": "International Consciousness" or "The Isolation of Modern Poetry?"

1. Of all Schwartz's peers, it was perhaps F. O. Matthiessen who addressed the question most directly, visiting Austria and Czechoslovakia in 1948 to conduct seminars on American Literature—a diplomatic as well as an educative enterprise—and explicitly endorsing Schwartz's belief in Europe as "the greatest thing in North America." Matthiessen recounts the experience in *From the Heart of Europe.*
2. William Phillips and Philip Rahv, "Literature in a Political Decade," in *New Letters in America,* ed. Horace Gregory and Eleanor Clark (New York: W. W. Norton, 1937), 172–180. Cited in Terry A. Cooney, *The Rise of the New York Intellectuals: Partisan Review and Its Circle, 1934–1945* (Madison, WI: University of Wisconsin Press, 1986), 92.
3. Cited in Alan M. Wald, *The New York Intellectuals: The Rise and Decline of the Anti-Stalinist Left from the 1930s to the 1980s* (Chapel Hill: University of North Carolina Press, 1987), 4.
4. Christopher Hitchens, "Bravo, Old Sport," *London Review of Books,* April 4, 1991.
5. Leon Trotsky, "Leon Trotsky to André Breton," *Partisan Review* 6, no. 2 (Winter 1939): 127.
6. See, for example, Edmund Wilson's piece on "Flaubert's Politics" in *Partisan Review* 4, no. 1 (December 1937). "In the case of Taine and Sainte-Beuve," Wilson says, Flaubert "came to deplore their preoccupation in their criticism with the social aspects of literature at the expense of all its other values; but he himself always seems to see humanity in social terms and historical perspective" (13). The *Partisan Review* editors would not publish literary works on the basis of their social ideology, but this does not mean that they would resist criticizing it in those terms.

7. William Phillips and Philip Rahv, "Editorial Statement," *Partisan Review* 4, no. 1 (December 1937): 4.

8. Irving Howe, "The New York Intellectuals," in *Decline of the New,* 223.

9. Ibid., 223.

10. Quoted in Cooney, *The Rise of the New York Intellectuals,* 182.

11. Delmore Schwartz, Delmore Schwartz Papers. Yale Collection of American Literature, Beinecke Rare Book and Manuscript Library, Box 7, Folder 425.

12. Delmore Schwartz, *Letters of Delmore Schwartz,* ed. Robert Phillips (Princeton: Ontario Review Press, 1984), 101.

13. Jim Keller, "Delmore Schwartz's Strange Times," in *Reading The Middle Generation Anew,* ed. Eric Haralson (Iowa City: University of Iowa Press, 2006), 158.

14. "The Poet as Poet" (1939), In *Selected Essays of Delmore Schwartz,* 80. Schwartz's emphasis.

15. Delmore Schwartz, "An Unwritten Book," In *Selected Essays of Delmore Schwartz,* 84, 86–87.

16. Helen Vendler, "Dear Delmore," *New York Review of Books,* April 11, 1985. Nor is internationalism's worth as self-evident today as it was for Schwartz. Charles Bernstein, for example, criticizes its tendency to remove poems "from the local contexts that give them meaning" and to undervalue "the untranslatable particularities not only of given poems but also of the selection of poets." ("Poetics of the Americas," *Modernism/Modernity* 3, no. 3 [1996]: 3).

17. Even more conspicuously, perhaps, since he is discussing his own country, Schwartz feels obliged, in a discussion of Faulkner's fictional Yoknapatawpha County, Mississippi, to say something of "the immense distance between the region of the critic and that of the author" ("The Fiction of William Faulkner," in *Selected Essays of Delmore Schwartz,* 283).

18. "T. S. Eliot as the International Hero" (1945), in *Selected Essays of Delmore Schwartz,* 123.

19. "Tradition and the Individual Talent," in *The Sacred Wood,* 41.

20. Delmore Schwartz Papers, Box 6, Folder 359.

21. Delmore Schwartz Papers, Box 4, Folder 245.

22. "The Vocation of the Poet in the Modern World" (1951), in *Selected Essays of Delmore Schwartz,* 22.

23. Delmore Schwartz, "The Present State of Poetry," in *Selected Essays of Delmore Schwartz,* 48. Perhaps it wasn't so "clear and explicit" then, but each of the writers considered in F. O. Matthiessen's *American Renaissance: Art and Expression in the Age of Emerson and Whitman* (1941)—the study that established the nineteenth-century US canon as we now know it—had a keen sense of vistas beyond their own nation. See, for example, Wai Chee Dimock's *Through Other Continents: American Literature across Deep Time* for a discussion of Thoreau's simultaneous reading of the Bible, the Bhagavad Gita, and other "scriptures of the several nations" (23). See also Colleen Glenney Boggs's consideration of Whitman and translation in *Transnationalism and American Literature: Literary Translation, 1773–1892,* and Paul Giles on how Hawthorne and Melville read

Dante, Chaucer, medieval Islamic legend, Shakespeare, and Ruskin (*The Global Remapping of American Literature*, 97–107). American experience has always been, to some extent, international.

24. Stephen Hahn, "The Isolation of Delmore Schwartz," *Columbia Literary Columns* 40, no. 1 (November 1990): 24.

25. Delmore Schwartz, "Ezra Pound and History" (1960), in *Selected Essays of Delmore Schwartz*, 116.

26. Ezra Pound, *Poems and Translations*, ed. Richard Sieburth (New York: Library of America, 2003), 549.

27. W. H. Auden, *Collected Poems*, ed. Edward Mendelson (London: Faber, 1976), 101.

28. Delmore Schwartz, "The Isolation of Modern Poetry," in *Selected Essays of Delmore Schwartz*, 3.

29. Bellow's Charlie Citrine describes Schwartz's alter ego, Humboldt, as "a pioneer in the use of this word," adding, "Sensibility later made it big" (*Humboldt's Gift*, 2). But Eliot had already made sensibility "big," and it was also widely used by Rahv and Phillips in the early years of *Partisan Review*. In a 1934 essay entitled "Sensibility and Modern Poetry," Phillips identified three types of sensibility: that of the writer, that of the literary work or form, and that of a tradition or historical period. He also described it "in Eliotic fashion as a medium or solvent by which specific opinions, programs, or ideologies are transformed by the writer into something more indirect, subtle, and affective" (see Harvey M. Teres, *Renewing the American Left: Politics, Imagination, and the New York Intellectuals* [Oxford: Oxford University Press, 1996], 43–44). Schwartz, for his own part, described sensibility as a "quasi-psychological term" signifying "the awareness of which a mind is capable" (Delmore Schwartz Papers, Box 6, Folder 357).

30. Eliot, "The Metaphysical Poets," in Eliot, *Selected Essays*, 286.

31. Delmore Schwartz, "Poetry and Belief in Thomas Hardy," in *Selected Essays of Delmore Schwartz*, 60.

32. Delmore Schwartz, "Rimbaud in Our Time," In *Selected Essays of Delmore Schwartz*, 57.

33. Delmore Schwartz, "The Writing of Edmund Wilson," in *Selected Essays of Delmore Schwartz*, 362.

34. Edmund Wilson, *Axel's Castle: A Study in the Imaginative Literature of 1870–1930* (1931), (London: Collins, 1969), 39.

35. Ibid., 34.

36. Schwartz's preferred definition of symbolism further stresses this process of "cultivation," an act of singularly self-conscious crafting. The movement, he says, "was a prolonged cultivation of the power of language for its own sake which eventuated in an emphasis upon the connotative usages of language to an exclusion, varying from author to author, of the denotative usages" ("The Writing of Edmund Wilson," 362).

37. Atlas, *Delmore Schwartz*, 159.

38. Wilson, *Axel's Castle*, 227.

39. Delmore Schwartz, "The Vocation of the Poet," in *Selected Essays of Delmore Schwartz*, 23.
40. See Atlas, *Delmore Schwartz*, 162 and *DS & JL Letters*, 212.
41. Delmore Schwartz, "Under Forty: A Symposium on American Literature and the Younger Generation of American Jews," *Contemporary Jewish Record* 7, no. 1 (February 1944): 14.
42. Benjamin Schreier, "Ethnic Poetics and the Irreversibility of 'Jewishness' in Delmore Schwartz," in *Studies in Irreversibility: Texts and Contexts*, ed. Benjamin Schreier (Newcastle: Cambridge Scholars Publishing, 2007), 68.
43. John Hollander, "The Question of American Jewish Poetry," in *What is Jewish Literature?*, ed. Hana Wirth-Nesher (New York: Jewish Publication Society, 1994), 43; Maeera Y. Shreiber, "Jewish American Poetry," in *The Cambridge Companion to Jewish American Literature,* ed. Michael P. Kramer and Hana Wirth-Nesher (Cambridge: Cambridge University Press, 2003), 150.
44. Schwartz, "Ezra Pound and History," 119. Schwartz is hopeful enough to believe that one can be anti-Semitic some of the time but not all the time, but does not cite any of the apparently philo-Semitic passages to which he refers.
45. Delmore Schwartz Papers, Box 6, Folder 359.
46. Ibid.
47. Ibid.
48. Ibid.
49. Anthony Julius, *T. S. Eliot, Anti-Semitism, and Literary Form* (Cambridge: Cambridge University Press, 1995), 2.
50. Ibid., 56.
51. Delmore Schwartz Papers, Box 6, Folder 359.
52. Schwartz, *Letters*, 261.
53. Delmore Schwartz Papers, Box 6, Folder 359.
54. Ibid.
55. Bryan Cheyette, *Constructions of 'the Jew' in English Literature and Society: Racial Representations, 1875–1945* (Cambridge: Cambridge University Press, 1993), 267.
56. Ibid. See also Rachel Blau DuPlessis's chapter on "'Wondering Jews': Melting-Pots and Mongrel Thoughts," in *Genders, Races and Religious Cultures in Modern American Poetry, 1908–1934* (Cambridge: Cambridge University Press, 2001). DuPlessis argues that, in conflating Jewish figures like Bleistein with the Black/Irish Sweeney, Eliot creates "a poetic mongrel" (152). Despite his disgust, she suggests, Eliot "wants to claim the passions and energies of their presence for his work and culture" (154).
57. Maud Ellman, "The Imaginary Jew: T. S. Eliot and Ezra Pound," in *Between "Race" and Culture*, 93.
58. Teres, *Renewing the American Left*, 205.
59. Howe, "The New York Intellectuals," 216.
60. Delmore Schwartz Papers, Box 4, Folder 263.
61. Delmore Schwartz, "Fiction Chronicle: The Wrongs of Innocence and Experience," *Partisan Review* 19, no. 3 (May–June, 1952): 358.

62. Delmore Schwartz Papers, "A Bitter Farce," in *The World Is a Wedding: And Other Stories*, 114.
63. We know from other stories—"New Year's Eve" and "America! America!"—that Fish is also a poet.
64. See Hugh Brogan, *The Penguin History of The United States of America*, revised ed. (London: Penguin, 2001), 554.

2   *In Dreams Begin Responsibilities*: "The Egocentric Predicament"

1. Schwartz, *In Dreams Begin Responsibilities*. Schwartz married Gertrude Buckman in 1938.
2. Schwartz regarded "Animula" as "perhaps the best of all [Eliot's] poems. Certainly it is his most direct, most lucid, and most concise statement of a vision of life" (Delmore Schwartz Papers, Box 6, Folder 360).
3. Richard J. Finneran, ed., *The Collected Works of W. B. Yeats, Volume One: The Poems* (Basingstoke: Macmillan, 1983; 2nd ed., 1991), 100. Finneran believes that the epigraph "might well have been written by Yeats [himself], possibly with the assistance of Ezra Pound" (636).
4. Sharon Cameron, *Lyric Time: Dickinson and the Limits of Genre* (Baltimore: Johns Hopkins University Press, 1979), 120.
5. Ibid., 120.
6. Theodor Adorno, "Lyric Poetry and Society," in *The Adorno Reader*, ed. Brian O'Connor, 213.
7. "Editorial Statement," in *Partisan Review* 4, no. 1 (December 1937): 3.
8. Christopher Ricks, *Allusion to the Poets* (Oxford: Oxford University Press, 2003), 2.
9. T. S. Eliot, "Philip Massinger," in *The Sacred Wood*, 106.
10. "*Primitivism and Decadence* by Yvor Winters" (1938), in *Selected Essays of Delmore Schwartz*, 343.
11. Cited in Richard McDougall, *Delmore Schwartz* (New York: Twayne Publishers, 1974), 20.
12. Delmore Schwartz, "Poet's Progress: Review of *Person, Place and Thing* by Karl Shapiro," *Nation*, January 9, 1943, 63–64.
13. Delmore Schwartz, "Anywhere Out of the World: Review of T. S. Eliot's *Four Quartets*," *Nation*, July 24, 1943, 102.
14. In "Father and Son," for example, when the son says "Father, you're not Polonius" (109) he sounds merely affected. This forced address is not rescued by other references to *Hamlet* elsewhere in the volume.
15. Eliot, "Philip Massinger," 106.
16. Edward Ford points this out in *A Reevaluation of the Works of American Writer Delmore Schwartz, 1913–1966*, 2. See also Guillaume Apollinaire, *Alcools*, ed. Garnet Rees (London: Athlone, 1975).
17. Delmore Schwartz, "Wallace Stevens: An Appreciation," In *Selected Essays of Delmore Schwartz*, 194.

18. Wallace Stevens, *Collected Poetry and Prose*, ed. Joan Richardson (New York: Library of America, 1997), 50.
19. Hart Crane, *Complete Poems and Selected Letters*, ed. Langdon Hammer (New York: Library of America, 2006), 44; William Wordsworth, "My Heart Leaps Up when I Behold," *The Major Works*, ed. Stephen Gill (Oxford: Oxford University Press, 2008), 246.
20. W. H. Auden, *The English Auden: Poems, Essays and Dramatic Writings, 1927–1939*, ed. Edward Mendelson (London: Faber, 1986), 84. One of Schwartz's reasons for admiring *The Orators* was that "the Id has insisted upon being heard, despite the deliberate plan of the poet." Auden's "irreducible subject, psychic illness" intrudes, breaking down the objective narrative and plot ("The Two Audens" [1939], in *Selected Essays of Delmore Schwartz*, 149).
21. Plato, *The Republic*, trans. R. E. Allen (New Haven: Yale University Press, 2006), 329.
22. Walter Benjamin, "The Work of Art in the Age of Mechanical Reproduction (1937)," in *Illuminations,* ed. Hannah Arendt (London: Pimlico, 1999), 229. Schwartz would not himself have read Benjamin, though he may have become aware of him later in his life through Hannah Arendt. However, as Elisa New has argued, "Schwartz's attention to mass culture puts him in intellectual relationship with thinkers like Benjamin, Adorno and Bloch," his elder contemporaries. New further suggests that "The Work of Art in the Age of Mechanical Reproduction" and "In Dreams Begin Responsibilities" "may be read to gloss one another: Schwartz dramatizes Benjamin; Benjamin lends theoretical sinew to Schwartz" (Elisa New, "Reconsidering Delmore Schwartz," *Prooftexts* 5, no. 3 [September 1985]: 252).
23. Sigmund Freud, "The Uncanny," in *The Uncanny*, trans. David McLintock (London: Penguin, 2003), 155.
24. Delmore Schwartz Papers, Box 6, Folder 359. Schwartz's emphases.
25. "Tradition and the Individual Talent," in *The Sacred Wood*, 49.
26. Laurence Goldstein, *The American Poet at the Movies: A Critical History* (Ann Arbor: University of Michigan Press, 1994), 99.
27. The inversion is perhaps more clear-cut in the posthumously published story, "The Heights of Joy." The financier, Hugo Bauer, on marrying the European star Magda Gehrhardt, realizes that he finds "his wife as an image in a film far more exciting than the actuality he possesse[s] so near him" (Delmore Schwartz, *Screeno: Stories & Poems* [New York: New Directions, 2004], 75). Gehrhardt is more real on the screen to him than she is in person, and the story vindicates this apparent delusion.
28. See Matthew Arnold, *The Poems of Matthew Arnold*, ed. Kenneth Allott, 1965; ed. Miriam Allott, 2nd ed. (London: Longman, 1979), 257.
29. New, "Reconsidering Delmore Schwartz," 253.
30. Ibid., 252.
31. See Irving Howe, *World of Our Fathers: The Journey of the East European Jews to America and the Life They Found and Made There* (1976) (London: Phoenix, 2000), 166.

32. "An Argument in 1934," *Kenyon Review* 4, no. 1 (Winter 1942): 69–70.
33. Percy Bysshe Shelley, *Poetical Works*, ed. Thomas Hutchinson (London: Oxford University Press, 1970), 443.
34. An earlier version of the poem is spoken by the character May in Schwartz's play, "Venus in the Back Room," in *Shenandoah and Other Verse Plays*, ed. Robert Phillips (Rochester, NY: BOA Editions Ltd., 2000), 137.
35. Stevens, *Collected Poetry and Prose*, 135.
36. Delmore Schwartz Papers, Box 6, Folder 357.
37. R. W. E. Nelson draws attention to how many of Schwartz's poems and stories—among them "The Sin of Hamlet," "The Track Meet," and "All of the Fruits Had Fallen"—similarly climax with moments of self-recognition occasioned by accidental glimpses of oneself in a mirror. At such moments, Nelson argues, the individual becomes aware "that man's essential condition is one of guilt and anxiety" (Richard William Eric Nelson, "Self-Reflections and Repetitions: A Study of the Writings of Delmore Schwartz," PhD diss., University of Durham, 1994, 16).
38. The first quotation is unattributed, but the view itself would seem to be derived from Descartes. Schwartz favors the unconventional transliteration "Trotzky" over the more usual "Trotsky."
39. Schwartz may not have read Heidegger in the original German, but knew about him from his former tutor at NYU, Sidney Hook, one of the first American scholars to write about him (albeit skeptically). See Martin Woessner, *Heidegger in America* (Cambridge: Cambridge University Press, 2011), 26–30. In a 1944 journal entry Schwartz accuses Heidegger of overemphasizing one emotion (anxiety) to the exclusion of others such as desire and gratification (*Portrait of Delmore: Journals and Notes of Delmore Schwartz: 1939–1959*, ed. Elizabeth Pollet [New York: Farrar, Straus and Giroux, 1986], 247).
40. Keller, "Delmore Schwartz's Strange Times," 158.
41. "The Commencement Day Address," in *In Dreams Begin Responsibilities and Other Stories*, 117. The story was published in Laughlin's *New Directions Anthology* 1938, but not collected until after Schwartz's death. It responds to Auden's "Address for a Prize-Day" at the start of *The Orators*, whose air-man protagonist claims that his true ancestor is not his father but his uncle. Duspenser's proposition explodes such a fantasy to the point that it represents an encumbrance rather than liberation, but it similarly diminishes the oppressive claims of one's biological father, releasing the individual from the confines of a singular family.
42. Czar Nicholas had four daughters and a son. "Brother" in Schwartz's poem, then, could be identified as Tsarevitch Aleksey, born in 1904. Schwartz would have known that the Tsarevitch was a hemophiliac, and therefore especially vulnerable; but it is the fates of the children rather than their specific identities that most matter here.
43. This line could invite a slightly misleading biographical reading. Schwartz's grandfather, like Noah Green in *Genesis*, in fact served under Nicholas I,

Nicholas II's grandfather. "Your" here refers to Russia and not specifically to Czar Nicholas II.

44. Cynthia Ozick, Introduction to *Screeno: Stories & Poems*, by Delmore Schwartz, 10.

45. Finneran, ed., *The Collected Works of W. B. Yeats*, 233.

46. Auden, *The English Auden*, 61.

47. Alfred North Whitehead, *Process and Reality: An Essay in Cosmology* (1929), corrected ed., ed. David Ray Griffin and Donald W. Sherburne (New York: The Free Press, 1978), II. ii. 64.

48. *Coriolanus* (1608), ed. G. R. Hibbard (London: Penguin, 1967), I.vi.69.

3 "The Land of the Old World Failure and the New World Success": *Genesis* and "America! America!"

1. Fitzpatrick, "Life, Work, Failure: Delmore Schwartz," 131; Ashbery, *The Heavy Bear*, 7.

2. At times of heightened emotion, Hershey too speaks in verse, "in his voice their voices echoing" (*G*, 95).

3. Thomas Hardy, *The Complete Poetical Works, Vol 4, The Dynasts, Parts First and Second*, ed. Samuel Hynes (Oxford: Clarendon Press, 1995), 16.

4. R. P. Blackmur, "Commentary by Ghosts," *Kenyon Review* 5, no. 3 (Summer 1943): 469.

5. Ashbery, *The Heavy Bear*, 7.

6. See James William Johnson, "Lyric," in *The New Princeton Encyclopedia of Poetry and Poetics* (Princeton: Princeton University Press, 1993).

7. See John. P. McWilliams, Jr. *The American Epic: Transforming a Genre, 1770–1860* (Cambridge: Cambridge University Press, 1989). McWilliams identifies Whitman's "Song of Myself" not as "the centrepiece of American epic verse," but as "the massive cause of its continuing impossibility" (McWilliams, *The American Epic,* 237) on the grounds that Whitman's impulse, no matter how radically extended, is lyrical.

8. Ashbery, *The Heavy Bear*, 7.

9. Adam Kirsch, *The Wounded Surgeon: Confession and Transformation in Six American Poets* (New York: W. W. Norton, 2005), 199, 200.

10. "Views of a Second Violinist," 27.

11. In "T. S. Eliot's Voice and his Voices," Schwartz advocates speaking of "open and closed versification" rather than of free or formal verse, going on to argue that open versification, of the kind often favored by Eliot, "includes all the closed forms of versification and the older open forms exemplified in the Bible, Whitman, Marianne Moore, and William Carlos Williams, without being committed to any particular one at any time" (142). Schwartz's own practice in *Genesis* is slightly different, since the open versification (the biblical prose) and the closed (the blank verse) are clearly distinct from each other, despite

occasional blurring. The biblical prose does not "include" the blank verse but complements it, and operates alongside it.

12. "T. S. Eliot's Voice and his Voices" (1954, 1955), in *Selected Essays of Delmore Schwartz*, 130.

13. Given that Hershey's mother's question is related indirectly, the question mark is unnecessary (as the comma at the end of the first sentence of the passage is also grammatically misleading). Schwartz's use of punctuation is casual throughout *Genesis*.

14. Howe, "Foreword to Atlas, ed.," ix.

15. Schwartz, "America! America!," 12. Schwartz's emphasis.

16. Delmore Schwartz, "The World Is a Wedding," in *In Dreams Begin Responsibilities and Other Stories*, 67.

17. Cynthia Ozick, "The Question of Our Speech: The Return to Aural Culture," in *Memory and Metaphor* (New York: Vintage, 1991), 164.

18. Delmore Schwartz, "On the Telephone," in *The Ego is Always at the Wheel*, 11.

19. Lowell, *Collected Poems*, 166.

20. Howe, "The New York Intellectuals," 242.

21. Lowell, *Collected Poems*, 179.

22. Ashbery, *The Heavy Bear*, 7.

23. Beyond the fact that "The Sea and the Mirror" and "Coriolanus and His Mother" both reinterpret Shakespeare plays from modern and meta-theatrical perspectives, there are tonal similarities. The rambling philosophizing of "Caliban to the Audience" recalls not just late Henry James but also Schwartz's prose interludes. Auden's Caliban's "All we have ever asked for is that for a few hours the curtain should be left undrawn, so as to allow our humble ragged selves the privilege of craning and gaping at the splendid goings-on inside" (Auden, *Collected Poems*, 425) is as eloquently colloquial, for example, as Schwartz's "Between the acts something must be done to occupy our minds or we might become too aware of our great emptiness" (*SK*, 92). Meanwhile, in the second part of "The Sea and the Mirror," Antonio's "I am I, Antonio / By choice myself alone" (Auden, *Collected Poems*, 412) resonates with the many statements of self-reliance made by Schwartz's Coriolanus.

24. John Haffenden, ed., *W. H. Auden: The Critical Heritage* (London: Routledge, 1983, repr. 1997), 371.

25. Delmore Schwartz Papers. Box 1, Folder 36.

26. F. Scott Fitzgerald, *The Great Gatsby*, ed. Ruth Prigozy (Oxford: Oxford University Press, 1998), 144.

27. Kirsch, *The Wounded Surgeon*, 203.

28. Berthold Schwartz, the inspiration for this name, is believed to have invented the cannon in the fourteenth century.

29. Delmore Schwartz, "Shenandoah," in *Shenandoah and Other Verse Plays*, 20.

30. Schwartz, "The World Is a Wedding," 83.

31. Schwartz, "America! America!," 21–22. The story first appeared, in a slightly different version with Shenandoah Fish named Belmont Weiss, in *Partisan*

Review 7, no. 2 (March–April 1940). It was collected in *The World Is a Wedding* in 1948.

32. Saul Bellow, *Herzog* (1964) (London: Penguin, 2001), 147.

33. Karl Marx, "Estranged Labor," in *Economic & Philosophic Manuscripts of 1844*, ed. Dirk J. Struik, trans. Martin Milligan (London: Lawrence & Wishart, 1970), 106.

34. Ibid., 109.

35. John Milton, *Paradise Lost*, ed. Alastair Fowler (London: Longman, 1971), 59.

4   "An Innocent Bystander": The City, *Vaudeville for a Princess*, and Schwartz's Postwar Cultural Criticism

1. Oswald Spengler, *The Decline of the West*, edited and abridged by Helmut Werner. English ed. edited by Arthur Helps, translated by Charles Francis Atkinson (New York: Oxford University Press, 1991), 20. Spengler's emphasis. *The Decline of the West* was first published in German in two volumes in 1918 and 1922. It was first published in English in 1926 and 1928, and in a one-volume edition in 1932.

2. Delmore Schwartz, "Memoirs of a Metropolitan Child, Memoirs of a Giant Fan," in *The Ego is Always at the Wheel*, 121.

3. Saul Bellow, "A Jewish Writer in America," *New York Review of Books*, October 27, 2011. Bellow disregards the fact that Spengler had grouped Muslims and early Christians among the "Magians" as well.

4. Delmore Schwartz Papers, Box 9, Folder 508, 379.

5. Delmore Schwartz Papers, Box 4, Folder 246. The lineation is as it appears in the manuscript.

6. The idea that the city does not exist in any unified sense beyond the imagination is one that would be increasingly taken up by thinkers in the decades that followed. Marshall McLuhan offers one of the most radical statements in his series of manifestos concerning new media, *Counterblast* (1954). He announces that "THE CITY no longer exists, except as a cultural ghost for tourists." The reason for this is that cosmopolitanism is no longer confined to conurbations, but is also the essential condition of any highway eatery "with its TV set, newspaper, and magazine." (*Essential McLuhan,* ed. Eric McLuhan and Frank Zingrone [Routledge: London, 1995], 210).

7. Sigmund Freud, *Civilization and Its Discontents* (1930), trans. David McLintock (London: Penguin, 2004), 7–11.

8. Allen Tate, "To Whom is the Poet Responsible?," *The Hudson Review* 4, no. 3 (Autumn 1951): 333. Tate's emphasis.

9. Theodor Adorno, "Cultural Criticism and Society," in *The Adorno Reader*, ed. Brian O'Connor (Oxford: Blackwell, 2000), 210.

10. Delmore Schwartz, "New Year's Eve," in *In Dreams Begin Responsibilities, and Other Stories*, 113.

11. Rolfe Humphries, for example, wrote that Schwartz's poetry "suffers its most severe criticism at the hands of the author's own prose...the verse tends to be solemn, owlish, abstract, tiresome, and, to my ear at least, entirely earless." Quoted in McDougall, *Delmore Schwartz*, 105.

12. Hugh Kenner, "Bearded Ladies & the Abundant Goat," *Poetry* 79, no. 1 (October 1951): 50.

13. The book is "suggested by [the then] Princess Elizabeth's admiration of Danny Kaye" (*V*). Robert Deutsch elucidates the "elaborate pun": Elizabeth Pollet, Schwartz's second wife, to whom the book is dedicated, is "the poet's true princess," while Schwartz conceives of himself as a Danny Kaye-like clown, a "heavy bear," in comparison to his beloved (Robert H. Deutsch, *The Poetry of Delmore Schwartz* [Potsdam, NY: Wallace Stevens Society Press, 2003], 102). Deutsch consistently misnames Schwartz's wife "Elizabeth Follet."

14. Bruce Bawer, *The Middle Generation: The Lives and Poetry of Delmore Schwartz, Randall Jarrell, John Berryman and Robert Lowell* (Hamden, CT: Shoe String, 1986), 132.

15. Ibid., 134.

16. William Shakespeare, sonnet 73 in *Complete Sonnets and Poems*, ed. Colin Burrow (Oxford: Oxford University Press, 2002), 527.

17. Morton Seiff, "Fallen David and Goliath America: The Battle Report of Delmore Schwartz," *Jewish Social Studies* 13, no. 4 (October 1951): 315.

18. Ibid., 315.

19. Schwartz, "Anywhere Out of the World," 102.

20. See, for example, David Chinitz, *T. S. Eliot and the Cultural Divide* (Chicago: University of Chicago Press, 2003) for an analysis of Eliot's engagement with popular culture.

21. Plato, *The Republic*, 179.

22. Ibid., 188–189.

23. Ibid., 191.

24. Faber Gottschalk, in the story "The Statues," finds it similarly impossible to articulate a feeling in which he has conviction but which is essentially indefinable. In defending a group of surreal snow statues against those who intend to remove them, he declares: "To anything which is beautiful, to anything which is true, to anything which is good we are committed, though the commitment jeopardizes our lives" (Delmore Schwartz, "The Statues," in *Screeno*, 98). However, like Christ's disciples, he pays for his glimpse of unspeakable beauty: after the statues melt, his quotidian life loses meaning and he dies by falling, or possibly jumping, "in front of an onrushing subway train" (100).

25. Walter Pater, *The Renaissance*, ed. Adam Phillips (Oxford: Oxford University Press, 1987), 80.

26. See "Notes toward a Supreme Fiction," in Stevens, *Collected Poetry and Prose*, 329–352, and Hugh Kenner, *A Homemade World: The American Modernist Writers* (New York: Knopf, 1975), 54.

27. Delmore Schwartz, "The Fabulous Example of André Gide" (1951), in *Selected Essays of Delmore Schwartz*, 249.

28. Dwight MacDonald, "The Bomb," in *The Responsibility of Peoples and Other Essays in Political Criticism*, 113.

29. Dwight MacDonald, "The Responsibility of Peoples," in *The Responsibility of Peoples*, 30–31.

30. Benedict Anderson, *Imagined Communities: Reflections on the Origin and Spread of Nationalism* (London: Verso, 2006 [1983]).

31. Dwight MacDonald, "The Germans—Three Years Later," in *The Responsibility of Peoples*, 71.

32. MacDonald, "The Bomb," 111–112.

33. Ibid., 112.

34. See Ralph Waldo Emerson, "The American Scholar," in *Selected Essays*, ed. Larzer Ziff, 83–105; MacDonald, "The Bomb," 113.

35. Dwight MacDonald, "I Choose the West," in *The Responsibility of Peoples*, 125.

36. Delmore Schwartz, "Our Country and Our Culture" (1952), in *Selected Essays of Delmore Schwartz*, 399.

37. Delmore Schwartz, "Novels and the News" (1959), in *Selected Essays of Delmore Schwartz*, 389.

38. Delmore Schwartz, "Some Movie Reviews" (1946–1956), in *Selected Essays of Delmore Schwartz*, 457.

39. Delmore Schwartz, "Film Review: The Country Girl," *New Republic*, April 4, 1955, 21.

40. Delmore Schwartz, "Film Review: *The Bridges at Toko-Ri*," *New Republic*, March 14, 1955, 28.

41. Delmore Schwartz, "Film Review: *Underwater!* and *The Blackboard Jungle*," in *New Republic*, April 11, 1955, 465.

42. Delmore Schwartz, "The Badness of Most Recent Films (1955)," from "Some Movie Reviews" (1946–1956) in *Selected Essays of Delmore Schwartz*, 476.

43. Delmore Schwartz, "The Man With the Golden Arm," *New Republic*, February 6, 1956, 22.

44. Delmore Schwartz, "Films and TV," from "Some Movie Reviews" (1946–1956) in *Selected Essays of Delmore Schwartz*, 467.

45. Delmore Schwartz, "Screeno," in *In Dreams Begin Responsibilities, and Other Stories*, 187.

46. Delmore Schwartz, "Survey of Our National Phenomena," in *The Ego is Always at the Wheel*, 106.

47. Schwartz, "The Present State of Poetry," 46.

5   *Summer Knowledge*: "Infinite Belief in Infinite Hope"

1. Delmore Schwartz, "Introduction," *What Is to Be Given: Selected Poems by Delmore Schwartz* (Manchester: Carcanet, 1976), viii.

2. Emerson, "Nature," In Emerson, *Selected Essays*, 39.

3. Many of these drafts are reproduced in Elizabeth Pollet's *Portrait of Delmore* (see, for example, 471–472), though further versions exist in the Schwartz archive. Given their tonal and stylistic consistency, it is likely that Schwartz planned to incorporate them into a single long poem.

4. There are unmistakable echoes of "Little Gidding" in these lines: "the end of all our exploring / Will be to arrive where we started / And know the place for the first time" (Eliot, *CPP*, 197). Schwartz's ambivalence about the *Four Quartets* did not preclude him from drawing upon them.

5. Hecht, "The Anguish of the Spirit and the Letter," 595.

6. Ibid., 597.

7. John Hollander, "Poetry Chronicle," *Partisan Review* (Spring 1960): 368. Laurence Goldstein, in his discussion of Schwartz's late poem "Love and Marilyn Monroe," also evokes Smart, suggesting that Schwartz's form is a means of identifying himself with a poet who was confronting insanity (Goldstein, *The American Poet at the Movies*, 11). Schwartz himself, in a scrawled manuscript, describes Smart as "the poor mad poet (crazy as a posse of foxes)" (Delmore Schwartz Papers, Box 4, Folder 263).

8. This remains so despite the fact that it is the East River, not the Hudson, that divides Brooklyn from Manhattan.

9. Walt Whitman, "Crossing Brooklyn Ferry," in *Leaves of Grass and Other Writings*, ed. Michael Moon (New York: W. W. Norton, 2002), 136–137.

10. "Assent," another word used frequently in the late poems, may also be suggested. See, for example, "the heights of assent" in "At a Solemn Musick" (*SK*, 148).

11. Ashbery, *The Heavy Bear*, 7.

12. Stevens, *Collected Poetry and Prose*, 14.

13. Ibid., 8.

14. Delmore Schwartz Papers, Box 8, Folder 470.

15. Delmore Schwartz Papers, Box 6, Folder 360. It is surprising that Schwartz here overlooks Pound's famous declaration: "To break the pentameter, that was the first heave" (Ezra Pound, "Canto LXXXI," in *The Cantos of Ezra Pound* [New York: New Directions, 1996], 538), with its suggestion that a departure from "the iambic norm" was a principle of the whole endeavor of literary modernism.

16. John Milton, *Complete Shorter Poems*, ed. John Carey (London: Longman, 1968), 2nd ed. (1997), 167–170.

17. Ibid., 167.

18. Many of Schwartz's lyrics of this period—like the earlier "Poems in Imitation of the Fugue Form"—aspire to the quality of music. "'I Am Cherry Alive,' the Little Girl Sang," "A Small Score," and "A Little Morning Music," in the section headed "Morning Bells," all draw attention to musical composition, while "Vivaldi" employs musical notation to delineate its tempo. Although Schwartz also revels in the spontaneity of birdsong, he is especially interested

in the ritualistic aspects of musical performance, something to which he draws attention by retaining Milton's archaic and solemnizing spelling of "musick" (only used for this poem) and through the systematic and formal manner in which he relates the musicians' proclamations.

19. *Paradiso* concludes: "But already my desire and my will / Were being turned like a wheel, all at one speed, // By the love which moves the sun and the other stars" (Dante, *The Divine Comedy*, ed. David H. Higgins, trans. C. H. Sisson [Oxford: Oxford University Press, 2008], 499).

20. Pound, *Poems and Translations*, 254.

21. Harold Bloom, "Introduction," in *American Religious Poems*, ed. Harold Bloom and Jesse Zuba (New York: Library of America, 2006), xxv, xxvii.

22. William Shakespeare, *The Complete Sonnets and Poems*, ed. Colin Burrow (Oxford: Oxford University Press, 2002), 373, 374. Burrow notes that when the poem first appeared it bore no title. "The Phoenix and the Turtle" was not used until 1807.

23. Whitman, *Leaves of Grass and Other Writings*, 31.

24. Stevens, *Collected Poetry and Prose*, 55.

25. In Shakespeare's "Let the Bird of Loudest Lay" the phoenix and the turtle dove, though separate, are made one through their chaste love, which only finds its true fulfillment in death. Schwartz's line "'Call us what you will: we are made such by love'" (*LL*, 61) from 'The Studies of Narcissus' makes direct reference to Donne's "The Canonization" in which two lovers are directly identified with the phoenix: "We die and rise the same, and prove / Mysterious by this love." (Donald R. Dickson, ed. *John Donne's Poetry* [London: Norton, 2007], 78).

26. John Milton, "Samson Agonistes," in *Complete Shorter Poems*, ed. John Carey (London: Longman, 1968; 2nd ed. 1997), ll. 1687–1707, 411–412.

27. Another late work that implicitly addresses the holocaust is the story "The Track Meet." Like many of the *Vaudeville for a Princess* poems, it is about witness: the narrator, in the company of an English visitor, Reginald Law, attends a track meet where he sees his five brothers (who are each named for the monarchs of Europe) triumph in the races only to be shot dead by a group of chorus girls. In his guilt at being unable to save them, he hopes that it is just a dream, only for Law to tell him that if it is a dream, it is worse, since that means that the evil he witnesses comes from himself, not from an external source.

28. Stevens, *Collected Poetry and Prose*, 33.

29. Ibid., 55.

30. Ibid., 12.

31. Ibid., 13.

32. *King Lear* in *The Riverside Shakespeare*, ed. G. Blakemore Evans et al, 1303–1359 (Boston: Houghton Mifflin, 1997), V.ii.9–11, 1339.

33. Some years earlier, F. O. Matthiessen had also used Edgar's lines (as marked by Herman Melville in his copy of *Lear*), as one of the epigraphs for *American Renaissance: Art and Expression in the Age of Emerson and Whitman*. For

Matthiessen, the years 1850–1855 were when literature in America became ripe.

34. Hecht, "The Anguish of the Spirit and the Letter," 597.

35. Amongst Schwartz's manuscripts there are also drafts of a poem to be titled "Vermeer's Officer and Laughing Girl" (Delmore Schwartz Papers, Box 4, Folder 236).

36. Some kinds of visual and concrete poetry would challenge this assumption. Schwartz, though innovative, never goes so far as to treat his pages as a canvas or his words as brushstrokes. Although its lines are long, the poem conforms to linear conventions.

37. Meyer Schapiro, "Seurat," in *Modern Art: 19th & 20th Centuries* (London: Chatto & Windus, 1978), 101.

38. Richard A. Johnson, "Summer Knowledge, Hard Hours," *The Sewanee Review* 76, no. 4 (Autumn 1968): 684.

39. See Brad Gooch, *City Poet: The Life and Times of Frank O'Hara* (New York: HarperPerennial, 1994), 186.

40. For O'Hara, responsibilities do not begin in dreams, but they do begin "in bed." (O'Hara, "Memorial Day, 1950," *Collected Poems*, ed. Donald Allen [Los Angeles: University of California Press, 1995], 17). Robert Phillips suggests that O'Hara sullies Schwartz's work in making such a statement (*LL*, "Foreword," xxii). David Lehman, meanwhile, argues in favor of O'Hara's relaxed tone and contentment in contrast to Schwartz's perpetual anxiety (Lehman, "Delmore, Delmore," 78). Neither accepts, however, that O'Hara's allusion is not necessarily hostile. If anything, O'Hara takes a Schwartz-like impulse—to address what love might mean, and how it might be negotiated, in the middle of the twentieth century, in the city—and comes up with a more optimistic answer than Schwartz himself ever discovered. Schwartz tries to seek the miraculous in everyday life; O'Hara does the same but finds it more easily, hearing music, for example, in the sewage and in the sound of a locomotive (O'Hara, *Collected Poems*, 18).

41. Brad Gooch claims that Schwartz was present at a party hosted by John Ashbery at which O'Hara first met the artist Larry Rivers (Gooch, *City Poet,* 174). Gooch also claims that Schwartz wrote a recommendation for O'Hara when he applied for his first position at the Museum of Modern Art (Gooch, *City Poet,* 207). If this was the case, then it is all the more surprising that Schwartz appears not to have had any other interaction with O'Hara.

42. O'Hara first saw *La Grande Jatte* at the Art Institute in Chicago in 1951—presumably on the same exhibition tour as Schwartz saw it in New York (Gooch, *City Poet,* 185).

43. Max Brod noted that Kafka often liked to quote Flaubert's remark, which the unmarried French novelist is reputed to have made on visiting a bourgeois family. See, for example, Ronald D. Gray, *Franz Kafka* (Cambridge: Cambridge University Press, 1973), 53.

Conclusion

1. Berryman, *The Dream Songs*, 304.
2. T. S. Eliot, *The Use of Poetry and the Use of Criticism: Studies in the Relation of Criticism to Poetry in England*, (2nd ed. London: Faber and Faber, 1964), 22.
3. Ibid., 149.
4. Ibid., 65, 25.
5. Kenneth Koch, "A Momentary Longing to Hear Sad Advice from One Long Dead," *A Possible World* (New York: Alfred A. Knopf, 2002), 9.
6. Howe, *World of Our Fathers*, 585; Howe, "The New York Intellectuals," 242.
7. Eliot, *The Use of Poetry and the Use of Criticism*, 26.
8. Eileen Simpson, *Poets in Their Youth: A Memoir* (New York: Vintage, 1983), 19.
9. Eliot, *The Use of Poetry and the Use of Criticism*, 23.
10. Berryman, *The Dream Songs* (282), 304.
11. Perloff, for example, reads "Tired and Unhappy, You Think of Houses" as a failed imitation of one of Eliot's "Preludes." She makes the questionable assumption that Schwartz is seeking an objective correlative for a very specific state of mind. Meanwhile, her objection to the poem being written in full sentences—evincing her own preference for the thoroughly fragmentary—suggests an unwillingness to read it on its own terms. (Marjorie Perloff, *21st-Century Modernism: The "New" Poetics* [Malden, MA: Blackwell, 2002], 160).
12. Stevens, *Collected Poetry and Prose*, 410.
13. *DS & JL Letters*, 8.
14. Auden, *Collected Poems*, 693.
15. Paul Muldoon, *Poems, 1968–1998* (London: Faber, 2001), 190.
16. Ibid., 192.
17. Joan Didion, *The Year of Magical Thinking* (London: Harper Perennial, 2006), 78.
18. Mutlu Konuk Blasing, *Politics and Form in Postmodern Poetry: O'Hara, Bishop, Ashbery, and Merrill* (Cambridge: Cambridge University Press, 1995), 120.

Bibliography

Primary Works by Delmore Schwartz

Schwartz, Delmore. "America! America!" In *In Dreams Begin Responsibilities, and Other Stories*, 10–33.

———. "An Argument in 1934." *Kenyon Review* 4 (Winter 1942): 62–74.

———. "Anywhere Out of the World: Review of T. S. Eliot's *Four Quartets*." *Nation*, July 24, 1943, 102–103.

———. "Auden and Stevens." *Partisan Review* 14 (Fall 1947): 528–532.

———. "A Bitter Farce." In *The World Is a Wedding: And Other Stories*, 104–121.

———. "The Child Is the Meaning of This Life." In *In Dreams Begin Responsibilities, and Other Stories*, 140–186.

———. "The Commencement Day Address." In *In Dreams Begin Responsibilities, and Other Stories*, 115–125.

———. *Delmore Schwartz and James Laughlin: Selected Letters*. Edited by Robert Phillips. New York: W. W. Norton, 1993.

———. Delmore Schwartz Papers. Yale Collection of American Literature, Beinecke Rare Book and Manuscript Library

———. *The Ego Is Always at the Wheel: Bagatelles*. Edited by Robert Phillips. New York: New Directions, 1986.

———. "Ezra Pound and History" (1960). In *Selected Essays of Delmore Schwartz*, 113–119.

———. "Ezra Pound's Very Useful Labors" (1938). In *Selected Essays of Delmore Schwartz*, 102–112.

———. "The Fabulous Example of André Gide" (1951). In *Selected Essays of Delmore Schwartz*, 246–254.

———. "Fiction Chronicle: The Wrongs of Innocence and Experience." *Partisan Review* 19 (May–June 1952): 354–359.

———. "The Fiction of Ernest Hemingway: Moral Historian of the American Dream" (1955). In *Selected Essays of Delmore Schwartz*, 255–273.

———. "The Fiction of William Faulkner" (1941). In *Selected Essays of Delmore Schwartz*, 274–289.

————. "Film Review: *The Bridges at Toko-Ri.*" *New Republic*, March 14, 1955, 28–29.

————. "Film Review: *The Country Girl.*" *New Republic*, April 4, 1955, 21.

————. "Film Review: *Underwater!, Blackboard Jungle.*" *New Republic*, April 11, 1955, 29–30.

————. "Film Review: *The Court Jester.*" *New Republic*, March 5, 1956, 21.

————. "Films–TV." *New Republic*, July 18, 1955, 21–22.

————. *Genesis.* New York: New Directions, 1943.

————. "The Grapes of Crisis" (1951). In *Selected Essays of Delmore Schwartz*, 377–385.

————. "The Heights of Joy." In *Screeno*, 63–88.

————. *In Dreams Begin Responsibilities.* New York: New Directions, 1938.

————. "In Dreams Begin Responsibilities." In *In Dreams Begin Responsibilities*, 11–20.

————. *In Dreams Begin Responsibilities, and Other Stories.* Edited by James Atlas. New York: New Directions, 1978.

————. "The Isolation of Modern Poetry" (1941). In *Selected Essays of Delmore Schwartz*, 3–13.

————. *Last and Lost Poems.* Edited by Robert Phillips. New York: Vanguard Press, 1979.

————. *Last & Lost Poems.* Edited by Robert Phillips. Revised ed. New York: New Directions, 1989.

————. *Letters of Delmore Schwartz.* Edited by Robert Phillips. Princeton: Ontario Review Press, 1984.

————. "The Literary Dictatorship of T. S. Eliot" (1949). In *Selected Essays of Delmore Schwartz*, 312–331.

————. "The Man With the Golden Arm." *New Republic*, February 6, 1956, 22.

————. "Memoirs of a Metropolitan Child, Memoirs of a Giant Fan." In *The Ego is Always at the Wheel*, 115–136.

————. "New Year's Eve." In *In Dreams Begin Responsibilities, and Other Stories*, 94–114.

————. "Novels and the News" (1959). In *Selected Essays of Delmore Schwartz*, 386–390.

————. "On the Telephone." In *The Ego is Always at the Wheel*, 11–15.

————. "Our Country and Our Culture" (1952). In *Selected Essays of Delmore Schwartz*, 399–403.

————. "The Poet as Poet" (1939). In *Selected Essays of Delmore Schwartz*, 72–80.

————. "Poet's Progress: Review of *Person, Place and Thing* by Karl Shapiro." *Nation*, January 9, 1943: 63–64.

————. "Poetry and Belief in Thomas Hardy" (1940). In *Selected Essays of Delmore Schwartz*, 58–71.

————. "The Poetry of Allen Tate" (1940). In *Selected Essays of Delmore Schwartz*, 153–172.

————. *Portrait of Delmore: Journals and Notes of Delmore Schwartz: 1939–1959.* Edited by Elizabeth Pollet. New York: Farrar, Straus and Giroux, 1986.

———. "The Present State of Poetry" (1958). In *Selected Essays of Delmore Schwartz*, 30–50.

———. "Primitivism and Decadence by Yvor Winters" (1938). In *Selected Essays of Delmore Schwartz*, 332–350.

———. "Rimbaud in Our Time" (1939). In *Selected Essays of Delmore Schwartz*, 53–57.

———. *A Season in Hell*. New York: New Directions, 1939.

———. "Screeno." In *In Dreams Begin Responsibilities, and Other Stories*, 140–186.

———. *Screeno: Stories & Poems*. New York: New Directions, 2004.

———. *Selected Essays of Delmore Schwartz*. Edited by Donald A. Dike and David H. Zucker. Chicago: University of Chicago Press, 1970.

———. *Selected Poems (1938–1958): Summer Knowledge*. New York: Doubleday, 1959. Republished New York: New Directions, 1967.

———. *Shenandoah and Other Verse Plays*. Edited by Robert Phillips. Rochester, NY: BOA Editions Ltd., 2000.

———. "Shenandoah." In *Shenandoah and Other Verse Plays*, 3–31.

———. "Some Movie Reviews" (1946–1956). In *Selected Essays of Delmore Schwartz*, 446–476.

———. "The Statues." In *Screeno*, 89–100.

———. *Successful Love, and Other Stories*. New York: Corinth Books, 1961.

———. "Survey of Our National Phenomena." In *The Ego is Always at the Wheel*, 103–112.

———. *Syracuse Poems, 1964*. Syracuse: Department of English, Syracuse University, 1965.

———. "T. S. Eliot as the International Hero" (1945). In *Selected Essays of Delmore Schwartz*, 120–128.

———. "T. S. Eliot's Voice and His Voices" (1954, 1955). In *Selected Essays of Delmore Schwartz*, 129–142.

———. "The Track Meet." In *In Dreams Begin Responsibilities, and Other Stories*, 126–139.

———. "The Two Audens" (1939). In *Selected Essays of Delmore Schwartz*, 143–152.

———. "Under Forty: A Symposium on American Literature and the Younger Generation of American Jews." *Contemporary Jewish Record* 7, no. 1 (February 1944): 12–14.

———. "An Unwritten Book" (1942). In *Selected Essays of Delmore Schwartz*, 81–101.

———. *Vaudeville for a Princess, and Other Poems*. New York: New Directions, 1950.

———. "Views of a Second Violinist" (1949). In *Selected Essays of Delmore Schwartz*, 24–29.

———. "The Vocation of the Poet in the Modern World" (1951). In *Selected Essays of Delmore Schwartz*, 14–23.

———. "Wallace Stevens: An Appreciation" (1955). In *Selected Essays of Delmore Schwartz*, 192–196.

———. *What Is to Be Given: Selected Poems by Delmore Schwartz*. Manchester: Carcanet, 1976.

———. *The World Is a Wedding: And Other Stories*. New York: New Directions, 1948.

———. "The World Is a Wedding." In *In Dreams Begin Responsibilities, and Other Stories*, 34–93.

———. "The Writing of Edmund Wilson" (1942). In *Selected Essays of Delmore Schwartz*, 360–374.

Other Works

Adams, James Truslow. *The Epic of America*. Garden City, NY: Garden City Books, 1933.

Adorno, Theodor. "Cultural Criticism and Society." In *The Adorno Reader*. Edited by Brian O'Connor, 195–210. Oxford: Blackwell, 2000.

———. "Lyric Poetry and Society." In *The Adorno Reader*, 211–229.

Anderson, Benedict. *Imagined Communities: Reflections on the Origin and Spread of Nationalism*. London: Verso, 2006.

Apollinaire, Guillaume. *Alcools* (1913). Edited by Garnet Rees. London: Athlone, 1975.

Arendt, Hannah. *The Portable Hannah Arendt*. Edited by Peter Baehr. London: Penguin, 2003.

Aristotle. *Poetics*. Edited by Stephen Halliwell. Cambridge, MA: Harvard University Press, 1995.

Arnold, Matthew. *The Poems of Matthew Arnold*. Edited by Kenneth Allott, 1965; 2nd ed. Edited by Miriam Allott. London: Longman, 1979.

Ashbery, John. *Collected Poems 1956–1987*. Edited by Mark Ford. New York: Library of America, 2008.

———. "In Discussion with Al Filreis, 26 March 2002." *Pennsound*. Accessed November 2, 2013. http://writing.upenn.edu/pennsound/x/Ashbery.php.

———. *The Heavy Bear: Delmore Schwartz's Life versus His Poetry: A Lecture Delivered at the Sixty-Seventh General Meeting of the English Literary Society of Japan on 21st May 1995*. Tokyo: English Literary Society of Japan, 1996.

Atlas, James. *Delmore Schwartz: The Life of an American Poet*. New York: Farrar, Straus and Giroux, 1976.

Auden, W. H. *The Age of Anxiety: A Baroque Eclogue*. Edited by Alan Jacobs. Princeton: Princeton University Press, 2011.

———. *Collected Poems*. Edited by Edward Mendelson. London: Faber, 1976.

———. *The English Auden: Poems, Essays and Dramatic Writings, 1927–1939*. Edited by Edward Mendelson. London: Faber, 1986.

Barrett, William. *The Truants: Adventures among the Intellectuals*. New York: Doubleday, 1982.

Bawer, Bruce. *The Middle Generation: The Lives and Poetry of Delmore Schwartz, Randall Jarrell, John Berryman and Robert Lowell*. Hamden, CT: Shoe String, 1986.

Bellow, Saul. "A Jewish Writer in America." *New York Review of Books*, October 27, 2011.

———. *Herzog* (1964). London: Penguin, 2001.

———. *Humboldt's Gift* (1975). London: Penguin, 1997.

Benjamin, Walter. "The Work of Art in the Age of Mechanical Reproduction (1937)." In *Illuminations*. Edited by Hannah Arendt, 211–244. London: Pimlico, 1999.

Berryman, John. "The Art of Poetry No. 16." *Paris Review* 53 (Winter 1972). Accessed November 2, 2013. http://www.theparisreview.org/interviews/4052/the-art-of-poetry-no-16-john-berryman.

———. *Collected Poems, 1937–1971*. Edited by Charles Thornbury. London: Faber, 1990.

———. *The Dream Songs*. London: Faber, 1990.

———. "The Imaginary Jew." In *The Freedom of the Poet*. Edited by Robert Giroux, 353–366. New York: Farrar, Straus & Giroux, 1976.

Bernstein, Charles. "Poetics of the Americas." *Modernism/Modernity* 3, no. 3 (1996): 1–23.

Blackmur, R. P. "Commentary by Ghosts." In *Kenyon Review* 5, no. 3 (Summer 1943): 467–471.

Blasing, Mutlu Konuk. *Politics and Form in Postmodern Poetry: O'Hara, Bishop, Ashbery, and Merrill*. Cambridge: Cambridge University Press, 1995.

Bloom, Harold. *The Anxiety of Influence: A Theory of Poetry*. Revised ed. Oxford: Oxford University Press, 1997.

Bloom, Harold, and Jesse Zuba, eds. *American Religious Poems*. New York: Library of America, 2006.

Boggs, Colleen Glenney. *Transnationalism and American Literature: Literary Translation 1773–1892*. London: Routledge, 2007.

Brogan, Hugh. *The Penguin History of the United States of America*. Revised ed. London: Penguin, 2001.

Cameron, Sharon. *Lyric Time: Dickinson and the Limits of Genre*. Baltimore: Johns Hopkins University Press, 1979.

Cooney, Terry A. *The Rise of the New York Intellectuals:* Partisan Review *and Its Circle, 1934–1945*. Madison, WI: University of Wisconsin Press, 1986.

Cheyette, Bryan. *Constructions of "The Jew" in English Literature and Society: Racial Representations, 1875–1945*. Cambridge: Cambridge University Press, 1993.

———, ed. *Between "Race" and Culture: Representations of "the Jew" in English and American Literature*. Stanford, CA: Stanford University Press, 1996.

Chinitz, David. *T. S. Eliot and the Cultural Divide*. Chicago: University of Chicago Press, 2003.

Crane, Hart. *Complete Poems and Selected Letters*. Edited by Langdon Hammer. New York: Library of America, 2006.

Dante. *The Divine Comedy*. Edited by David H. Higgins. Translated by C. H. Sisson. Oxford: Oxford University Press, 2008.

Deutsch, Robert H. *The Poetry of Delmore Schwartz*. Potsdam, NY: Wallace Stevens Society Press, 2003.

Dickson, Donald R., ed. *John Donne's Poetry*. London: Norton, 2007.

Didion, Joan. *The Year of Magical Thinking*. London: Harper Perennial, 2006.

Dike, Donald A., and David H. Zucker. Preface to *Selected Essays of Delmore Schwartz*, vii–xiv.

Dimock, Wai Chee. *Through Other Continents: American Literature across Deep Time*. Princeton: Princeton University Press, 2006.

Donoghue, Denis. "The American Style of Failure." *The Sewanee Review* 82, no. 3 (Summer 1974): 407–432.

DuPlessis, Rachel Blau. *Genders, Races and Religious Cultures in Modern American Poetry, 1908–1934*. Cambridge: Cambridge University Press, 2001.

Dunn, Douglas. Introduction to Schwartz, *What is to Be Given*, vii–xix.

Eliot, T. S. *The Complete Poems and Plays*. London: Faber, 1975.

———. "The Metaphysical Poets." In Eliot, *Selected Essays*, 281–291.

———. "Philip Massinger." In *The Sacred Wood*, 104–121.

———. *The Sacred Wood: Essays on Poetry and Criticism* (1928). London: Faber, 1997.

———. *Selected Essays*. London: Faber and Faber, 3rd ed. 1951, repr. 1999.

———. "Tradition and the Individual Talent." In *The Sacred Wood*, 39–49.

———. *The Use of Poetry and the Use of Criticism: Studies in the Relation of Criticism to Poetry in England*. 2nd ed. London: Faber and Faber, 1964.

Ellman, Maud. "The Imaginary Jew: T. S. Eliot and Ezra Pound." In *Between "Race" and Culture*, 84–101.

Emerson, Ralph Waldo. "The American Scholar." In *Selected Essays*. Edited by Larzer Ziff, 83–105. London: Penguin, 1982.

———. "Nature." In Emerson, *Selected Essays*, 35–82.

Fitzgerald, F. Scott. *The Great Gatsby*. Edited by Ruth Prigozy. Oxford: Oxford University Press, 1998.

Fitzpatrick, Catherine. "Life, Work, Failure: Delmore Schwartz." *Cambridge Quarterly* 42, no. 2 (2013): 112–133.

Ford, Edward. *A Re-evaluation of the Works of American Writer Delmore Schwartz, 1913–1966*. Lewiston: NY: Edwin Mellor Press, 2005.

Freud, Sigmund. *Civilization and its Discontents* (1930). Translated by David McLintock. London: Penguin, 2004.

———. "The Uncanny" (1919). In *The Uncanny*. Translated by David McLintock. London: Penguin, 2003.

Frost, Robert. *The Poetry of Robert Frost*. Edited by Edward Connery Lathem. London: Vintage, 2001.

Goldstein, Laurence. *The American Poet at the Movies: A Critical History*. Ann Arbor: University of Michigan Press, 1994.

Gooch, Brad. *City Poet: The Life and Times of Frank O'Hara*. New York: HarperPerennial, 1994.

Gray, Richard. *American Poetry of the Twentieth Century*. New York: Longman, 1976.

Gray, Ronald D. *Franz Kafka*. Cambridge University Press: Cambridge, 1973.

Haffenden, John. *The Life of John Berryman*. London: Routledge & Kegan Paul, 1982.

———, ed. *W. H. Auden: The Critical Heritage*. London: Routledge, 1983, repr. 1997.

Hahn, Stephen. "The Isolation of Delmore Schwartz." *Columbia Literary Columns* 40, no. 1 (November 1990).

Hardy, Thomas. *The Complete Poetical Works. Vol. 4, The Dynasts, Parts First and Second*. Edited by Samuel Hynes. Oxford: Clarendon Press, 1995.

Hecht, Anthony. "The Anguish of the Spirit and the Letter." *Hudson Review* 12, no. 4 (Winter 1959–1960): 593–603.

Herbert, George. *The Complete English Works*. Edited by Ann Pasternak Slater. London: Everyman, 1995.

Herd, David. *John Ashbery and American Poetry*. Manchester: Manchester University Press, 2000.

Hitchens, Christopher. "Bravo, Old Sport." *London Review of Books*, April 4, 1991.

Hollander, John. "Poetry Chronicle." *Partisan Review* 27, no. 2 (Spring 1960): 363–368.

———. "The Question of American Jewish Poetry." In *What is Jewish Literature?* Edited by Hana Wirth-Nesher. New York: Jewish Publication Society, 1994.

Hook, Sidney. "Imaginary Enemies, Real Terror." *The American Scholar* 47, no. 3 (Summer 1978): 406–412.

Howe, Irving. *Decline of the New*. London: Victor Gollancz, 1971.

———. Foreword to Atlas, ed., *In Dreams Begin Responsibilities, and Other Stories*, vii–xiii.

———. "The New York Intellectuals." In *Decline of the New*, 211–265.

———. *World of Our Fathers: The Journey of the East European Jews to America and the Life They Found and Made There* (1976). London: Phoenix, 2000.

Humphries, Rolfe. "A Verse Chronicle." *Nation* 171, November 25, 1950, 490.

Johnson, James William. "Lyric." In *The New Princeton Encyclopedia of Poetry and Poetics*. Princeton: Princeton University Press, 1993.

Julius, Anthony. *T. S. Eliot, Anti-Semitism, and Literary Form*. Cambridge: Cambridge University Press, 1995.

Jumonville, Neil, ed. *The New York Intellectuals Reader*. London: Routledge, 2007.

Kazin, Alfred. *New York Jew*. London: Secker and Warburg, 1978.

Kirsch, Adam. *The Wounded Surgeon: Confession and Transformation in Six American Poets*. New York: W. W. Norton, 2005.

Keller, Jim. "Delmore Schwartz's Strange Times." In *Reading The Middle Generation Anew*. Edited by Eric Haralson, 153–182. Iowa City: University of Iowa Press, 2006.

Kenner, Hugh. "Bearded Ladies and the Abundant Goat." *Poetry* 79 (October 1951): 50–53.

———. *A Homemade World: The American Modernist Writers*. New York: Knopf, 1975.

Koch, Kenneth. *A Possible World*. New York: Alfred A. Knopf, 2002.

Lehman, David. "Delmore, Delmore: A Mournful Cheer." In *The Line Forms Here*. Ann Arbor: University of Michigan Press, 1991, 65–81.

Lowell, Robert. *Collected Poems*. Edited by Frank Bidart and David Gewanter. London: Faber, 2003.

MacDonald, Dwight. "The Bomb." In *The Responsibility of Peoples*, 103–115.

———. "Delmore Schwartz (1913–1966)." In *Selected Essays of Delmore Schwartz*, xv–xxi.

———. "The Germans—Three Years Later." In *The Responsibilities of Peoples*, 71–75.

———. "I Choose the West." In *The Responsibility of Peoples*, 121–125.

———. *The Responsibility of Peoples and Other Essays in Political Criticism*. London: Victor Gollancz Ltd., 1957.

———. "The Responsibility of Peoples." In *The Responsibility of Peoples*, 9–45.

Marx, Karl. "Estranged Labor." In *Economic & Philosophic Manuscripts of 1844*. Edited by Dirk J. Struik. Translated by Martin Milligan, 106–119. London: Lawrence & Wishart, 1970.

Matthiessen. F. O. *American Renaissance: Art and Expression in the Age of Emerson and Whitman*. London: Oxford University Press, 1941; repr. 1980.

———. *From the Heart of Europe*. New York: Oxford University Press, 1948.

McDougall, Richard. *Delmore Schwartz*. New York: Twayne Publishers, 1974.

McLuhan, Eric, and Frank Zingrone, eds. *Essential McLuhan*. Routledge: London, 1995.

McWilliams, John P., Jr. *The American Epic: Transforming a Genre, 1770–1860*. Cambridge: Cambridge University Press, 1989.

Merrill, James. *The Changing Light at Sandover*. New York: Alfred A. Knopf, 2003.

Milton, John. *Complete Shorter Poems*. Edited by John Carey. London: Longman, 1968; 2nd ed. 1997.

———. *Paradise Lost*. Edited by Alastair Fowler. London: Longman, 1971.

Muldoon, Paul. *Poems, 1968–1998*. London: Faber, 2001.

Nelson, Richard William Eric. "Self-Reflections and Repetitions: A Study of the Writings of Delmore Schwartz." PhD diss., University of Durham, 1994.

New, Elisa. "Reconsidering Delmore Schwartz." *Prooftexts* 5, no. 3 (September 1985): 245–262.

O'Connor, William Van. "The Albatross Was Intended to Fly." *Poetry* 79 (October 1951): 55–59.

O'Donnell, G. M. "Delmore Schwartz's Achievement." *Poetry* 54 (May 1939): 105–108.

O'Hara, Frank. *Collected Poems*. Edited by Donald Allen. Los Angeles: University of California Press, 1995.

Olson, Charles. "Projective Verse." In *A Charles Olson Reader*. Edited by Ralph Maud, 39–49. Manchester: Carcanet, 2005.

Ozick, Cynthia. Introduction to *Screeno: Stories & Poems*, by Delmore Schwartz, 7–16.

————. "The Question of Our Speech: The Return to Aural Culture." In *Memory and Metaphor by Cynthia Ozick*, 146–172. New York: Vintage, 1991.

Pater, Walter. *The Renaissance*. Edited by Adam Phillips. Oxford: Oxford University Press, 1987.

Perloff, Marjorie. *21st Century Modernism: The "New" Poetics*. Malden, MA: Blackwell, 2002.

Phillips, Robert. "Foreword to the Original Edition (1979)." In *Last & Lost Poems*, by Delmore Schwartz, xi–xxiii.

————. Introduction to *The Ego Is Always at the Wheel*, by Delmore Schwartz, ix–xii.

————. "Preface to the Paperback Edition (1989)." *Last & Lost Poems*, by Delmore Schwartz, xxv–xxvi.

Phillips, William. *A Partisan View: Five Decades of the Politics of Literature*. New Brunswick, NJ: Transaction Publishers, 1983.

Phillips, William, and Philip Rahv. "Editorial Statement." *Partisan Review* 4, no. 1 (December, 1937): 3–4.

————. "Literature in a Political Decade." In *New Letters in America*. Edited by Horace Gregory and Eleanor Clark. New York, 1937.

Plato. *The Republic*. Translated by R. E. Allen. New Haven: Yale University Press, 2006.

Pound, Ezra. *ABC of Reading* (1934). London: Faber, 1991.

————. *The Cantos of Ezra Pound*. New York: New Directions, 1996.

————. *Poems and Translations*. Edited by Richard Sieburth. New York: Library of America, 2003.

Rainey, Lawrence. *Institutions of Modernism: Literary Elites and Public Culture*. London: Yale University Press, 1998.

Ricks, Christopher. *Allusion to the Poets*. Oxford: Oxford University Press, 2003.

Russell, Bertrand. *History of Western Philosophy*. 2nd ed. London: Routledge, 1961.

Schapiro, Meyer. "Seurat." In *Modern Art: 19th & 20th Centuries*, 101–110. London: Chatto & Windus, 1978.

Schreier, Benjamin. "Ethnic Poetics and the Irreversibility of 'Jewishness' in Delmore Schwartz." In *Studies in Irreversibility: Texts and Contexts*. Edited by Benjamin Schreier, 61–82. Newcastle: Cambridge Scholars Publishing, 2007.

————. "Jew Historicism: Delmore Schwartz and Overdetermination." *Prooftexts* 27, no. 3 (2007), 500–530.

Seiff, Morton. "Fallen David and Goliath America: The Battle Report of Delmore Schwartz." *Jewish Social Studies* 13, no. 4 (October 1951): 311–320.

Shakespeare, William. *Complete Sonnets and Poems*. Edited by Colin Burrow. Oxford: Oxford University Press, 2002.

————. *Coriolanus* (1608). Edited by G. R. Hibbard. London: Penguin, 1967.

————. *King Lear*. In *The Riverside Shakespeare*. Edited by G. Blakemore Evans, et al., 1303–1359. Boston: Houghton Mifflin, 1997.

Shapiro, Karl. *Collected Poems 1940–1978*. New York: Random House, 1978.

Shapiro, Karl. "The Death of Randall Jarrell." In *Creative Glut: Selected Essays of Karl Shapiro*. Edited by Robert Phillips, 154–177. Oxford: Oxford Publicity Partnership, 2004.

Shelley, Percy Bysshe. *Poetical Works*. Edited by Thomas Hutchinson. London: Oxford University Press, 1970.

Shreiber, Maeera Y. "Jewish American Poetry." In *The Cambridge Companion to Jewish American Literature*. Edited by Michael P. Kramer and Hana Wirth-Nesher, 149–169. Cambridge: Cambridge University Press, 2003.

Simic, Charles. "All Gone into the Dark." *London Review of Books,* September 9, 2010, 12.

Spengler, Oswald. *The Decline of the West*. Edited and abridged by Helmut Werner. English ed. Edited by Arthur Helps. Translated by Charles Francis Atkinson. New York: Oxford University Press, 1991.

Stevens, Wallace. *Collected Poetry and Prose*. Edited by Joan Richardson. New York: Library of America, 1997.

———. *Letters of Wallace Stevens*. Edited by Holly Stevens. New York: Knopf, 1981.

Tate, Allen. "To Whom is the Poet Responsible?" *The Hudson Review* 4, no. 3 (Autumn 1951): 325–334.

Teres, Harvey M. *Renewing the American Left: Politics, Imagination, and the New York Intellectuals*. Oxford: Oxford University Press, 1996.

Trilling, Lionel. "The Function of the Little Magazines." In *The Liberal Imagination: Essays on Literature and Society*, 89–99. Oxford: Oxford University Press, 1951.

Trotsky, Leon. "Leon Trotsky to André Breton." *Partisan Review* 4, no. 2 (Winter 1939): 126–127.

———. *Literature and Revolution*. Ann Arbor: University of Michigan Press, 1960.

The Velvet Underground. "European Son (to Delmore Schwartz)." *The Velvet Underground & Nico*. Verve Records, 1967.

Vendler, Helen. "Dear Delmore." *New York Review of Books*, April 11, 1985.

Wald, Alan M. *The New York Intellectuals: The Rise and Decline of the Anti-Stalinist Left from the 1930s to the 1980s*. Chapel Hill: University of North Carolina Press, 1987.

Wilson, Edmund. *Axel's Castle: A Study in the Imaginative Literature of 1870–1930* (1931). London: Collins, 1969.

———. "Flaubert's Politics." *Partisan Review* 4, no. 1 (December, 1937): 13–24.

Whitehead, Alfred North. *Process and Reality: An Essay in Cosmology* (1929). Corrected ed. Edited by David Ray Griffin and Donald W. Sherburne. New York: The Free Press, 1978.

Whitman, Walt. *Leaves of Grass and Other Writings*. Edited by Michael Moon. New York: W. W. Norton, 2002.

Woessner, Martin. *Heidegger in America*. Cambridge: Cambridge University Press, 2011.

Wordsworth, William. *The Major Works*. Edited by Stephen Gill. Oxford: Oxford University Press, 2008.

Yeats, W. B. *The Collected Works of W. B. Yeats, Volume One: The Poems*. Edited by Richard J. Finneran. Basingstoke: Macmillan, 1983; 2nd ed., 1991.

Index

Titles of books, poems and essays, when discussed at any length, are noted under the names of their respective authors.